Types,
Psalms and
Prophecies

Types,
Psalms
and
Prophecies

Being a Series
of Old Testament Studies

by

David Baron

Author of
"The Ancient Scriptures for the Modern Jew",
"Rays of Messiah's Glory",
"The Visions and Prophecies of Zechariah"

Keren Ahvah Meshihit

TYPES, PSALMS AND PROPHECIES

BY
DAVID BARON

ISBN 978-965-447-046-9

First edition © 1906
This edition © 2000
by
Keren Ahvah Meshihit
P. O. Box 10382
91103 Jerusalem, Israel

Printed in Israel
by Yanetz Ltd. Jerusalem
September 2013

See our Catalog in website to order books:
www.kerenahvah.org

הודפס בישראל, תשרי תשע״ד

PREFACE TO THE THIRD EDITION

IT IS eighteen years since this book was first published—
a second edition of it being printed before the end of
that same year. The character of this series of "Old
Testament Bible Studies" is described in the preface to
the first edition, to which I would draw the reader's attention.

I have carefully gone through the proofs of this new
edition, but have made only very slight alterations and
corrections. Did time and strength permit, I would
have re-written and slightly condensed two or three of
the chapters, particularly the expositions of Psalms xxxiii.,
lxiii., and the first part of Psalm lxv., which were originally
shorthand notes of addresses only slightly revised. But
this is impossible at present, owing to the strain of many
tasks and duties, so I let them stand in their original
form.

There is much expository matter in this volume, and
my own faith has been strengthened and my spirit re-
freshed in going through its pages again after all these
years since the book was first written.

In sending it forth on its mission I cannot but render
praise to God for condescending to make use of my unworthy effort to open up some of the "wonderful things"
contained in His Holy Word, and for the spiritual help,
as well as instruction, which many—according to their
own testimony—have already found in these pages. To
His blessing I still commend it.

DAVID BARON.

EN-HAKKORE,
NORTHWOOD, MIDDLESEX,
March 1924.

PREFACE

THE following chapters consist of a selected series of Old Testament Bible Studies, most of which have appeared in parts in "The Scattered Nation," the quarterly magazine of The Hebrew Christian Testimony to Israel, and which I have again and again been asked to gather into a more permanent form. They are all revised, and three or four of them are here written out in full for the first time, while the whole section entitled "The Sacred Calendar of the History of Redemption" is altogether new.

While fully conscious of the inadequacy of my effort, and the imperfection both in style and composition, I yet humbly believe that there is a blessing in these pages for such as still esteem the law of God's mouth to be better than thousands of gold and silver, and who desire to get a closer insight into those "wonderful things" which holy men of old spake as they were moved by the Holy Ghost. And I am the more confident in my hope, since, even in the disjointed fragmentary form in which some of these chapters appeared in the pages of a quarterly magazine, they proved a help and blessing to some of God's people, as a number of letters which have reached me from time to time from Christians in different parts have borne witness.

It is my deep conviction that the continuous systematic unfolding of the Holy Scriptures, in which their true connection and interdependence, and their literal sense, and historical concrete basis are shown before any figurative or practical application of them is made, is the great need in the teaching and preaching of the present day, and that it is chiefly to the almost exclusively fragmentary, vague, disjointed, *textual* manner in which the Bible is being dealt with, that the lamentable lack of depth and backbone in the Christianity of the present day is due.

It is also owing chiefly to this cause, and to the neglect, or misinterpretation of typology and prophecy, and the ignoring of the position of Israel in relation to the purposes of God as revealed in the Scriptures, that the Old Testament has become "as the words of a book that is sealed" to the majority of professing Christians, and that the most destructive and unjustifiable theories and speculations in reference to the early records of Israel's history, which form the basis on which the redemption scheme more fully unfolded in the New Testament rests, are readily accepted by many Christians.

My humble aim, therefore, for many years past has been to unfold connectedly whole Scriptures, and thus to let the sacred oracles speak for themselves. And to those who have read my books, "The Ancient Scriptures and the Modern Jew," "Rays of Messiah's Glory," etc., I shall not appear as altogether a stranger in this field.

In this series of selected Types, Psalms, and Prophecies, my readers will find a great variety of truths handled, and though they deal only with a few of the Divine Oracles, yet Scripture being organically interdependent, the true understanding of even one of its integral parts is a great help to the right interpretation of the whole.

I have, as will be observed in the course of these studies, consulted and gladly availed myself of help from many sources, both English, German, and Hebrew, but my chief guide has been the Hebrew Bible itself, with the letter of which I have been familiar from my childhood in the old, pious Jewish home, but the spiritual understanding of which was hid from me until, nearly thirty years ago,[1] the light of the Cross broke upon my heart, when all at once in its light I began to see light. While giving the primary sense and prophetic significance of these great Scriptures, my aim has been to make these expositions *practically and spiritually helpful to the ordinary English Christian reader,* and for this reason I have avoided as far as possible minute critical points, or the use of Hebrew or other foreign words. Nor could I enter always into the reasons for preferring, not without careful and prayerful consideration, some renderings of the original text to others. I will only here state that while the whole Scripture, which in each case stands at the head of the chapter in which it is treated, is given for convenience sake in paragraph form from the English Revised Version, in the exposition itself I have always had the Hebrew text before me, and have sought to bring out the different shades of meaning which cannot well be reproduced in any one translation.

It is the prayer of my heart that at least in some little way these pages may conduce to the glory of the God of Israel, and of His Anointed, and may prove a help to the understanding of the sacred oracles which alone are able to make men wise unto salvation.

1906   DAVID BARON.

---

[1] This was written in 1906.

CONTENTS

I

II

III

IV

V

VI

VII

VIII

IX

X

APPENDICES

I

THE SACRED CALENDAR OF THE HISTORY OF REDEMPTION

LEVITICUS XXIII

"And the Lord spake unto Moses, saying, Speak unto the children of Israel, and say unto them, The set feasts of the Lord, which ye shall proclaim to be holy convocations, even these are My set feasts. Six days shall work be done; but on the seventh day is a sabbath of solemn rest, an holy convocation; ye shall do no manner of work: it is a sabbath unto the Lord in all your dwellings.

These are the set feasts of the Lord, even holy convocations, which ye shall proclaim in their appointed season. In the first month, on the fourteenth day of the month at even, is the Lord's passover. And on the fifteenth day of the same month is the feast of unleavened bread unto the Lord: seven days ye shall eat unleavened bread. In the first day ye shall have an holy convocation: ye shall do no servile work. But ye shall offer an offering made by fire unto the Lord seven days: in the seventh day is an holy convocation: ye shall do no servile work.

And the Lord spake unto Moses, saying, Speak unto the children of Israel, and say unto them, When ye be come into the land which I give unto you, and shall reap the harvest thereof, then ye shall bring the sheaf of the first-fruits of your harvest unto the priest; and he shall wave the sheaf before the Lord, to be accepted for you: on the morrow after the sabbath the priest shall wave it. And in the day when ye wave the sheaf, ye shall offer a he-lamb without blemish of the first year for a burnt offering unto the Lord. And the meal offering thereof shall be two-tenth parts of an ephah of fine flour mingled with oil, an offering made by fire unto the Lord for a sweet savour: and the drink offering thereof shall be of wine, the fourth part of an hin. And ye shall eat neither bread, nor parched corn, nor fresh ears, until this selfsame day, until ye have brought the oblation of your God: it is a statute for ever throughout your generations in all your dwellings.

And ye shall count unto you from the morrow after the sabbath from the day that ye brought the sheaf of the wave offering; seven sabbaths shall there be complete: even unto the morrow after the seventh sabbath shall ye number fifty days; and ye shall offer a new meal offering unto the Lord, ye shall bring out of your habitations two wave loaves of two tenth parts of an ephah:

they shall be of fine flour, they shall be baken with leaven, for first-fruits unto the Lord. And ye shall present with the bread seven lambs without blemish of the first year, and one young bullock, and two rams: they shall be a burnt offering unto the Lord, with their meal offering, and their drink offerings, even an offering made by fire, of a sweet savour unto the Lord. And ye shall offer one he-goat for a sin offering, and two he-lambs of the first year for a sacrifice of peace offerings. And the priest shall wave them with the bread of the first fruits for a wave offering before the Lord, with the two lambs: they shall be holy to the Lord for the priest. And ye shall make proclamation on the self-same day; there shall be an holy convocation unto you: ye shall do no servile work: it is a statute for ever in all your dwellings throughout your generations.

And when ye reap the harvest of your land, thou shalt not wholly reap the corners of your field, neither shalt thou gather the gleaning of thy harvest: thou shalt leave them for the poor, and for the stranger; I am the Lord your God.

And the Lord spake unto Moses, saying, Speak unto the children of Israel, saying, In the seventh month, in the first day of the month, shall be a solemn rest unto you, a memorial of blowing of trumpets, an holy convocation. Ye shall do no servile work: and ye shall offer an offering made by fire unto the Lord.

And the Lord spake unto Moses, saying, Howbeit on the tenth day of this seventh month is the day of atonement: it shall be an holy convocation unto you, and ye shall afflict your souls; and ye shall offer an offering made by fire unto the Lord. And ye shall do no manner of work in that same day; for it is a day of atonement, to make atonement for you before the Lord your God. For whatsoever soul it be that shall not be afflicted in that same day, he shall be cut off from his people.

And whatsoever soul it be that doeth any manner of work in that same day, that soul will I destroy from among his people. Ye shall do no manner of work: it is a statute for ever throughout your generations in all your dwellings.

It shall be unto you a Sabbath of solemn rest, and ye shall afflict your souls: in the ninth day of the month at even, from even unto even, shall ye keep your sabbath.

And the Lord spake unto Moses, saying, Speak unto the children of Israel, saying, On the fifteenth day of this seventh month is the feast of tabernacles for seven days unto the Lord. On the first day shall be an holy convocation; ye shall do no servile work. Seven days ye shall offer an offering made by fire unto the Lord: on the eighth day shall be an holy convocation unto you; and ye shall offer an offering made by fire unto the Lord: it is a solemn assembly; ye shall do no servile work."

I

THE SACRED CALENDAR OF THE HISTORY OF REDEMPTION

THIS chapter may well be styled "The Sacred Calendar of the History of Redemption," for not only are each of the "feasts," or special "assemblies," or "appointed seasons" of meeting between. the Lord and His people, as the Hebrew words *"mo'adei Yehovah"* may be rendered, considered separately, full of emblematic and spiritual teaching, but taken together they form a series of striking symbolic prophecies, some fulfilled, some yet to be fulfilled, and thus *foretell* as well as set forth the great plan of Redemption. "It is beautifully supposed by some," observes Dr. Andrew Bonar, "that *Israel's Feasts* represent the *course of time*—this earth's days, from creation to the final end. The Lamb slain (Passover) commences it, and the. eighth day of the happy Feast of Tabernacles is its close; while *the Sabbath*, the rest—God's rest in Himself, and His creatures rest around Him—both *precedes* and *follows* this *course of time*." [2]

---

[2] "And that this meaning was intended from the first, not only in reference to the Passover, but to all the feasts, appears from the whole design of the Old Testament, and from the exact correspondence between the types and the antitypes. Indeed, it is, so to speak, impressed upon the Old Testament by a law of internal necessity. For when God bound up the future of all nations in the history of Abraham and his seed He made that history prophetic, and each event and every rite became, as it were, a bud, destined to open in blossom and ripen into fruit on that tree under the shadow of which all nations were to be gathered."—*Edersheim*.

This beautiful "supposition" will grow into a certainty to every intelligent and devout student of Scripture, who cannot but find accumulating evidence as he proceeds that these "feasts," like Israel's ceremonial and ritual in general, are not of man's origination, but appointed and ordered by Him who is infinite in knowledge, and who knows the end from the beginning.

"For these rites and ceremonies must, every one of them, be regarded as predictions of those things they typified.

"Every well-established type is an instance of fulfilled prophecy; and when we view them all combined, we have a congeries of prophecies manifestly fulfilled, and affording an amount of accumulated evidence which must be convincing to any candid mind. In all the necessary elements of prophetic evidence, the argument derived from these types is remarkably certain and facile. Their antiquity or priority in point of time to their antitypes is undoubted, it is admitted on all hands. They were celebrated by successive generations, for centuries before those things which answered to them appeared to human observation, or could be known in any other way, than by Divine revelation.

"Their fulfilment, also, is equally certain; we compare the antitypes with the types and find them answer, the one to the other, in an immense variety of particulars. It is utterly impossible that this agreement should be the result of accident; it is so minute, and carried out into such numerous ramifications, that it exceeds even the credulity of infidelity itself to ascribe it to anything but design." [3]

But not only are the "feasts" and every detail of the ceremonial to be observed at those appointed seasons full of meaning, but the *very order* in which they stand in the

[3] J. B. Lowe, B.A., "The Annual Festivals of the Jews."

sacred calendar, is, I believe, significant as setting forth the order of sequence in which the various stages of God's great redemption scheme were to unfold themselves in the course of the ages.

It will be impossible for us to enter fully into this vast theme, nor do I purpose even to touch here on the significance of the various accompanying sacrifices and offerings which formed part of the ritual at these "solemn assemblies." All I intend, by God's help, to do, is to trace in mere outline the leading truths connected with the "feasts" themselves.

There are seven "appointed seasons," and they are all included in the first seven months of the Jewish year.[4]

THE SABBATH

But before these great annual occasions of Jehovah's "trystings" with His people are enumerated, we have the reiteration of the command in reference to the weekly

---

[4] "The symbolical character which is to be traced in all the institutions of the Old Testament appears also in the arrangement of its festive calendar. Whatever classification of the festivals may be proposed, one general characteristic pervades the whole. Unquestionably, the number seven marks in Scripture the sacred measurement of time. The Sabbath is the seventh of days; seven weeks after the commencement of the ecclesiastical year is the Feast of Pentecost; the seventh month is more sacred than the rest, its 'firstborn' or 'new moon' being not only devoted to the Lord like those of the other months, but specially celebrated as the 'Feast of Trumpets,' while three other festivals occur within its course—the Day of Atonement, the Feast of Tabernacles, and its Octave. Similarly, each seventh year is Sabbatical, and after seven times seven years comes that of Jubilee. Nor is this all. Seven days in the year may be designated as the most festive, since in them alone 'no servile work' was to be done, while on the so-called minor festivals (Moed Katon), that is, on the days following the first of the Passover week, and of that of Tabernacles, the diminution of festive observances and of restrictions on labour marks their less sacred character."—*Edersheim.*

seventh-day Sabbath: *"Six days shall work be done, but on the seventh day is the sabbath of rest* [*or 'a sabbath of solemn rest,' as the Revised Version has it, the words in the Hebrew literally meaning 'a sabbath of sabbatism'*], *an holy convocation: ye shall do no manner of work; it is a sabbath unto Jehovah in all your dwellings"* (ver. 3).

It has been well observed that it is the manner of Scripture, often to be noticed, especially in the prophetic parts, to give us a glimpse of the goal and end before speaking of the *process* by which the blessed consummation will be brought about. Now the end of redemption as far as man and this earth are concerned is the Sabbatic period, in which all the redeemed family shall at last fully enjoy "God's Sabbatism," and creation itself shall be delivered from the bondage of corruption into the glorious liberty of the children of God. And of this rest which yet remaineth for the people of God, and of the time when the last vestiges of the havoc wrought by sin shall have disappeared, and the whole creation shall cease to travail and to groan, the weekly Sabbath was appointed by God as a prophecy and pledge. It was indeed instituted in the first instance as a memorial of God's finished work in creation, because in it He had rested from all His work which God created and made (Gen. ii. 2, 3). And in Israel subsequently it was appointed by God not only as a perpetual testimony to Himself as the creator, but in addition also, as a weekly memorial of their redemption from the bondage of Egypt, as we read in Deut. v. 12-15: "Keep the sabbath day to sanctify it, as Jehovah thy God hath commanded thee. . . . And remember that thou wast a bondman in the land of Egypt, and Jehovah thy God brought thee out thence by a mighty hand and by a stretched out arm: *therefore Jehovah thy God commanded thee to keep the sabbath day."* But from the time sin entered into the world, and creation was marred by the Fall, beneficent indeed to man as the appointment of a seventh-day rest from his physical toil still remained, neither God nor man could longer find true rest in an earth brought under the curse. Nor did Israel enter into God's rest when they were brought out of Egypt, for that redemption, as already seen by their own prophets and psalmists, was itself only *typical,* pointing in a variety of ways to the great spiritual redemption from the bondage to sin and Satan which alone could bring true rest unto our souls and fit man to enjoy God's Sabbatism.

The Sabbath day, therefore, became to the spiritually enlightened in Israel chiefly a symbol and pledge of God's promised rest to His people, and to the earth in the future, and to this day in their *mizmorim,* or hymns sung in every pious Jewish home on Friday evenings, at the ushering in of the Sabbath, there are touching references to the glorious future time when, under Messiah's sway, the earth shall find rest, and to the blessed day "which shall be all Sabbath"—in allusion to the very ancient Jewish division of the course of time into a week of millenniums, viz., two thousand years "without law," two thousand years under the law; two thousand years the days of Messiah; and the last the seventh as earth's Sabbath. It is, however, important, to remember that the weekly seventh-day Sabbath is essentially connected with the old marred creation, with the imperfect Mosaic dispensation, and with the mere typical redemption from Egypt.

But from the beginning there was the promise of a new creation, of a more perfect dispensation than that of the law, and of the greater deliverance than that from Egypt; and it was but meet, when the promises were at last fulfilled in the advent of the Redeemer, the true Joshua, through whom alone we enter into rest, that the weekly

Sabbath should henceforth be associated not with the imperfect, or even with the merely typical, but with the perfect and the eternal. The greatest honour bestowed on the Sabbath of the old creation was that our Lord Jesus, after pouring out His soul as a ransom for us, made it the one complete day of His rest in death in proof that His work was accomplished, and the sore travail of His soul for our redemption ended; "but when He rose, the sanctity and hallowment of that primeval Sabbath passed on with Him into the new day—even that day of resurrection-rest into which He entered as 'the first-begotten from the dead,' 'the beginning of the (new) creation of God.'

"With His resurrection the seventh-day Sabbath of the old creation expired, transmitting its sanctity and its privileges to the new Sabbath—the first day, which became our day of rest in the power of a new creation. 'If any man be in Christ (to him there is) a new creation. Old things have passed away, behold, all things have become new.' Such is our condition, as viewed in Christ our Representative and Forerunner. Surely, a new Sabbath day befits those of whom such things can be spoken.

"How necessarily, therefore, must the seventh-day Sabbath, seeing that it was bound up with the old creation, resign its claims to that new day on which the Head and Representative and Forerunner of the redeemed rose to take the Headship of the new creation of God. In the types of Israel, the special honour attaching to the eighth day had long been indicated. It was the day appointed for circumcision, that great type of separation from the flesh unto God, according to the power of the resurrection of Christ.[5] On the eighth day the firstborn were to be given unto God.

---

[5] See Col. ii. 11.

"On the eighth day the priests (their consecration having been perfected) entered on their ministrations in the Tabernacle. So also the Pentecostal day, on which the Holy Ghost was sent down as the witness of the resurrection-glory of Jesus, was an eighth day. It followed the last of the seventh-day sabbaths that completed the seven weeks numbered from the day of the offering of the firstfruits. The eighth day was 'the great day' of the Feast of Tabernacles.[6]

"In these, and other instances, the eighth day is singled out for special honour. It was thus honoured in type, because it was to be honoured by the great fact of the resurrection of our Substitute. That marked it especially as the day of result—a day that, following on and springing out of the series of days that had preceded, embodied in itself and made manifest the consequences of the agencies that had in those days operated. In relation to the past, it was an eighth day; in relation to that which was to succeed, a first day. But it could not have been that which it was as the first day, except it had been, as the eighth day, connected with the days that had preceded. What would resurrection have brought to us if there had not been previous redemption?"[7]

We are sometimes challenged by Jews and others to produce any direct New Testament warrant for the change of day from the seventh to the first, but though it is true that no such formal ordinance was given, it cannot be said that the New Testament is silent respecting the sanctification of the new day, "for habitual Apostolic action is equivalent to Apostolic commandment." "This day," says Bishop Pearson, "did the Apostles from the beginning most religiously observe, by their meeting together for

---

[6] See John vii. 37 and Lev. xxiii. 36.
[7] "Thoughts on Scriptural Subjects," by Benjamin Wills Newton.

holy purposes, and to perform religious duties. The first observation was performed providentially, rather by the design of God than any such inclination or intention of their own: for the same day, saith the Evangelist (that is the day on which Christ rose from the dead), at evening, being the first day of the week, the disciples were assembled for fear of the Jews. The second observation was performed voluntarily, for after eight days again His disciples were within, and Thomas with them. The first day of the week, when Christ rose, by the providence of God the disciples were together, but Thomas was absent; upon the first day of the next week they were all met together again in expectation of our Saviour, and Thomas with them.

"Again, when the day of Pentecost was fully come, which was also the first day of the week, they were all with one accord in one place; and having received the promise of the Holy Ghost, they spake with tongues, preached the Gospel, and the same day were added unto them about three thousand souls. The same practice of convening we find continued in the following years; for upon the first day of the week, when the disciples came together to break bread, Paul preached unto them; and the same Apostle gave express command concerning the collection for the saints both of the Churches of Galatia and of Corinth: 'upon the first day of the week, let every one of you lay by him in store, as God hath prospered him.'

"From this resurrection of our Saviour, and the constant practice of the Apostles, this first day of the week came to have the name of the Lord's day, and is so called by St. John, who says of himself in the Revelation, 'I was in the Spirit on the Lord's day.'

"And thus the observation of that day, which the Jews did sanctify, ceased, and was buried with our Saviour; and in the stead of it, the religious observation of that day on which the Son of God rose from the dead, by the constant practice of the blessed Apostles, was transmitted to the Church of God, and has continued in all ages.

"This day, thus consecrated by the resurrection of Christ, was left as the perpetual badge and cognisance of His Church. As God spake by Moses to the Israelites, 'Verily My sabbath shall ye keep, for it is a sign between Me and you throughout your generations, that ye may know that I am the Lord that doth sanctify you'; thereby leaving a mark of distinction upon the Jews, who were by this means known to worship that God whose Name was Jehovah, who made the world, and delivered them from the hands of Pharaoh; so we must conceive that He hath given us this day as a sign between Him and us for ever, whereby we may be known to worship the same God Jehovah, who did not only create heaven and earth in the beginning, but also raised His eternal Son from the dead for our redemption. As, therefore, the Jews do still retain the celebration of the seventh day of the week, because they will not believe any greater deliverance wrought than that of Egypt: as the Mohammedans religiously observe the sixth day of the week in memory of Mohammed's flight from Mecca, whom they esteem a greater prophet than our Saviour: as these are known and distinguished in the world by these several celebrations of distinct days in the worship of God; so all who profess the Christian religion are known publicly to belong unto the Church of Christ by observing the first day of the week, upon which Christ did rise from the dead, and by this mark of distinction are openly separated from all other professions."

THE PASSOVER

After the glimpse of the blessed goal foreshadowed by the weekly sabbath—not only the millennial sabbath of this earth, but the still more perfect eternal sabbatism of God, which awaits the redeemed family in the new heavens and the new earth in which shall dwell peace and righteousness forevermore—we have, I believe, in the series of the annual festivals themselves, which like the whole of Israel's divinely appointed ritual, were "a shadow of good things to come" (Heb. x. i.), the process prefigured in prophetically chronological order, as to how and by what different stages this blessed consummation shall finally be brought about.

First in order stands the Passover.

"These are the feasts [or 'appointed seasons' or 'solemn assemblies'] of Jehovah, even holy convocations which ye shall proclaim in their appointed season. In the first month, on the fourteenth day of the month at even, [or 'between the two evenings' [8]*] is Jehovah's Passover [or 'Passover unto Jehovah']"* (vers. 4, 5).

The history of redemption begins with the Passover. It is the first and "beginning of months," and commencing of days in the history of the redeemed family (Exod. xii. 2). But let me remind you that redemption has not only a beginning, but also a *prelude.* The prelude to the typical redemption from Egypt was Pharaoh's tyranny, Egyptian bondage, and God's promises and covenant with Abraham long before Israel went there (Gen. xv.), so that it is with right the Psalmist sings that it was in remembrance of His "holy word" of covenant and promise, and of

---

[8] According to the Samaritans, the Karaite Jews, and many modern interpreters, this means between actual sunset and complete darkness (or, say, between 6 and 7 p.m.); but from the contemporary testimony of Josephus, and from Talmudical authorities, there cannot be a doubt that, at the time of our Lord, it was regarded as the interval between the sun's commencing to decline and its actual disappearance. This allows a sufficient period for the numerous lambs which had to be killed, and agrees with the traditional account that on the eve of the Passover the daily evening sacrifice was offered an hour, or, if it fell on a Friday, two hours, before the usual time.

"Abraham His servant," that, when the fulness of time came, He brought forth His people from the land of Egypt with joy, and His chosen with singing (Psa. cv. 42, 43) And so the antitypical redemption, too, has its prelude. Sin introduced into the world by the Great Adversary; the Fall which brought man to ruin and wretchedness; and, blessed be God! the great covenant of grace, and the eternal counsels of peace and salvation to man between the Father and the Son, "before the foundation of the world" (Eph. i. 3-9). But of the prelude and of the goal of God's great redemption scheme the Bible gives us only glimpses, while it is occupied chiefly with the record— both prophetic and historic—of its process.

The ground and means of God's great salvation for man is the Lamb slain, the blood shed. Christ crucified is the very foundation-stone of redemption; and of this great and central truth the paschal lamb, which is the central object in the Passover, is one of the most perfect types to be found in Scripture. And it is interesting to observe that already in the Old Testament the daily sacrifice, and especially the *paschal* lamb, is regarded as a type of the Messiah—the pure, innocent, and suffering servant of Jehovah, upon whom the Lord lays the iniquity of us all, and who, "for us men" and our salvation, "is led *as a lamb to the slaughter,* and as a sheep before her shearers is dumb, so He openeth not His mouth" (Isa. liii.).

We cannot, of course, enter fully into the many points in which the paschal lamb sets forth the Person and atoning work of Messiah, but we may look just in passing at some of the instructions contained in Exodus xii., which gives us the account of the original institution of the ordinance. There we read first of all: "Speak ye unto all the congregation of Israel, saying, In the tenth day of this month they shall take to them every man a lamb ac-

cording to their father's house, a lamb for an house. . . .
And ye shall keep it until the fourteenth day of the same
month, and the whole assembly of the congregation of
Israel shall kill it at even" (vers. 3, 6)—which instruction
has generally been taken by commentators to foreshadow
the short interval of as many days between Christ's public
entry into Jerusalem and His crucifixion.

But there is probably also a deeper truth presented to
us here, that, namely, referred to by the Apostle Peter,
who, with the Passover type in his mind, tells us that redemption was no afterthought or remedy of an unseen evil
devised by God at the time of its arising, and that we were
not redeemed with corruptible things, with silver or gold,
from the vain manner of life handed down by our fathers,
but with the precious blood of Christ "as of a lamb without
blemish and without spot, *who was foreknown* [*or 'fore-
ordained'*] *indeed before the foundation of the world, but
was manifested at the end of the times* for us who by
Him do believe in God" (1 Pet. i. 18-20), which becomes
still more striking if we compare it with the words of the
same apostle in his second Epistle, who reminds us that
"one day is with the Lord as a thousand years, and a
thousand years as one day," and that the Lord is not slack
concerning His promise, as some men count slackness (2
Pet. iii. 8, 9)—in the light of which we may surely say that
it is no mere chance that Christ, the true Lamb of God,
who was "ordained" from the foundation of the world,
was actually manifested and slain for us at the end of four
millennial days, reckoned from the beginning of months,
and commencing of the days of human history, when the
first promise of a coming Redeemer was given, immediately
after the Fall in the Garden of Eden (Gen. iii. 15).

Then we read that the paschal lamb must be not only
"a male of the first year," a foreshadowing that the Christ
should pour out His soul unto death for us in the prime

of His life, but that, like all the animal sacrifices presented to God, the lamb must be "without blemish" (Exod. xii. 5), which gloriously received its fulfillment in the absolute moral perfection of the great antitype, the Lamb of God, of whom the Prophet Isaiah, in that great prophecy of the sufferings of the Messiah and of the glory which should follow, already says that "He had done no violence" (in His outward life), "nor was any deceit found in His mouth" (or inward being) (Isa. liii. 9), and who, as we have just been reminded by Peter, was the "Lamb without blemish" (in Himself) and "without spot" (or "unaffected by any impression of sin from without"), so that He can be the Saviour of others, and by His "precious blood" atone and cleanse from all sin.

The paschal lamb slain, they must take a bunch of hyssop and dip it in the blood and strike with it the lintel and the two side-posts of their dwellings, and not venture outside their blood-besprinkled doors until the morning; for that night was to be a night of judgment; Jehovah would pass through the land of Egypt and smite all the firstborn, both man and beast, from the firstborn of Pharaoh that sat on his throne, to the firstborn of the captive that was in the dungeon—for God is no respecter of persons, and only those sheltered under atoning blood—those for whom a ransom was provided in the slain lamb—would be passed over and sheltered from avenging justice.

There is no need for me to enlarge on the fact that Egypt, in its hostility to God and His people, and lying under curse and judgment, is regarded in Scripture as the type of "this present evil world," but I venture to quote here a passage from a suggestive little book by another Hebrew Christian writer in elucidation of some of these points: "Christ our Passover," he says, "has now been slain for us. The door of the sanctuary has been sprinkled, and opened wide to every one who is willing to enter and walk in the new and living way. Let him who is anxious to secure for his never-dying soul the love of God, and eternal life, provide for himself the blood of the Lamb, by joining the household and family of God. But the door of his heart and conscience must first be sprinkled by means of a bunch of hyssop, which is humility. As the proud and haughty ones are compared, in Scripture, to the lofty cedars of Lebanon, the humble, poor, and contrite ones are denoted by the hyssop, which was the smallest of plants, and was found growing on rocks and in the midst of ruins.

"The spiritually poor and needy, the meek and broken-hearted, can alone partake of the Feast of the Paschal Lamb. Humility is the bunch of hyssop which is dipped in the blood of the humble Jesus, and sprinkles it on the door-posts of the conscience and heart. When this is done to any one he may join the family, assembly, and Church of the firstborn. He may feed in safety upon the body of the Lamb, in the house of God, and, although thousands fall at his side, and tens of thousands at his right hand, the Lord looks upon the blood on the door-posts of his heart, and wards off from him the arm of the destroyer."[9]

Remember also, dear reader, that the blood was only to be sprinkled on "the two side-posts and on the upper door-post," but not on the threshold; and take care that you do not, by hardness of heart and contempt for this, the only means of God's great salvation, crucify to yourself the Son of God afresh, and thus trample His much more "precious blood" underfoot.

But once sheltered under its blood, Israel was called to feed on the lamb thus slain. *"And they shall eat the flesh in that night, roast with fire, and unleavened bread; with bitter herbs they shall eat it. Eat not of it raw,*

---

[9] Benjamin Weiss, in "A Christian Jew on the Old Testament."

*nor sodden at all with water, but roast with fire; its head
with its legs, and with the inwards thereof"* (Exod. xii.
8, 9), instructions full of spiritual significance when viewed
in the light of the antitypical fulfilment, for He who saves
His people by His blood, Himself becomes their spiritual
meat and drink, and says to all who would follow Him
through the wilderness into the promised land of rest: "As
the living Father has sent Me, and I live by the Father,
even so *he that eateth Me,* the same shall live by Me."
And again, "Whoso eateth My flesh, and drinketh My
blood, hath eternal life . . . for My flesh is meat indeed,
and My blood is drink indeed"—glorious spiritual realities symbolled forth by those blessed emblems of His
broken body and shed blood which He gave to His disciples
on that Passover night on which He was betrayed, when
He transformed the paschal supper into the communion
feast which the Church was to observe all through her
wilderness experience "till He come."

"And mark, my brethren, the whole of the paschal lamb
was eaten; not one particle of it was to be left; they
were expressly commanded to consume it all.

"It is thus the Saviour gives Himself altogether to be
His people's food; it is not a part, but the whole of a
precious Christ that is provided for us. All the holiness
of His life, all the devotedness of His death, all the efficacy
of His blood, all the power of His resurrection, the dignity
of His ascension, the influence of His intercession, and the
glory of His coming again; everything He does, He has,
He is, the whole is given unto us to feast upon; and we
need it all. I cannot spare a single particle of this provision—not the smallest fibre. I must have Him all to
meet the exigency of my case, the necessities of my soul.
I apprehend, my brethren, that if we know anything of
Jesus, as we ought to know, we shall be anxious to know
all about Him; we shall find the whole that God has

written needful to satisfy the cravings of our soul, needful
to compensate the exhaustion of a trying pilgrimage." [10]
Nor are the manner as to how, and the *adjuncts* with which
the paschal lamb was to be eaten without significance. It
was to be "roast with fire," which foreshadowed the sufferings of our Redeemer when He became "The sacrifice of
Jehovah's Passover" (Exod. xii. 27), and endured for us
not only the reproach and shame and agony heaped upon
Him by the wicked hands of men, but the righteous anger
against sin of Him who in His Divine essence and absolute
holiness is not only the God of love, but a "consuming
Fire."

Of the "unleavened bread" in relation to the Passover
we shall have occasion to speak further on, but the "bitter
herbs," or simply "bitters," as it is in the Hebrew, was
intended not only to remind them of their past afflictions in
Egypt, as has been suggested, but are emblematic of the
sorrow for sin, and of the bitter trials and conflicts both
within and without, peculiar only to those who have been
brought out of Egypt and who feed on the Paschal Lamb.
"By Christ's atoning blood," writes the Hebrew Christian
brother whom I have already quoted, "Christians are
reconciled to their heavenly Father, and their good and
kind Shepherd spreads a magnificent table for them, in
the presence of their deadliest enemies. They enjoy happiness and felicity, which the world can neither give nor
take away. Rising from the table they return into the
camp of their enemies to difficulties and trials, afflictions
and sore temptations. They have still to withstand the
sharp arrows of the Egyptians and to cross a Red Sea.
They have to traverse a wilderness, where there is no
water. They have to fight against an Amalek, and pass
over a Jordan, before they can come into the glorious

---

[10] J. B. Lowe, B.A., "The Annual Festivals of the Jews."

promised land, the spiritual Zion, and heavenly Jerusalem, where they will enjoy their Passover without bitter herbs, and abide for ever in the presence of the Lamb of God."

There are many other ways in which the Passover foreshadows the glorious Person and work of the Redeemer, the true "Lamb [11] of God, which beareth away the sin of the world," on which I cannot touch, but I must bring to your mind one more apparently very insignificant injunction, on the fulfillment of which, however, in the history of our Lord, great emphasis is laid in the New Testament, because in God's overruling providence it served to deepen and confirm the conviction in the minds of the apostles that Jesus of Nazareth was indeed the foretold Messiah of Israel, since not only His atoning death itself, *but the very manner* of that death, and each of the details and incidents connected with it, were in accordance with the predictions of prophets and seers centuries in advance.   How unlikely it would have seemed from the human point of view that the Messiah, upon whom all the hopes of the nation were set, should be put to death at

---

[11] "For other reasons also the paschal lamb was specially suited to be typical of Christ. It was a sacrifice, and yet quite out of the order of all Levitical sacrifices. For it had been instituted and observed before Levitical sacrifices existed; before the Law was given, nay, before the Covenant was ratified by blood. In a sense it may be said to have been the cause of all the later sacrifices of the Law, and of the Covenant itself. Lastly, it belonged neither to one nor to another class of sacrifices; it was neither exactly a sin offering nor a peace offering, but combined them both. And yet in many respects it quite differed from them.

"In short, just as the priesthood of Christ was a real Old Testament priesthood, yet not after the order of Aaron, but after the earlier, prophetic and regal order of Melchizedek, so the sacrifice also of Christ was a real Old Testament sacrifice, yet not after the order of Levitical sacrifices but after that of the earlier prophetic Passover sacrifice, by which Israel had become a royal nation."—*Edersheim.*

all; and if He were put to death that it should be, not by the Jewish mode of stoning, but by the more barbarous Gentile Roman method of crucifixion; but once the light of fulfilment was thrown on those most unlikely and astounding events in Jewish history, it became manifest that all these things happened "that the Scriptures might be fulfilled," and that they could only have been brought about by the overruling and controlling power of Him "who sees the end from the beginning, and from ancient times the things that are not yet done, saying, My counsel shall stand, and I will do all My pleasure" (Isa. xlvi. 10).

The apparently insignificant point to which I refer, is the injunction about the paschal lamb, which in the Hebrew is expressed in four words, "And a bone of Him shall ye not break" (Exod. xii. 46; Num. ix. 12).

Now this is the New Testament history and commentary on its fulfilment:—"The Jews, therefore, because it was the preparation, that the bodies should not remain on the cross upon the sabbath (for the day of that sabbath was a high day), asked of Pilate that their legs might be broken, and that they might be taken away. The soldiers, therefore, came and brake the legs of the first, and of the other which was crucified with him: but when they came to Jesus, and saw that He was dead already, they brake not His legs: howbeit one of them with a spear pierced His side, and straightway there came out blood and water. And he that hath seen hath borne witness, and his witness is true: and he knoweth that he saith true, that ye also may believe. *For these things came to pass, that the scripture might be fulfilled, A bone of Him shall not be broken.*

"And again another scripture saith, They shall look on Him whom they pierced" (John xix. 31-37).

The late Dr. Adolph Saphir beautifully observed, that with his eyes fixed on the dying Saviour, and in the **light** of what he had just witnessed, the Apostle John sees how Christ and His cross are not only the centre, but the Alpha and Omega, the Beginning and End, of Israel's history. The commencement of Israel's national history was the exodus from Egypt, of which the Passover was the perpetual memorial, but here is the true Passover, and it was to Him that the paschal lamb pointed all along when it was said, *"A bone of Him shall not be broken."*

And what is to be the end of Israel's history? It is graphically described in the last chapters of the prophecy of Zechariah. There we read of Israel's final repentance when the Spirit of Grace and supplication shall be poured upon them; of their sorrow and anguish over their "only one" whom they brought forth in travail, in whom was all their hope and salvation, and whom they yet pierced and crucified; of how that same long-rejected "pierced" One shall yet appear a second time for their salvation, and usher in that long-looked-for day, to which all the holy prophets bore witness, namely, when Jehovah shall be King over all the earth, when "the Lord shall be One and His Name One." But here is the One in whom all these glorious future events are centred, and through whom alone they shall be consummated when again that "other Scripture," in those very prophecies of Zechariah, shall be fulfilled, which saith, *"They shall look on Him whom they have pierced."*

The Feast of Unleavened Bread

Next in order and in closest association with the Passover [12] stands the Feast of Unleavened Bread.

"And on the fifteenth day of the same month is the

---

[12] In Matt. xxvi. 17, Mark xiv. 12, the Passover is called the first day of unleavened bread, because of its very close connection with it. On the evening of the Passover the feast did actually begin.

*feast of unleavened bread unto Jehovah: seven days ye
shall eat unleavened bread. In the first day ye shall have
an holy convocation: ye shall do no servile work. But ye
shall offer an offering made by fire unto the Lord seven
days: in the seventh day is an holy convocation; ye shall
do no servile work"* (vers. 6-8).

Here again the very order in which this feast stands is
of great significance. In more modern times, practically
since the destruction of the second Temple, when the
offering of the paschal lamb was no more possible, the
Passover and the feast of unleavened bread became con-
founded in the mind of the Jews, and the terms are used
by the Rabbis interchangeably, but originally and in the
Divine plan they were distinct, though in the most intimate
possible relation with one another.

The fullest explanation of the feast of unleavened bread,
and of its relation to the Passover, is given by the Apostle
Paul in 1 Cor. v. 6-8. "Know ye not," he says, "that a
little leaven leaveneth the whole lump? Purge out therefore the old leaven, that ye may be a new lump, as ye are
unleavened. *For even Christ our Passover is sacrificed
for us: therefore let us keep the feast, not with the old
leaven, neither with the leaven of malice and wickedness;
but with the unleavened bread of sincerity and truth."*

Here we see how the two stand related to one another
as *cause and effect,* and that if the paschal lamb sets forth
Christ our Passover slain for us in order to bring us
pardon, peace, and new life, the feast of unleavened bread
was designed to prefigure the holiness of the new life, and
the fellowship with God which must characterise the redeemed.

There is no true holiness or "doing right" in God's
sight, until we behold the "dear dying Lamb," and know
what it means to be redeemed with "precious blood,"
for even "the good works" of the unregenerate man, as

Augustine expressed it long ago, are in God's sight only
so many "splendid sins," but from the moment the paschal
lamb was slain, and the offerer identified himself with the
offering, the Jew had to put away all leaven from his
dwelling, and we read that "Whosoever eateth leavened
bread from the first day until the seventh day, that soul
shall be cut off from Israel."

So it is in the scheme of the greater spiritual redemption. It is the Lamb of God that bears away our sins,
and brings us pardon and reconciliation with God, but
"let every one that nameth the name of Christ depart
from iniquity" (2 Tim. ii. 19); or as the apostle, with the
Old Testament type in his mind, expresses it, "For Christ
also our Passover was sacrificed for us, therefore [or 'so
that'] we should keep the feast," namely, of unleavened
bread.

Of the essential ideas connected with the keeping of a
feast I shall have occasion to speak further on, but no
one can *enjoy* the feast of the Lord if he does not first
"purge out the old leaven." What is leaven? Actual
material leaven consists of a microscopic vegetable fer-
ment, which is characterised chiefly by the rapidity of its
growth and diffusiveness, so that it permeates the whole
lump into which it is put, and nothing is able to stop its
growth except fire—a fit emblem, therefore, of corruption, of which it is the figure in every place in which it is
mentioned in the New Testament.[18]

---

[18] I know there are some true and prominent servants of Christ
who make an exception of the reference in Matt. xiii. 33, where
they think leaven is used in a good sense as a figure merely of
rapid permeation, but this view is bound up with what I believe
to be an erroneous interpretation of the series of parables in that
chapter. It seems to me that none of those who heard the Lord
use that word could have understood anything good by it, especially
in view of the definitions which He Himself gave of leaven in His
other teachings.

Here in 1 Cor. v. the apostle speaks of it as the "old leaven," which answers to the *"old man"* with its corrupt deeds (Eph. iv. 22) of our former condition, and proceeds further to define it as "the leaven of *malice and wickedness,"* which embraces both "the evil habit of mind and outward manifestation of the same in word or deed." But the Lord Jesus Himself speaks of three kinds of leaven, against which He warns His disciples, and it is only if all these be "purged out" from our individual lives, and from the corporate life of a Church, that we know the blessedness of keeping the Lord's feast.

(*a*) In Luke xii. 1 we read, "In the mean time, when there were gathered together an innumerable multitude [literally 'the myriads'] of people, insomuch that they trode one upon another, He began to say unto His disciples first of all, *Beware ye of the leaven of the Pharisees, which is hypocrisy."* There were, doubtless, many noble exceptions among the Pharisees—men who, like Paul, had a great and true zeal for God, though not according to knowledge, and of whom it could be said "that according to the law they were blameless"; but the Pharisees for the most part, and Pharisaism as a system, were characterised by unreality and hypocrisy. And is not this insidious and hateful leaven found in lesser or greater degree in our hearts too? Is our Christian profession and walk in relation to God and man characterised in the fullest degree by the "unleavened bread of *sincerity"*—(the Greek word for which expresses literally "a thing which, when examined by the sunlight, is found to be pure and unadulterated")—and "truth"—that is, exact conformity to fact and reality as opposed to everything unreal and untrue?

And when we look away from our individual life to the life of the professing Church, alas! how permeated it is by the leaven of hypocrisy, especially in these days when outward profession is not only no longer accompanied by risks and dangers, but is even in certain circles advantageous and fashionable. Oh, how much of "religion" there is in Christendom, but how little of God and of true holiness there is in it all! And this outward profession of "a form of godliness but denying the power thereof" is to characterise more and more the last days (1 Tim. iv. 1-2; 2 Tim. iii. 5), when this awful leaven of hypocrisy will reach its climax in the false, feigned worship which will be paid by man to the Christ and to Antichrist, from which only the elect will be saved.

(b) In Matt. xvi. 11 the Lord warns the disciples to beware "of the leaven of the Pharisees and of the Sadducees," which is "their doctrine." Now the teaching of these two sects was on many essential points quite different, but in God's sight equally pernicious. It is impossible to enter here into an examination of these doctrines, and as a matter of fact there were different shades of views among the followers of each of these two great parties, but the chief errors of the Pharisees were that they laid equal, yea, even greater stress, on the "oral law" or traditions of men than on the word of God; and that in consequence of departing in spirit from God's self-revelation through Moses and the prophets, they became ignorant of the righteousness of God and invented a whole system of outward religiousness by which man was to go about to establish his own righteousness. And as to the Sadducees, it is not an injustice to them to say that the chief error in their teaching lay in its tendency to *rationalism*, and that their opposition to Pharisaism went the length not only of rejection of the traditions of the elders, but to a large extent also of the supernatural element in holy Scripture, so that though some of them would have protested against being classed in this category, the definition given of them as a whole in Acts xxiii. 8 is true, and they did practically teach that "there is no resurrection, neither angel, nor spirit." I may observe in passing that we have still to do with these two parties or elements in the Jewish nation, and that in modern Judaism we have on the one hand Rabbinism, which in its doctrines and practices is a continuation and development of Pharisaism in the time of Christ; while on the other hand, in the so-called "reform," or "progressive" movement so extensively spread on the Continent, and especially in the extremer forms which that movement is assuming in America, we have represented the ancient system and principles of the Sadducees.

And, my friends, is not this same pernicious leaven of both the Pharisees and of the Sadducees permeating the professing Church at the present time? Is not the greater part of Christendom at this present day exalting human traditions—its Christian Talmud—on to the same level—yea, even above—the inspired words of prophets and apostles and of Christ Himself? And has not the "simplicity of the Gospel" itself been changed by Christian Rabbis into a system of religiousness by which men go about to establish for themselves a righteousness before God by mere outward rites and observances?

And as to the doctrine of the Sadducees, alas! Christendom, and so-called "Protestant" Churches not excepted, is full of it; and it is sad and humiliating to look abroad and to see the desperate, but, thank God, fruitless attempts to strip the Christ of His Divine attributes, and the sacred Scriptures of their supernatural element, on the part even of some who claim to be Christian leaders and teachers.

(c) In Mark viii. 15 the Lord charged His disciples also, saying, "Take heed, beware . . . of the leaven of Herod"—which doubtless includes the Herodians of whom we read in different places in the Gospel narrative, and who, though a political rather than a religious party, were as much envenomed against the lofty claims and spiritual teaching of our Lord Jesus as the scribes and Pharisees, with whom, though naturally detesting one another, they were ready to take counsel how to destroy Him. The Herodians were supporters of Herod's dynasty, created by Cæsar, and their one care was to avoid all occasions of offence to the Romans. "They regarded the teaching of Christ as of a revolutionary character, and they strove hard to convict Him of seeking to establish a kingdom that would be subversive of Cæsar's, the more so that they saw He despised them as merely self-seeking politicians." In reality neither Herod nor Cæsar were anything to them, and they only cared for the comfortable position they held under the arrangement between these two potentates. And is not this Herodian leaven of compromise, selfish expediency, opportunism, and worldliness permeating the professing Church of Christ today?

Alas! there is much truth in the lament which I heard many years ago from the lips of a great Scotch divine: "The Church speaks of converting the world, but, alas! the world has long ago converted the Church," and again, "I looked for the Church and found it in the world; I looked for the world, and found it in the Church."

Now to all these evil principles and evil practices, and whether in relation to the Church corporately, or in relation to our own individual lives, the words of the apostle must be applied, "Purge out therefore the old leaven, that ye may be a new lump"—as a necessary preparation for keeping the feast.

In this admonition the apostle refers most probably to the custom of *bedikath chamets*—the ceremony of "searching for leaven," which is known to have existed in the time of Christ, and which still exists among the Jews in all the lands of their dispersion. I well remember the interest with which as a boy I used to follow about my father on the evening before the 14th of Nisan, as with lighted wax candle in hand, after uttering the prayer, "Blessed are thou Jehovah our God, King of the universe, who hast sanctified us by Thy commandments and commanded us to remove the leaven," he proceeded to search all likely and unlikely places all over the house for leaven, picking up a few crumbs of bread which had been purposely dropped here and there before, and gathering the whole into a large wooden spoon, and tying it together ready for the ceremonial burning before noon next day, ending the whole by uttering the formula in the Chaldaic language, "All the leaven in my possession, that which I have seen, and that which I have not seen, be it null, be it accounted as the dust of the earth."

I had no idea then of the typical or moral significance of this ceremonial, and I have often thought since how comparatively easy it is for the Jew to get rid of the material leaven, but what a much more formidable and difficult matter it is to get rid of the insidious leaven of corruption in our hearts. Nor can it be accomplished by one act, for who even among the holiest of God's saints can say in the fullest sense, and once for all, while still in this body of humiliation, "I have made my heart clean, I am pure from my sin"? Is it not rather that the more we seek to walk in the full light of His holiness, the more also the darkness of our own hearts is revealed to us? But let us see to it at least that we walk in sincerity and truth, and that we can at all times look up to the searcher of hearts and say, "Search me, O God, and know my heart: try me, and know my thoughts: and see if there be any way of wickedness [or of 'grief'] in me, and lead me in the way everlasting."

The spiritual reality of the Feast of Unleavened Bread will be exhibited by Israel on a national scale when, after they shall look upon Him whom they have pierced, and

behold as the Jewish Apostle John did at the foot of the
cross, and as Paul in the passage we were considering,
that their Messiah Jesus was their true Passover sacrificed
for them, they shall be known as *"the holy people"* with
Kodesh l'Yehovah—"Holiness to Jehovah"—written upon
all they are and have,' yea, even upon the very bells of
their horses (Zech. xiv. 20; Isa. lxii. 12).

"In those days, and in that time, saith Jehovah, the iniquity of Israel shall be sought for, and there shall be none;
and the sins of Judah, and they shall not be found: for
I will pardon them whom I reserve" (Jer. l. 20).

The Presentation of the "Omer" or Sheaf of First-Fruits

Next in order to the Passover and the Feast of Unleavened Bread, we have in the chapter which we are considering the significant ceremonial of the presentation of
the *Omer*—or "Sheaf of First-fruits."

*"And Jehovah spake unto Moses, saying, "Speak unto
the children of Israel, and say unto them, When ye be
come into the land which I give unto you, and shall reap
the harvest thereof, then ye shall bring the sheaf of the
first-fruits of your harvest unto the priest: and he shall
wave the sheaf before Jehovah, to be accepted for you: on
the morrow after the sabbath the priest shall wave it . . .
and ye shall eat neither bread, nor parched corn, nor fresh
ears, until this selfsame day, until ye have brought the
oblation of your God: it is a statute forever throughout
your generations in all your dwellings"* (vers. 9-14).

It is an ancient subject of controversy as to whether
the first day of the week or the second day of the Feast
of Unleavened Bread is meant by the expression "the
morrow after the sabbath"; but the first view, which

was the one adopted by the Sadducees in the time of Christ, and by the Karaite Jews at the present day, is doubtless an erroneous one, and rests on a misinterpretation of the word "Sabbath," which is used not only of the weekly rests, but also of the first and last days of the great festivals and of the Day of Atonement. As Dr. Edersheim observes, "The testimony of Josephus, of Philo, and of Jewish tradition, leaves no room to doubt that in this instance we are to understand by the Sabbath the 15th day of Nisan on whatever day of the week it might fall." The general impression one would get from the words of Scripture is that a *sheaf* of the first ripe ears of the early barley harvest was thus "presented" or waved before the Lord, and this was probably the case originally and in the ritual of the first Temple. In the second Temple, however, the ceremonial observed in connection with the presentation of the *Omer* was of a different and more elaborate nature. The following description of it in the Talmud, as summarised by Dr. Edersheim, will, no doubt, interest my readers:

"Already on the 14th of Nisan, the spot whence the first sheaf was to be reaped had been marked out by delegates from the Sanhedrin, by tying together in bundles, while still standing, the barley that was to be cut down. Though, for obvious reasons, it was customary to choose, for this purpose the sheltered Ashes-valley across Kedron, there was no restriction on that point provided the barley had grown in an ordinary field—of course in Palestine itself—and not in garden or orchard land, and that the soil had not been manured nor yet artificially watered.[14] When the time for cutting the sheaf had arrived, that is,

---

[14] The field was to be ploughed in the autumn, and sowed seventy days before the Passover.

on the evening of the 15th of Nisan (even though it were a Sabbath),[15] just as the sun went down, three men, each with a sickle and basket, formally set to work. But in order clearly to bring out all that was distinctive in the ceremony, they first asked of the bystanders three times each of these questions: 'Has the sun gone down?' 'With this sickle?' 'Into this basket?' 'On this Sabbath (or first Passover Day)?'—and, lastly, 'Shall I reap?' Having each time been answered in the affirmative, they cut down barley to the amount of one ephah, or ten omers, or three seahs, which is equal to about three pecks and three pints in our English measure. The ears were brought into the court of the Temple, and thrashed out with canes or stalks, so as not to injure the corn; then 'parched' on a pan perforated with holes, so that each grain might be touched by the fire, and finally exposed to the wind. The corn thus prepared was ground in a barley-mill, which left the hulls whole.

"According to some, the flour was always successively passed through thirteen sieves, each closer than the other. The statement of a rival authority, however, seems more rational—that it was only done till the flour was sufficiently fine, which was ascertained by one of the 'Gizbarim' (treasurers) plunging his hands into it, the sifting process being continued so long as any of the flour adhered to the hands. Though one ephah, or ten omers, of barley was cut down, only one omer of flour, or about 5.1 pints of our measure, was offered in the Temple on the second Paschal, or 16th day of Nisan. The rest of the flour might be redeemed,

---

[15] There was a controversy on this point between the Pharisees and the Sadducees. The article in Kitto's Cycl. erroneously names the afternoon of the 16th. of Nisan as that on which the sheaf was cut. It was really done after sunset on the 15th, which was the beginning of the 16th of Nisan.

and used for any purpose. The omer of flour was mixed with a 'log,' or very nearly three-fourths of a pint of oil, and a handful of frankincense put upon it, then waved before the Lord, and a handful taken out and burned on the altar. The remainder belonged to the priest." [16]

Now there is no doubt that in this presentation of the very earliest natural produce of the ground, Israel was taught to acknowledge God's power and bountifulness, and thus by a representative "first-fruits" to consecrate to Him the whole harvest—for all these Jewish festivals, although they commemorated the covenant dealings of God with His people, were also in connection with the natural seasons of the year—with the harvests which God gave unto His people—with the outward blessings with which He surrounded them.

But here, as is so often the case in Scripture, the earthly and visible is the symbol of greater and deeper spiritual realities. There is another harvest field for the first ripe fruit of which the Lord of the harvest had long been waiting—an harvest of which *"Christ is the first-fruits"* (1 Cor. xv. 23), and the whole redeemed family—"all they that are Christ's" perfected in resurrection glory "at His coming," shall be the fulness.

And it was on the third day after the Paschal lamb was slain (when the corn of wheat was cast into the ground to die that it may bear all this glorious harvest) that He rose again and stood forth as "the Branch of Jehovah for beauty and for glory, and (as) the fruit of the earth[17] for

---

[16] Edersheim, "The Temple and its Ministry."

[17] The construction of the Hebrew in Isa. iv. 2 demands that the expression, "The fruit of the earth," should be regarded as another title of "the Branch of Jehovah." It is one of the most remarkable prophecies of the mystery of the Divine and human

excellency and for comeliness" to His redeemed people;
and when after His resurrection He ascended to His Father and our Father, to His God and our God, it was not
only "to be accepted for us" (Lev. xxiii. 11), and there
evermore to appear in the presence of God for us (Heb.
ix. 24), but also as the pledge and earnest of the resurrection of His people.

"Does any one feel a doubt upon this subject? does it
seem 'a thing impossible that God should raise the dead'?
We appeal to the fact—'the best attested fact in history,'
as a famous Lord Chancellor well said—that Jesus rose
from the dead. The faith which realises this fact gives to
the soul the blessed persuasion that 'He who has raised up
the Lord Jesus, shall also raise us up by Jesus.'

"Of this the Holy Ghost bears witness also, in the passage quoted above. For after that he had said before,
'If Christ be not raised, then is your faith vain, ye are yet
in your sins,' the apostle goes on to say, *But now is
Christ raised from the dead, and become the first-fruits
of them that slept.* For since by man came death, by man

---

natures of the Messiah in the Old Testament. The following passage is from a sermon by Dr. Saphir: "Exactly as the type had
prefigured it, so was He offered up unto God. And on the morrow
after the Sabbath Day He came forth the Sheaf, the Branch out
of the earth. He grew up as it were before Jehovah. Such a man
God had never seen before. Oh, what a contrast between the first
Adam and the last Adam! 'The first Adam a living soul; the
last Adam a quickening spirit.' Suffering and death were behind
Him. He had died once unto sin, but now He lived unto God.

"Here is the glorious Head of humanity coming forth out of the
earth, a Sheaf waved from the earth unto God, that He might sit
at the right hand of the Father. Oh, how beautiful is the Passover
fulfilled unto us! Christ our Passover is offered; Christ the
first-fruits of the dead is risen. We are brought out of Egypt, the
house of bondage. We have been redeemed with the precious
Blood of the Lamb of God."

came also the resurrection of the dead. For as in Adam all die, even so in Christ shall all be made alive' (1 Cor. xv. 21, 22). In other words, Jesus stands to us in the relation of our covenant Head. As by virtue of our connection with the first Adam, we are subject to death and corruption, which we derive from him; so by virtue of our connection with the second Adam, we are made partakers of His life and immortality, which we derive from Him. 'He is the Head of the body, the Church; who is the beginning, the first-begotten from the dead' (Col. i. 18). In Him is life. He is the living one, the Prince of life. The Church in the person of the Saviour is made alive forevermore; and this life is not to be confined to Him, it is derived from Him unto all His people: because He lives they shall live also. He has a legal *right* to bestow this life upon them, because He was dead; He has *power* to impart it to them, because He is alive. Did He enter the gates of death as the covenant Head of the Church? In the same character He issued from them; and thus when He arose, it was as though every member of His body, great and small, had risen along with Him."

PENTECOST

The glad season of the grain harvest lasted seven weeks, and was closed with the Feast of Pentecost on which another "first-fruits" was presented to the Lord.

"And ye shall count unto you from the morrow after the Sabbath, from the day that ye brought the sheaf of the wave-offering; seven Sabbaths shall there be complete: even unto the morrow after the seventh Sabbath shall ye number fifty days; and ye shall offer a new meal-offering unto Jehovah. Ye shall bring out of your habitations two wave loaves of two tenth parts of an ephah: they shall

be of fine flour; they shall be baken with leaven, for first-fruits unto Jehovah" (Lev. xxiii. 15-18).

Ancient Jewish tradition already universally received at the time of Christ regarded the Day of Pentecost [18] as the anniversary of the giving of the law from Mount Sinai, and the prayers and *Machzor,* or liturgy, for that day are full of very touching, and also of some absurd references and legends, associating this festival with that solemn event. One beautiful observation of Maimonides is worth quoting, as it shows a recognition of the purpose God had in view in redeeming Israel out of Egypt, viz., "that they might observe His statutes, and keep His laws," and so be the centre in which the holiness of Jehovah might be displayed in the sight of the nations. "Just as one who is expecting the most faithful of his friends," he observes, "is wont to count the days and hours to his arrival, so we also count from the Omer (sheaf of first-fruits) of the day of our Exodus from Egypt to that of the giving of the law, which was the object of our Exodus, as it is said, 'I bare you on eagles' wings, and brought you

---

[18] Pentecost is designated by different names in the Scriptures. It is called *Hag ha-Kazir,* "Feast of Harvest" (Exod. xxiii. 16) ; *Hag ha-Shabuoth,* "Feast of Weeks" (Exod. xxxiv. 22; Deut. xvi. 10; 2 Chron. viii. 13) ; *Yom ha-Bikkurim,* "Day of First-fruits" (Num. xxviii. 26). In later and Rabbinic literature it is also called "Feast of the Fiftieth Day"; *"Hag atzeret,"* or simply *"Atzeret,"* "Feast of the Conclusion," or "Conclusion" (*i.e.,* of the Passover Season) ; and in reference to the prevailing belief that it was the anniversary of the giving of the law, it is called "The Day" (or season) "of the Giving of the Law."

The term "Whit-Sunday," *i.e.,* "White Sunday," is, of course, entirely of Christian origin, and is traced to the fact that in the early times of the Church those newly baptized appeared in the assemblies during the interval between Easter and Pentecost, and especially on the last Sunday of the seventh, clothed in white garments—emblematic of the purity and righteousness they had received, and, so to say, put on when they were new-born in Christ.

to myself.' And because this great manifestation did not last more than one day, therefore we annually commemorate it only one day." If this tradition be accepted, then one of the Christian meanings of this feast has been well expressed by a Hebrew Christian master, to whom I have already expressed my indebtedness.

"If Jewish tradition," he says, "connected the 'feast of first-fruits' with the 'mount that might be touched,' and the 'voice of words which they that heard entreated that the word should not be spoken to them any more,' we have in this respect also come unto Mount Zion, and to the better things of the New Covenant. To us the Day of Pentecost is, indeed, the 'feast of first-fruits,' and that of the giving of the better law, 'written, not in tables of stone, but on the fleshy tables of the heart,' 'with the Spirit of the living God.' For (on that same day), as the worshippers were in the Temple, probably just as they were offering the wave-lambs and the wave-bread, the multitude heard that 'sound from heaven, as of a mighty rushing wind,' which drew them to the house where the apostles were gathered, there to hear, 'every man in his own language,' 'the wonderful works of God.' And on that Pentecost day, from the harvest of first-fruits, not less than three thousand souls added to the Church were presented as a wave-offering to the Lord. The cloven tongues of fire and the apostolic gifts of that day of first-fruits have, indeed, long since disappeared. But the mighty rushing sound of the Presence and Power of the Holy Ghost has gone forth into all the world." [19]

Though not definitely stated in Scripture, there seems much probability in the Jewish association of Pentecost with the law-giving, but we are particularly concerned

---

[19] Edersheim.

with the ceremonial which constituted the peculiar feature
of that feast, for which modern Judaism has no explanation
beyond the visible and literal—that it was an acknowledgment, namely, of the mercies of Jehovah in giving them
"that good land," and in causing it to be fruitful, though
if that be all, it may well be asked why there should be a
different kind of first-fruits, and a different ceremonial
with the presentation of the first-fruits of the wheat harvest, than that presented from barley harvest.

In the light of the New Testament this second "first-
fruits" is full of typical and prophetic significance. The
true corn of wheat having fallen into the ground and died,
it brought forth much fruit, and the result, as set forth
in this type, is bread—two loaves, which are waved and
presented to Jehovah—for "not only is our Lord Jesus the
true meal-offering in whom the Father ever finds delight,
and who exhibited in the earth the habits and ways of
heaven, but His people also are constituted a new meal-
offering unto God, that in them too traits of heavenly
character might be found, and that so, the earth, sown with
seed from the harvest-field of Israel, might never be des-
titute of some fruit meet for the garners of heaven." [20]

It is not improbable that this type was in the mind of
the Apostle James when, writing of the election from
among the nations, he says: Of "His own will begat He
us with the word of truth, that we should be a *kind of
first-fruits of His creatures*"—for the preparation and presentation of the loaves are indeed emblematic of the Church,
and set forth that part of God's eternal counsel which is
being accomplished in this present dispensation—that is,
the period between Christ's resurrection and ascension,
and His coming again in His great power and glory.

---

[20] B. W. Newton, "Thoughts on Scriptural Subjects."

But let us note particularly two or three significant points in connection with this "new meal-offering" as a figure of the Church.

I. In contrast to the *Omer*, or "sheaf of first-fruits," presented on the 16th of Nisan, the *bikkurim* (as this second first-fruits are called) consisted of *two loaves.*

Of the *duplicate* character of this emblem different explanations have been given, but it seems to me clear that it sets forth beautifully that which may be said to constitute the particular feature of the Church of this present dispensation, namely, the two formerly irreconcilable elements—the Jew and the Gentile—made one in Christ.

This great truth is set forth here in type and figure and, as was the case with all the other Old Testament types, could not have been understood until it was fulfilled through Christ—for this mystery, or God's secret, which could not have been known apart from revelation, namely, that Gentiles should not only be "partakers of the same promise in Christ" with Jews, but made *"fellow-heirs and of the same body"*—was not made known in other ages and generations unto the sons of men, as it is in the New Testament revealed unto His holy apostles and prophets by the Spirit; and, as a matter of fact, until Christ broke down the middle wall of partition, and consecrated a new and living way for both Jew and Gentile through the veil of His rent flesh, no Gentile, even if he was circumcised, and became a proselyte, and surpassed the most pious in Israel in piety and learning, was ever received on terms of absolute equality, and regarded as altogether one with the congregation of Israel. "For two thousand years the knowledge of God and the ordinances of true religion were confined exclusively to the land of Israel; the nations of the earth (with a few individual exceptions) having rejected the opportunities which had been granted to them, were left to reap the consequences of their own apostasy, and given over to a reprobate mind. God's mercies in the meantime were richly lavished on the Jews; they were the chosen depositories of these mercies—'The adoption, and the glory, and the covenants, and the giving of the law, and the service of God, and the promises,' all pertain to them (Rom. ix. 4).

"And the ceremonial ordinances, while themselves a portion of these mercies, served also as a fence, or enclosure, outside of which, instead of the green pastures of covenanted privileges, were only the sterile wastes of human ignorance and sin. But with the present dispensation, a new order of things commences; the Saviour having in His own person taken human nature up to heaven, received of the Father the promise of the Holy Ghost, and standing now as the representative of 'all the seed,' whether they be Jews or Gentiles, He heads up all in one body unto God. There is then, you see, a unity, and yet a diversity, in the Christian Church; a unity because it is one Church; a diversity because it consists of two component parts, the Jew and the Gentile. 'For He is our peace, who hath made both one, and broken down the middle wall of partition between us; having abolished in His flesh the enmity, even the law of commandments contained in ordinances; for to make in Himself of twain one new man, so making peace; and came and preached peace to you which were afar off, and to them that were nigh. For through Him we both have access by one Spirit unto the Father' " (Eph. ii. 14-18).[21]

This, then, is what I believe to be the most probable significance of the *duplicate character* of this first-fruits. As these two loaves combined to make up one offering and were waved *as one* in the presence of God, so the

---

[21] Josiah B. Lowe, B.A., "The Annual Festivals of the Jews."

believing Jew and the believing Gentile, washed in the same blood, sanctified and indwelt by the same Spirit which teaches both alike to cry "Abba, Father," and presented by the One Great High Priest, are made equally acceptable, and are consecrated *as one offering* to the service of God.

II. Another peculiarity connected with the presentation of the *bikkurim* was that expressed in the words *"They shall be baken with leaven."* This is remarkable, especially in the light of the express injunction given to Israel to exclude leaven from their sacrifices (Exod. xxxiv. 25), but it only supplies us with another instance of the *minuteness* with which these types are regulated because of their rich symbolical significance.

Leaven, as was shown in a previous section, signifies corruption. From every sacrifice and offering therefore which set forth the perfect servant of Jehovah, the true Lamb of God, leaven was rigidly excluded. Thus with the *Omer,* or sheaf offered on the 16th of Nisan, which presented Christ in resurrection, the true first-fruits and meal-offering, there was no leaven, for nothing even suggestive of corruption could be associated with the only sinless One, in whom there was no guile nor was any deceit found in His mouth. But it is otherwise with His people. The Church is indeed "elect through sanctification of the Spirit unto obedience and sprinkling of the blood of Jesus Christ." We are as believers possessed of a new life, and whatever our previous life may have been, are now washed and sanctified and justified in the Name of our Lord Jesus, and by the Spirit of our God, and are designated by Him as "saints"; but who, even of the holiest of God's people, can take his place before Him as *altogether* sinless? Oh no, my friends, whatever our attainments in character and holiness, "if we say that we have no sin, we deceive ourselves, and the truth is not in us," and the more we seek by His grace to follow Him fully, and in the power of His Spirit to keep our hearts pure and our hands clean—in short, to "walk in the light as He is in the light"—the more conscious we become of the contrast between us and Him *in whom "there is no darkness at all."* For the same reason also there is no sin-offering connected with the sheaf which prefigured Christ; but with the two loaves there is the express command that apart from the other accompanying offerings there should be one he-goat for a sin-offering, which again teaches us that the Church, though called and qualified by the power of the Holy Ghost to serve, does, nevertheless, need at every moment of its service, the protection of sacrifice—"even that once-offered sacrifice in which the virtue and efficacy of all the offerings here enumerated were combined, and under the shelter of which, the Church, presented as the new meal-offering in the earth, abides. In the one oblation presented on the Cross, it has provided for it a fragrance and acceptableness which it can never find in its own leavened self."

I have said that that which is typified by Pentecost is spread over the whole of this Christian dispensation, though a striking fulfilment took place at the inauguration fifty days after Christ's resurrection, when the first Christian Pentecost "was now fully come." Perhaps that which is specially set forth by the actual *presentation* and waving of the loaves will be fulfilled at the close of this dispensation, when all the first-fruits from among men being gathered, and the number of the elect completed, Christ shall "present to Himself a glorious Church, not having spot, nor wrinkle, nor any such thing; but that it should be holy and without blemish" (Eph. v. 26, 27); but even then she will be so, not because He found her so, or because of her absolute purity while on earth, but because He sanctified and cleansed her with the washing of water by the Word, and made her perfect in the beauty and comeliness *which He did put upon her.*

III. Let us remember also that just as the *Omer* presented on the morrow after the Passover, setting forth Christ as "the first-fruits of them that slept," was a pledge and earnest of the *bikkurim* presented on Pentecost which prefigured the Church in its elective character as the first-fruits from among men, so this second first-fruits are in themselves also a prophecy and pledge of the fuller harvest yet to be gathered in "the dispensation of the fulness of the times," of which Scripture speaks, and of which I shall have occasion to write when dealing with the Feast of Tabernacles. The blessing which has come to the world with the first advent of our Saviour has been wonderful, but it has been so far only partial in degree and extent.

Indeed, unbelieving men sometimes taunt us with the little that the Gospel has accomplished, and maintain that Christianity has proved a failure; and "truly if, as is supposed by some, the Scriptures held out the expectation that the Gospel was to go on gradually extending, until the world was converted, there were some appearance of reason in the imputation. For when we contemplate the condition of the world after eighteen centuries, how far are we from seeing these expectations realised! Consider how small a proportion of the human race are even professedly believers in Jesus. In the wide wastes of heathen, Mohammedan, and Jewish ignorance that present themselves, how insignificant in point of extent and numbers is professing Christendom! And then contemplate this favoured field of Gospel culture itself, and what a spectacle does it present to the enlightened mind! Alas! how few, comparatively, profess 'the truth as it is in Jesus.' Again, consider the condition of professing Protestantism; look at our own highly favoured land, the most enlightened in the world, and ask, is this a Christian nation? Does it even deserve the name? or does it show any signs of approximation to such a happy state? My brethren, it is sufficient merely to glance at the state of things around us to feel persuaded that to whatever climax the world is progressing, it is not to one of righteousness and obedience to the Gospel."

But if we look into the Scriptures and around us at the condition of the world, we see that the Gospel has and does accomplish just that which God said it would accomplish in this present age. "A remnant according to the election of grace" was to be saved out of Israel (Rom. xi. 5). And the Gentiles, or the other nations of the earth, we read that God hath visited *"to take out of them a people for His name"* (Acts xv. 14). These two, reconciled in one body unto God through the Cross were to form His *Ecclesia*—His Church—the Bride, or body of Christ, "the fulness of Him that filleth all in all." And as the Scriptures have foretold so it is: Israel as a nation still rejects Christ, but are there not thousands of Jews who receive Him and become sons of God through believing in His Name? The nations of the earth still for the most part sit in darkness and under the shadow of death, but wherever the Gospel is preached are there not some who are visited by God's Spirit and "taken out" to be His? Nor does this truth of the elective character of this dispensation tend to slacken zeal or depreciate missionary labour as some suppose. Oh no, "this Gospel of the Kingdom *must* first be preached as a witness unto all nations," the whole of God's great harvest-field, consisting of all kindreds, peoples, and tongues, *"must"* first be traversed for the gathering in of "the first ripe ears" to constitute a glorious first-fruits, and then—

"After these things I will return,
And I will build again the tabernacle of David which is fallen,
And I will build again the ruins thereof,

And I will set it up;
That the residue of men may seek after the Lord,
And all the Gentiles upon whom My Name is called, saith the
    Lord, who maketh these things known from the beginning
    of the world" (Acts xv. 16-18, R.V.).

Then, not only shall all in Israel know God, from the least unto the greatest of them, but *all* the nations shall walk in the light of Jehovah.

The Meeting of Type and Antitype in Point of Time

So far we have dealt with prophetic types which have already received their fulfilment in the Christian dispensation. "Christ our Passover," to whom the Paschal lamb had so long pointed, has already been slain for us; the Omer sheaf, which was both a type and prophecy, "that He should be the first that should rise from the dead" (Acts xxvi. 23), received its glorious fulfilment when *on the third day* He rose again, and became the first-fruits of them that slept; and with the Day of Pentecost there commenced the gathering out of the first-fruits from among men of all nations who by one Spirit are formed into one new body, in which there is neither Jew nor Gentile, and who in the power of a new life are called into fellowship with God, and to keep the feast with the unleavened bread of sincerity and truth. But it is very interesting also to observe that in so far as this sacred calendar of the History of Redemption has already run its course, not only do type and antitype answer to one another in a most striking manner, and in a variety of ways which preclude the possibility of their fulfilment being brought about by anything but design, but they have also *synchronised as near as possible in point of time.*

Was it mere chance that when the hour was at last come for the Lamb of God to be offered for the sin of the world that it should have fallen on the Jewish Pass-over?[22] And when He whom the pangs of death could not hold emerged again from the grave, victorious over death, to be the beginning of a new spiritual harvest unto God from among men, was it mere accident that it should have been at the time, or within a few hours, that the priests and leaders of Israel were busied in preparing and presenting in their Temple the Omer of first-fruits?

And again, was it mere chance that it was not till "the Day of Pentecost *was fully come*" (Acts ii. 1) that there came a sound from heaven as of a rushing, mighty wind, to inaugurate the new dispensation, and the Spirit of God fell on that cosmopolitan crowd so that "about three thousand souls" were added to the company of the apostles and disciples to form a new meal-offering unto Jehovah— "a kind of first-fruits of His creatures"? (Jas. i. 18). And, finally, is it again mere chance that since these manifest fulfillments came *the very possibility* of continuing these types and ceremonies has been removed, for the Temple has been destroyed, and the Jewish people has since then been banished from their land and scattered into all parts of the earth, so that though they continue to observe what they call "Passover" in commemoration of the Exodus (though they are now in a longer captivity, and almost greater bondage than in Egypt), and though they abstain for that week from literal leaven, and have turned the Feast of Pentecost entirely into a festival in commemoration of the giving of the law, because in their dispersion it has lost its true significance to them— *there is no longer a paschal lamb, nor the Omer sheaf, nor the bikkurim loaves?*

---

[22] See Appendix II. dealing with the Actual Day of the Crucifixion and the "Three Days and Three Nights."

The Christian cannot but perceive in all this not only the prophetic character of Israel's types and ceremonies "which demanded equally with oral predictions the prescience of Him to whom alone are known all His works from the beginning of the world," but that *"Christ is all,"* and that from the very beginning the very election and call of Israel, and all their Divinely ordained ritual and services, had Him, and the great spiritual redemption which He was to accomplish, for their centre and goal.

The Interval Between the Fulfilled and Unfulfilled Feasts

We come now to that part of the Sacred Calendar in the History of Redemption, the fulfilment of which is, as I believe, yet in the future; and in dealing with these remaining "feasts" I must be very brief: first, because this chapter has already grown to larger proportions than was my intention in the first instance; and secondly, because in dealing with unfulfilled prophecies it becomes us to be much more careful and diffident than when writing of things which have already come to pass.

From Pentecost and the presentation of the *bikkurim* (first-fruits) on the 6th of the month Sivan, till the 1st of Tishri, a period of nearly four months out of the seven, the sacred calendar is (with the exception of the celebrations of the New Moons) a blank.[23]

---

[23] There are, of course, the Fast of the 4th and the Fast of the 5th Month, the first on the 17th of Tammuz, to commemorate the taking of Jerusalem by Nebuchadnezzar, and later by Titus; and the second on the 9th of Ab, in commemoration of the twofold destruction of the Temple; but they are not included in our sacred calendar, nor were they of Divine appointment. See "The Arrangement of the Jewish Calendar," Appendix I., at the end of the book.

Was it intended as a hint in its prophetic significance of the long interval which, according to the foreknowledge of God, was to be covered by this present dispensation— the period, namely, during which God does not manifestly interpose, but by the gracious operations of His Spirit is gathering out a people unto Himself, "a multitude which no man can number," not only out of all peoples and kindreds and tongues, but *in all the intervening centuries,* to be "a kind of first-fruits unto Himself" before the remaining part of His purpose in relation to the nations *as nations* can be accomplished?

At this point in our chapter there occurs a little paragraph which is also not void of spiritual significance: *"And when ye reap the harvest of your land, thou shalt not make clean riddance of the corners of thy field when thou reapest, neither shalt thou gather any gleaning of thy harvest: thou shalt leave them unto the poor, and to the stranger: I am Jehovah your God"* (ver. 22).

"In this manner" it is true "that *love to man* was taught in these thanksgiving feasts, at the very time that *love to God,* who so kindly gave them their plenty, was called forth and increased," [24] but it may be a hint also that *during this period* which was to follow Pentecost the harvest of spiritual blessing was no longer to be monopolised by Israel. "First, indeed, the riches of Israel's harvest-field was devoted to the supply of Israel itself. The early teaching of the apostles, and all the early attention of the Pentecostal Church, was directed towards Israel. Samaria, indeed, was visited by Peter and John, and Peter was caused (though he did it with slow and hesitating hand) to open to the Gentiles the door of fellowship in Israel's blessings. Nevertheless Peter and John are distinctively described as ministers to the circumcision

---

[24] Dr. Andrew Bonar.

(Gal. ii. 7). They avowedly devoted themselves to the service of Israel. To Israel, seeing that the Pentecostal harvest was from their land reaped, the fulness of the resulting plenty was first presented."

But this ordinance given to Israel of not making a "clean riddance" in gathering in their harvest was also not forgotten: "The watchful care of the great Head of Israel secured its observance. The poor exiled Israelite and the distant Gentile stranger were not forgotten. The Pentecostal harvest was well-nigh ended in the land of Israel, when a late outstanding ear was gathered, and not appropriated to Israel but devoted to the need of the dark Gentile world." The Apostle Paul was that outstanding ear late gathered. He was to be for a seed of blessing to the whole Gentile world. It might almost be said that he carried with him the power of that promise yet to be fulfilled to Israel: *"I will sow her unto Me in the earth"* (Hos. ii. 23). Under his ministry fields that ripened for a new harvest unto God sprang up everywhere among the Gentiles, where formerly no fruit had been; and thus even they who had been outcast and unclean became another new meat-offering consecrated unto the Lord. This was the thought in which the Apostle's soul rejoiced when he spoke of himself as the minister of Jesus Christ unto the Gentiles, ministering the Gospel of God, "that the offering up (ἡ προσφορα) of the Gentiles might be acceptable, being sanctified by the Holy Ghost." To us that blessing descends; we, too, through God's marvellous grace, become partakers of Israel's blessing, and are made, like them, a new meat-offering unto God. Through him the fountains of blessing that had been opened in Israel's land were caused to flow down unto the dark Gentile world. The Apostle's soul appreciated the blessing of his calling. It was his joy to

say, "Rejoice, ye Gentiles, with His people." [25] This
same very able expositor might well ask: "What if
the fields of Israel had never been whitened with the
Pentecostal harvest? Those precious stores of spiritual
food opened by the ministry of Jewish apostles would
in that case never have been ours. If they had never
preached the gospel of salvation as recorded in the Acts,
or ministered to the Churches those truths which we find
in their epistles, what would have become of us? Where
would have been our food?"

THE BLOWING OF TRUMPETS

The long gap—the prolonged period of silence—comes
to an end with the 1st of Tishri, the seventh or last month
in the sacred cycle, in the first twenty-one or twenty-two
days of which all the remaining great events in the prophetic calendar are crowded. *"And the Lord spake unto
Moses, saying, Speak unto the children of Israel, saying,
In the seventh month, in the first day of the month, shall
be a solemn rest unto you, a memorial of blowing of
trumpets, an holy convocation. Ye shall do no servile
work: and ye shall offer an offering made by fire unto
the Lord"* (Lev. xxiii. 23-25).

The "blowing of trumpets" was a great institution in
Israel, and was used:

1. For the calling together of special solemn assemblies;

2. As signals for the breaking up and journeys of the
camp;

3. As sound of alarm in time of danger;

4. And especially on new moons and the great festivals
when the trumpets were to be blown "over your burnt-

---

[25] "Thoughts on Scriptural Subjects."

offerings, and over your sacrifices of peace-offerings . . .
for a memorial before your God." [26]

Now there was no doubt a certain retrospective and
commemorative significance in this institution, reminding
Israel of the covenant relationship on which God had
entered with them at Sinai,[27] for it is interesting to observe that the first mention of the trumpet is in connection

---

[26] See the whole passage, Num. x. 1-10.

[27] The Synagogue has from ancient times observed the 1st of
Tishri as the New Year, that is the commencement of the Civil
Year, and asserts that thus the year began in the earliest times
long before the religious year, commencing with Nisan (Passover)
was instituted with the Exodus. Even Josephus (Ant. i. 3. 3)
asserts that while Moses appointed Nisan to be the first month
for the sacred festivals and solemnities, he preserved the original
order of the months for buying and selling, and for the transaction of other business. But there is no basis for all this in the
Old Testament.

The Rabbis really recognise four beginnings of the year from
different standpoints: (1) the 1st Nisan (first month) for *regnal*
dating; (2) the 1st Tishri (seventh month) as *agricultural* New
Year for the beginning of harvest; (3) the 1st Elul (sixth month)
for reckoning *tithes of the cattle* (Rabbi Eleazar, however, would
reckon these from the 1st of Tishri); and (4) the 1st, or, according to Bet Hillel, the 15th of Shebat (eleventh month) as *the
New Year for trees.*

The 1st Tishri is generally considered by the Rabbis as the beginning of creation, and the Mishna, which devotes a whole tractate to this feast called Rosh-ha-Shanah (New Year), speaks of it
especially as a day of judgment, when all the children of men pass
for judgment before the Creator, as sheep pass for examination
before the shepherd. Three books, says the Talmud, are opened on
Rosh-ha-Shanah before the Creator, wherein the fate of the wicked,
the righteous, and those of an intermediate class (not utterly
wicked) are recorded. The names of the righteous are immediately inscribed, and they are at once sealed to live (or "to life");
the middle class are allowed a respite of ten days till the Day of
Atonement, to repent and become righteous; whilst the wicked are
at once blotted out of the book of the living. For this reason the
ten intervening days are called "Terrible Days," and "Days of
Repentance."

with that solemn transaction when the signal was, *"When the trumpet soundeth long* they shall come up to the mount"; and again, *"And when the voice of the trumpet sounded long and waxed louder and louder* Moses spake, and God answered him by a voice" (Exod. xix. 13-19).

And to this commemorative sense the reference in the 81st Psalm—the special Psalm which in the ritual of the second Temple was used on the Feast of Trumpets—would seem to point.

> *"Blow up the trumpet in the new moon,*
> *At the full moon on our solemn feast-day,*
> *For it is a statute for Israel,*
> *An ordinance of the God of Jacob.*
> *He appointed it in Joseph for a testimony*
> *When He went out over the land of Egypt*
> *(Where) I heard a language that I knew not."*

But the object of it is expressly stated to have been "for a memorial, that they might be remembered before Jehovah," it being specially added, "I am Jehovah your God." "It was, so to speak, the host of God assembled, waiting for their Leader; the people of God united to proclaim their King. At the blast of the priest's trumpets they ranged themselves, as it were, under His banner, and before His throne, and this symbolical confession, and proclamation of Him as 'Jehovah their God' brought them before Him 'to be remembered' and 'saved.' " [28]

But it is of special importance to remember that the Feast of Trumpets stands at the head and in special relation to the solemn events which were coming on in this seventh or last month of the sacred cycle, even as the Passover stands at the head of the series of fulfilled "feasts" which begin in the first month and end with Pentecost.

---

[28] Edersheim.

"In Leviticus, the term 'memorial' does not anywhere mean the keeping in memory of a thing past. Many have erred from overlooking the sense of the term. It is, in fact, a ceremonial or tabernacle term, signifying something done in order to call attention to something yet remaining. It should be rendered 'a reminding' of something present, or of something just at hand, rather than 'memorial,' which suggests the past. In Hebrew the term is Zichron, from the same root as Ha-mazchirim (Isa. lxii. 6), 'Ye who are the remembrancers of the Lord,' reminding Him of what is to be done. So also Exod. iii. 15, 'This is My Name for ever, and My memorial' (zichri)—q.d., to remind My people of what I still am, and may be expected to do. So also Acts x. 4, 'Thy prayers and thine alms are come up for a memorial before God'—to remind Him what to do for thee. The word may in other connections call attention to the past, but the above is sufficient proof of its very usual sense in calling attention to things coming on and not yet actually arrived. It was in this sense that Maimonides understood this Feast of Trumpets. It awakened, he thought, the people to repentance, in prospect of the Day of Expiation." [29]

---

[29] Dr. Andrew Bonar, "Commentary on Leviticus."

In fact, the commentator of Maimonides makes use of the following words to denote the meaning of the blowing of trumpets: "Rouse ye, rouse ye, from your sleep, you who mind vanity, for slumber most heavy has fallen upon you. Take it to heart, before whom you are to give an account in the Judgment." "May not some such formula have been anciently used in the synagogue, and may not the remembrance of it have been present to the mind of the apostle when he wrote (Eph. v. 14), 'Awake, thou that sleepest, and arise from the dead, and Christ shall give thee light'? If so, we may possibly find an allusion to the appearance of the new moon, specially to that of the seventh month, in these words of one of the preceding verses: 'For ye were sometimes darkness but now are ye light in the Lord; walk as children of light.' "—Edersheim, "The Temple and its Ministry."

In connection with its future or prophetic significance it is important to bear in mind that the Feast of Trumpets was appointed for the 1st of the *seventh* month, and as the trumpet was blown on *every* new moon, it was really "the seventh trumpet" that was heard by Israel on that day. In brief, prophetically regarded, the Feast of Trumpets may be viewed as foreshadowing that "Day" when God shall break the long silence of this dispensation, and by manifest acts of His interposition call the attention of His Church and Israel, as well as of the nations, to the most solemn last events of the age, which, though characterised by most terrible judgments, shall culminate in the antitypical Feast of Tabernacles, when God's harvest, including the vintage, shall at last have been reaped and gathered, and when He, as undisputed Lord, shall be King over all the earth, and Jehovah shall be One, and His Name One (Zech. xiv. 9). And if I am asked what are the special future events which will be ushered in by the antitypical "Feast of Trumpets," I would mention particularly—

(*a*) The regathering of scattered Israel preparatory to the solemn events which shall issue in their national conversion in their own land, when "it shall come to pass in that day that a *great trumpet shall be blown,* and they shall come which were ready to perish in the land of Assyria, and they that were outcasts in the land of Egypt; and they shall worship Jehovah in the holy mountain at Jerusalem" (Isa. xxvii. 13).

(*b*) And this gathering of Israel nationally will be but the earthly counterpart of that other yet more stupendous and blessed event, which is the hope of the Church in the New Testament, when "He shall send His angels *with a great sound of a trumpet,* and they shall gather His elect from the four winds, from one end of heaven to the other" (Matt. xxiv. 31). Yea, when the *Lord Himself* shall descend from heaven with a shout, with the voice of the archangel, *and with the trump of God,* and the **dead** in Christ shall rise first: then we that are alive and **remain** shall be caught up together with them in the clouds **to** meet the Lord in the air, and so shall we be ever with the Lord" (1 Thess. iv. 16, 17).

The Day of Atonement

We now come to what must be regarded as the most solemn day in the whole sacred cycle.

"And the Lord spake unto Moses, saying, Howbeit on the tenth day of this seventh month is the Day of Atonement: it shall be an holy convocation unto you, and ye shall afflict your souls: and ye shall offer an offering made by fire unto the Lord. And ye shall do no manner of work in that same day; for it is a day of atonement to make atonement for you before the Lord your God. For whatsoever soul it be that doeth any manner of work in that same day, that soul will I destroy from among his people. Ye shall do no manner of work: it is a statute for ever throughout your generations in all your dwellings. It shall be unto you a Sabbath of solemn rest, and ye shall afflict your souls; in the ninth of the month at even, from even unto even, shall ye keep your Sabbath" (Lev. xxiii. 26-32, R.V.).

It is both impossible and unnecessary to enter here into the full significance of *"The Day,"* as the Rabbis have styled the Day of Expiation and "Cleansing" (Lev. xvi. 30), in order to distinguish it, and to emphasise its prominence and importance above all other days of the year. Every Christian who is at all instructed in the Word of God knows that the true Day of Atonement is the Day of Calvary, and that the sin-offerings which formed the centre of the whole solemn ritual, as described in the sixteenth chapter of this same book, received their true fulfilment when He who knew no sin was made sin for us, that we might be made the righteousness of God in Him; and that the entrance of the High Priest on that one day within the veil, "not without blood," was a type of our Lord Jesus Christ who "with His own blood" entered not into the holy places made with hands, which were only figures of the true, but into heaven itself, now to appear in the presence of God for us (Heb. ix.) ; [30] but it is noteworthy that in this sacred calendar which we are considering (Lev. xxiii.) it is not the sacrificial ritual and high-priestly service appointed for that day which are brought before us, but the *affliction of soul on the part of the people,* who are commanded to treat this day as "a Sabbath of Sabbaths," not, as in the case of the other holy convocations, to rejoice in their feast, but by withdrawing from all their ordinary avocations to give themselves up wholly to penitence and sorrow in immediate view of the Atonement which by God's gracious appointment was being accomplished for them. It must be borne in mind also that the Day of Atonement (or, literally, *Atonements, Yom Kippurim,* Lev. xxiii. 27), was a day for expiation and cleansing, not so much of the individual as of the people as a whole. It was Israel's *national* day of reconciliation, and hence points to an event in Israel's history yet unfulfilled and future.

"In common with the two other festivals of the seventh month," to use the words of an old writer, "the Day of Atonement is designed to shadow forth the future dealings of God with them, and will have its accomplishment in that day, when they shall *as a nation* be brought to repentance for their sins, and faith in the blood of the Lamb." Such a day of the affliction of their soul on a scale and in degree as never before is clearly indicated in the prophetic Scriptures, and synchronises with the day when

---

[30] In Chap. II. of this book, in the exposition of Psa. xxxii., the reader will find the solemn ceremonial of the Day of Atonement fully described.

"the iniquity of the land shall be removed in one day"
(Zech. iii. 9).

"And I will pour upon the house of David and upon
the inhabitants of Jerusalem the spirit of grace and supplication, and they shall look upon Me whom they have
pierced, and they shall mourn for Him as one mourneth
for his only son, and shall be in bitterness for him as one
that is in bitterness for his firstborn. *In that day there
shall be a great mourning in Jerusalem . . . every family
apart and their wives apart. In that day there shall be a
fountain opened to the house of David, and to the inhabitants of Jerusalem for sin and for uncleanness*" (Zech.
xii. 10-14; xiii. 1).

But, again, I may be asked, how can this be reconciled
with the statement that the true Day of Atonement is the
Day of Calvary, and was not the "fountain for sin and
uncleanness" opened when our Saviour was nailed to the
cross, and when the soldier with the spear pierced His
side and forthwith there came out blood and water?
Yes, my dear friend, but to the sinner actually and experimentally, the Day of Calvary is the day when his eyes
are opened to the true meaning *to himself* of the great
redeeming work there accomplished, and when the Spirit
of God *applies* Jesu's blood and righteousness and high-
priestly intercessions to his own need. Thus "in that day"
it will be with Israel nationally.

A simple illustration from the experience of Hagar
in the wilderness of Beer-sheba may help us to understand
this. When the water in her bottle was spent and she put
down the lad, as she thought, to die, she herself went to
a distance, and in the anguish of her spirit lifted up her
voice and wept. But God heard not only her voice but
the voice of the lad, and had pity on them. *"And God
opened her eyes, and she saw a well of water."* The well
was most probably there all the time, but her eyes, dimmed

by her very sorrow and tears, could not see it, and it was to her, as she was filling her skin bottle, as if the well had just sprung up. So it will be with Israel. The fountain for sin and for uncleanness has been opened in the wounds of their Messiah nineteen centuries ago, but "in that day" when the Spirit of grace and of supplication is poured out upon them as a nation, *the eyes of the blind shall be opened*" (Isa. xxxv.), and the Spirit of God will apply to their hearts and consciences as a people the great redeeming work accomplished on Calvary, and the words used in connection with the Day of Atonement shall receive a fulfilment as never before: *"For on this day He shall atone for you to cleanse you from all your sins; before Jehovah ye shall be clean"* (Lev. xvi. 30, Hebrew).

On that day the High Priest, as described fully in another part, entered twice within the veil—first, with the blood of the sin-offering for himself and his house, and then a second time with the blood of the goat of the people's sin-offering on which the lot fell "la-Yehovah"; and it was not till He came forth a second time, and the remaining part of the ceremonial was gone through, that the people could rejoice in the knowledge that atonement was fully accomplished, the whole of which, in this sense also, may be regarded as a figure of the work of Christ in relation to the Church and to Israel. For Himself, the Holy One needed not as the Aaronic priests to offer sacrifice, but for those who in this interval, and in a special sense, constitute His redeemed family, atonement is fully accomplished, not only as an objective fact, but as a blessed subjective reality; and in proof. that it is not only "finished," but accepted, the Great High Priest after His Resurrection showed Himself again, "but not to all the people" (Acts x. 41), but only to His own family of faith.

But in relation to Israel the High Priest may still be regarded as inside the veil, or in the Holy Place, and the people as "waiting without" marvelling that He tarries so long (Luke i. 10, 21), but soon He will come forth again, in the hour of their deepest sorrow and humiliation, to cleanse them before Jehovah, so that they shall be known and called in all the earth as "The holy people, The Redeemed of the Lord," that He may be glorified (Isa. lxii. 12).

Finally, "when the High Priest came forth from the sanctuary and appeared again unto the people, he first despatched the scapegoat bearing all their iniquities into the wilderness, and then united with them in offering the burnt-offering unto the Lord. And such shall be the result of the second advent of our Saviour. Then shall sin be completely put away, and every trace of it removed for ever. In one sense sin is already put away—it is no more imputed unto them who believe in Jesus; but sin itself remaineth, yea, and will remain, until He comes again. But then it shall be for ever banished, and all its consequences shall be removed for ever. Then *there shall be no more sin,'* nothing of it shall remain but the blessed consciousness that we are redeemed from its power and its curse. And then, too, *shall Jesus and His people unite to offer the burnt-offering unto God.* Then in the midst of His redeemed He shall head up all their pure and holy service; and blessed and consecrated by the presence of incarnate Godhead, the untiring energies of the redeemed people shall be for ever consuming, yet unconsumed, upon the altar of eternal love." [31]

It was on the evening also of the Day of Atonement, after the complete cycle of seven sevens of years were fulfilled, that the "Jubilee" was proclaimed (Lev. xxv. 9, 10), which was the signal of liberty, not only to the people but *for the land itself,* which that year was neither

---

[31] J. B. Lowe, B.A., "The Annual Festivals of the Jews."

to be ploughed, sown, nor reaped, the typical significance of which was already discerned by the prophets in the Old Testament, who rejoiced in spirit, and by faith greeted from afar the time when, after Israel's iniquity shall have been purged, Messiah will not only "proclaim liberty to the captives," [32] but when the earth itself shall at last enjoy her rest, and the whole creation, which has been groaning and travailing in pain together until now, shall at last be delivered from the bondage of corruption into the glorious liberty of the children of God.

THE FEAST OF TABERNACLES

We now come to the last of the "Solemn Assemblies" in the sacred cycle, "The Feast," as it is sometimes called (1 Kings viii. 2, and elsewhere), "the season of our joy," as it became known later in the Jewish liturgy, or, more significant still, the "Hag-Yehovah," *the Feast of Jehovah*, as it is emphatically called in the chapter we are considering (ver. 39).

Now primarily this was, above all the other feasts, the harvest festival of joy and thanksgiving, in celebration not only of the full ingathering of the "labours of the field," but also of the fruit and of the vintage, and is therefore pre-eminently styled "the Feast of Ingathering." [33]   It had, moreover, a clear retrospective or commemorative significance, as is plainly stated in the command that they should dwell in booths: "And ye shall take you on the first day the fruit of the goodly trees, branches of palm trees and boughs of thick trees, and willows of the brook, and ye shall rejoice before Jehovah your God seven days

---

[32] The very words used in Isa. lxi. 1 are taken from the command in reference to the Jubilee in Lev. xxv. 9, 10.

[33] Exod. xxiii. 16, xxxiv. 22 ; Deut. xvi. 13.

. . . ye shall dwell in booths seven days . . . *that your generations may know that I made the children of Israel to dwell in booths when I brought them out of the land of Egypt: I am Jehovah your God"* (vers. 40-43)—an ordinance well calculated indeed to keep alive in their mind the grateful remembrance of the God of Israel, who sustained them miraculously in the wilderness, and led them by the hand of Moses, Aaron, and Joshua safely into the promised land.

The Rabbis in later times regarded the *Sukkah* (tabernacle), in which they dwelt during the feast, as more especially symbolical of the cloud of glory which hovered over the Tabernacle, and which led and shielded Israel by day and illumined them by night in their forty years' wilderness wanderings,[34] but even the Mishna and the Talmud single out this feast from all the others as being of an *anticipative* or prophetic character, while Christian scholars and Bible students are in agreement that there is nothing in this dispensation to answer to the Feast of Tabernacles. No, its fulfilment is yet in the future, when, after Israel's national Day of Atonement shall have come to pass, and the nation which was destined of God from the beginning to be the channel of blessing to the world shall have been reconciled and cleansed, and equipped by the power of God to go forth on its mission of spreading the knowledge of their Messiah over the whole earth, the great "Feast of Ingathering" shall take place, and "all peoples" shall sit down to the "feast of fat things, yea, a feast of wines on the lees, of fat things full of marrow," which Jehovah of Hosts has prepared for them on Mount Zion.[35] And that this is no mere fanciful interpretation

---

[34] Orah Hayyim, 625, 1.

[35] Isa. xxv. "That these are not ideal comparisons, but the very design of the Feast of Tabernacles, appears not only from the

must be clear to every one acquainted with the writings of the prophets, in which there are so many allusions to this feast as to justify the observation of a true master in Israel that "the fulfilment of its types seemed to be the goal of all their desires."

But perhaps the most striking reference to the Feast of Tabernacles in the prophetic Scriptures is to be found in the prophecies of Zechariah. In the twelfth and thirteenth chapters of that book we have graphic predictions, which read almost like history instead of prophecy, of the solemn events which will accompany and follow Israel's restoration to their land, culminating, as I have already shown, in their great Day of Atonement—when the spirit of grace and of supplication shall be poured upon them, and they shall look unto Him whom they have pierced and mourn, and when the fountain shall be opened unto them for sin and for uncleanness. The blessed results of Jehovah's recognising them again as "My people," and their saying "Jehovah is my God" (Zech. xiii. 9), is to be seen in the fourteenth chapter, where it is proclaimed that "Jehovah shall be King over all the earth; in that day shall Jehovah be One and His Name One. . . . And it shall come to pass that every one that is left of the nations which came against Jerusalem *shall go up from year to year to worship the King Jehovah of Hosts and to keep the Feast of Tabernacles*"—for Jerusalem shall then be the metropolis of God's kingdom on earth, and the joy and blessedness foreshadowed by that feast shall, in the

---

language of the prophets and the peculiar services of the feast, but also from its position in the Calendar, and even from the names by which it is designated in Scripture. Thus in its reference to the harvest it is called 'Feast of Ingathering'; in that to the history of Israel in the past, the 'Feast of Tabernacles'; while its symbolic bearing on the future is brought out in its designation as emphatically *'the* feast,' and 'the Feast of Jehovah.' "—*Edersheim.*

millennial period, not only be the portion of saved Israel, but shall also pervade all the nations of the earth.

Though not part of the original Mosaic appointment, the ceremonial service for this feast which was in practice in the Temple, was also designed to point and emphasise its symbolic and prophetic significance. I will mention only two or three features of that ritual.

I. *Simchat-bet-ha-Sho'ebah*—literally, "Joy of the House of drawing . . . (the water)," or, the Ceremonial of the Water Libation.[36]

Every morning of the feast, while the morning sacrifice was being prepared, a joyous procession, accompanied by music, and headed by a priest bearing a golden pitcher, measuring just a little over two pints, made its way from the Temple courts to the Pool of Siloam. At the same time another procession went to the place in the Kedron valley called Moza, or Colonia, whence they brought willow branches, which they bound on either side of the altar of burnt-offering, "bending them over towards it so as to form a kind of leafy canopy."

Then the ordinary sacrifice proceeded, "the priest who had gone to Siloam so timing it that he returned just as his brethren carried up the pieces of the sacrifice to lay them on the altar. As he entered by the 'Water Gate,' which obtained its name from this ceremony, he was received by a threefold blast from the priests' trumpets." Amid great demonstrations of excitement and joy this water was poured into a silver basin, or tube, on the altar,

---

[36] Those of my readers who are able to read Rabbinic literature will find the ceremonial described fully both in the "Jerusalem" and Babylonian Talmuds, tractate Sukkah, and also in the Tosefta to Sukkah. To the general reader I would recommend Dr. Edersheim's "The Temple and its Ministry," where full descriptions are given.

simultaneously with the prescribed libation of wine, which was poured into another tube, the people shouting the while to the priest who was pouring the water, "Lift your hand," so that the assembled worshippers might be assured that the function had been properly performed, for Alexander Jannæus, the Maccabean King and High Priest, who held the views of the Sadducees on this subject, had shown his contempt of the Pharisees on one occasion by pouring the water on the ground instead of on the altar, for which he was pelted by the people with their etrogim (citrons), and might have lost his life but for the interposition of his foreign bodyguard, who on that occasion slaughtered 6,000 Jews in the Temple courts.

On the seventh day, called the "Hoshanna rabba," the great Hosanna, the joy and excitement of the people reached their climax. "The joyous crowds of worshippers on that day, seen from one of the flat roofs of Jerusalem overlooking the Temple area, would resemble a forest in motion, for all carried palm branches in their hands which were more than a man's height in length. Great silence would fall on the assembled throng as the choir of Levites commenced to sing the Hallel (the specially prescribed 'Praise' for the great festivals, consisting of Psalms cxiii.-cxviii.), to each line of which the people had to respond with 'Hallelujah.' Soon the whole crowd fell into order, and, led by the priests, marched in procession round the altar. Seven times they encompassed it. As the singers reached verses 25 to 29 of Psalm cxviii., and joined in the words, 'Anna Adonai [37] Hoshi'ah-na!' ('Hosanna—make Thy salvation now manifest, O Lord'), 'Anna Adonai Hatzlicha-na!' ('O Lord, send now prosperity!') the people waved their palm branches and accompanied the song

---

[37] The name "Jehovah" was not pronounced, "Adonai" (Lord) being substituted for it.

with loud exclamations of joy. And as they reached the words, 'Blessed is He that cometh in the Name of Jehovah,' the godly and spiritual among them would in their hearts greet the coming Messiah and King to whom they well new that these words applied." [38]   Indeed, the joy accompanying this ceremonial was so great that it became a proverb. "He that hath not seen *Simchat-bet-ha-Sho'-ebah,* the joy of the drawing (and the pouring) of the water hath not seen joy in his life."   Now, though the Rabbis attached a symbolic significance to the ceremonial in connection with the dispensation of the rain, the amount of which for the year they imagined was determined by God at this feast, and perhaps also a commemorative sense, as reminding them of the wonders God wrought for them in the wilderness in giving them water out of a rock, the main reference according to themselves, as already said, was to the future blessings to be bestowed on them in Messiah's time, and especially pointed to the pouring out of the Spirit; as is to be inferred from the singing by the multitude of Isa. xii. 3, and from the distinct statement in the Talmud (Jer. Sukkah V. also Tosefta Sukkah IV.). "Why is it called *Bet-ha-Sho'eba?* . . . Because of the pouring of the Holy Spirit, according to what is said: 'With joy shall ye draw water out of the wells of salvation.'"   Now, in a limited though very blessed degree this has already been fulfilled, for it was in reference to this ceremonial of the pouring of water that our Lord Jesus "on the last day—the great day of the feast"—stood and cried, saying, "If any man thirst let him come unto Me and drink. He that believeth on Me, as the Scripture hath said, out of his belly shall flow rivers of living water; and

---

[38] "The Ancient Scriptures and the Modern Jew," by David Baron. See also the chapter in this book "The Commencement of the Hallel."

this He spake of the Spirit which they that believed on Him were about to receive"; in accordance with which when once Jesus was glorified, on being raised from the dead and taken up to the right hand of God, the Spirit came down from heaven like a rushing mighty wind, and the Church of this dispensation was formed, every living member of which knows experimentally of the indwelling of this blessed heavenly Paraclete.

In its fulness, however, such a prophecy as Isa. xii. and the wonderful prediction of Joel: "And it shall come to pass afterward that I will pour out My Spirit *upon all flesh,*" shall only be realised subsequent to Israel's great national. Day of Atonement.   Then "the ransomed of Jehovah shall return, and come to Zion with songs and everlasting joy upon their heads; they shall obtain joy and gladness, and sorrow and sighing shall flee away" (Isa. xxxv. 10).   Then shall Israel nationally experience the truth of Christ's word, "But the water that I shall give him shall be in him a well of water springing up unto eternal life"; and then also "shall living waters go out from Jerusalem" for the quickening and refreshing of the whole world (Zech. xiv. 8).

Another feature in the Temple service of the Feast of Tabernacles also deserves mention because of its rich symbolic import.

At the conclusion of the first day of the feast the worshippers congregated in the Court of the Women, where a great illumination took place. Four huge golden lamps or candelabras were there, each with four golden bowls against which rested four ladders. Four youths of priestly descent ascended these with large pitchers of oil from which they filled each bowl. The old worn breeches and girdles of the priests served for wicks to these lamps. So great and brilliant was the light that, according to a saying, "there was not a court in Jerusalem that was not lit

up by it." Around these great golden burning lamps a
sacred dance took place, in which even the chassidim
(saints) and "the men of deed" or prominent leaders of
the people, with flaming torches in their hands danced
before the people, and sang before them hymns and songs
of praise. "The Levites also with harps, and lutes, and
cymbals, and trumpets, and instruments of music without
number, stood upon the fifteen steps which led down from
the Court of Israel to that of the Women, according to the
number of the fifteen 'Songs of Degrees' in the Book of
Psalms." [39]

Now this illumination too was regarded as of the same
twofold symbolic significance as the pouring of the water.
It reminded them of the past when God led them in the
wilderness with the cloud of glory and the pillar of fire—
of the Shekinah glory which dwelt in the first Temple, but
was, alas, already absent in the second; but it also, and
chiefly, was meant to remind them of the Messianic
promises in the future when the light of Jehovah should
arise upon their land and people.

Now this too, has in a partial degree, been already
fulfilled, for He who cried, "If any man thirst let him
come unto Me and drink," at this same feast, and in reference to this illumination, again spake unto them saying,
*"I am the Light of the world; he that followeth Me
shall not walk in darkness, but shall have the Light of
Life";* and since then hundreds of millions who have
heard His voice, and have followed in His steps, have had
their hearts and souls, their present and their future
eternity, illumined by His Gospel. But while this is so,
Israel, *as a nation,* still walks in darkness, and the other
peoples of the earth are still covered by the shadow of
death—until the Sun of Righteousness shall arise with

---

[39] Edersheim.

healing in His wings, and the word shall go forth: "Arise, shine, for thy light is come, and the glory of Jehovah is risen upon thee." Then *"nations,"* as nations, *"shall come to thy light;* and kings to the brightness of thy glory" (Isa. lx. 1-3), and the promise confirmed by the oath of Him who cannot lie shall be fulfilled—"As truly as I live, all the earth shall be filled with the glory of Jehovah" (Num. xiv. 21). The Feast of Tabernacles was the only one that had an octave, "the last and great day of the feast," the *Atzereth*—"conclusion," or *"crowning feast* of all the feasts of the year," as Philo, the Alexandrian, called it, on which Israel dwelt no longer in booths to remind them of the wilderness, but returned to their homes to rejoice there, and to begin, so to say, a cycle beyond the one of seven which they had just completed.

Now the eighth day in Scripture is the *Resurrection Day,* and points, I believe, to the Eternal Day, after the cycle of time in which the history of the earth, as set forth in the sacred Calendar of the History of Redemption shall have been finished—"when the *consummation* of earthly rest shall synchronise with the *commencement* of heavenly glory"—when a great voice out of the throne shall go forth, saying: *"Behold, the tabernacle of God is with men, and He shall dwell with them, and they shall be His people.* And God Himself shall be with them and be their God. And God shall wipe away every tear from their eyes, and there shall be no more death, neither sorrow, nor crying, neither shall there be any more pain, for the former things have passed away" (Rev. xxi. 1-8).

"Then," to conclude with the words of an old divine, "the mystery of the water which was poured upon the sacrifices shall be fulfilled, when He who is the Alpha and the Omega, shall proclaim, *It is done. I will give to him that is athirst to drink of the water of life freely.* Then He who, at the Feast of Tabernacles, invited sinners to come to Him and drink, shall lead His redeemed people *by living fountains of water, and make them drink of the river of His pleasures.* Then, too, the symbol of the palm branches shall be accomplished in the final victory of the redeemed over Death and Hades; and they shall realise the blessed fulfillment of the promise, 'He that overcometh shall inherit all things; and I will be his God, and he shall be My son.' Then, too, shall be *the Great Hosanna* when that great multitude which no man could number, out of all nations, and kindred, and people, and tongues 'shall stand before the throne of God, and *before the Lamb,* clothed with white robes, *and palms in their hands,*' and shall 'cry with a loud voice, saying, Salvation to our God which sitteth upon the throne, and unto the Lamb' " (Rev. vii. 9, 10).

ESSENTIAL IDEAS CONNECTED WITH ISRAEL'S FEASTS AND THEIR SPIRITUAL REALISATION IN THE NEW TESTAMENT

I cannot leave the glorious subject which we have been considering without adding a few simple, practical words on the spiritual application of the "Feasts of the Lord" to Christians, beyond what has already been unfolded in the course of our study.

The literal observance of these feasts, which Judaising teachers tried to introduce into the Christian Church, was a perversion of Christian truth, because they failed to perceive their highly symbolic and prophetic character as "shadows of good things to come," and it was to those who had been misled by such teachers that the Apostle wrote, *"I am afraid of you"* (Gal. iv. 10).

Even the observance, or non-observance, of special "Christian" days in commemoration of the various stages of Christ's redeeming work on earth, is dealt with in the New Testament as one of the non-essentials, with regard to which believers are exhorted patiently to bear without judging one another (Rom. xiv. 5, 6); but if we have, indeed, tasted and known that the Lord is gracious, and can say, "Even Christ our Passover is sacrificed for us," every day of our life ought to be characterised as the keeping of a feast. And if we want to know what is implied in the words, "Let us keep the feast," the answer will be found in the essential ideas underlying, not only the feast of Unleavened Bread, which in that passage was more particularly in the Apostle's mind, but all the feasts of Israel. I will only name two or three of the chief characteristics here as briefly as possible.

I. These feasts of Jehovah were, in the first instance, *seasons of rest.* In Exod. xii. 16 we read that "no manner of work" was to be done in them, which, in Lev. xxiii. 7, is explained as "no servile" (or *"slavish"*) work, *i. e.,* nothing implying hard toil, bondage, or degradation. That did not imply idleness or inactivity. No; God's demand from Pharaoh was, "Let My people go *that they may serve Me"* (Exod. viii. 1); and on their weekly Sabbaths and annual feasts they were to be set free from their ordinary occupations and engagements so as *to have leisure for God,* and attend to *His* worship and *His* service. This blessedness is to be ours now *all our life.* "Come unto Me, all ye that labour and are heavy laden, and *I will give you rest";* but not that we may henceforth be at leisure to please ourselves. No, *"take My yoke upon you,* and learn of Me, for I am meek and lowly in heart, and ye shall find rest unto your souls." He frees us from the bondage of sin and care, and gives us rest from our evil dispositions, that we may attain to the highest rest of fellowship with Him in suffering and service.

Let us, therefore, who believe, seek to enter more fully now into His rest, and we shall experience—yea, even in the midst of toil, and in spite of the strife of tongues, and

the tumult of the peoples by which we may be surrounded—that peace of God "which passeth all understanding."

"Him that is of a steadfast mind [or more literally,
'of a mind,' or 'spirit,' or 'disposition which *leans,*' *i. e.*,
on God] Thou wilt keep [or 'preserve'] in peace—peace,
because he trusteth in Thee" (Isa. xxvi. 3, Hebrew).

II. "Thou *shalt rejoice in thy feast,*" and not only so,
but the feast was to be a season of *all-pervading joy.*
"Thou shalt rejoice before Jehovah thy God, thou, and
thy son, and thy daughter, and thy manservant, and thy
maidservant, and the Levite that is within thy gates, and
the stranger, and the fatherless, and the widow, that are
in the midst of thee," ending up with the emphatic command, "Thou shalt *surely* [or more literally, 'Thou shalt
only'] rejoice" (Deut. xvi. 11-15).

There is a question asked in the Talmud why God
appointed Israel so many feasts, and the answer is, because God wanted His people to be a *joyous people.*
And if Israel under the old covenant was called to rejoice, how much more ought we to "keep the feast" in
this sense, who have been blessed of God with all spiritual
blessings in heavenly places in Christ Jesus, and to whom
the Man of Sorrows, who yet, in a special sense, was
"anointed with the oil of joy above His fellows," said, not
only, "Peace I leave with you," but also, "These things
have I spoken unto you that *My joy* might remain in
you, and that *your joy might be full*" (John xv. 11).
Therefore, "Rejoice in the Lord *alway;* again I say [or,
'I will always say,' it matters not what my or your outward
circumstances may be], *Rejoice*" (Phil. iv. 4).

III. But *rest* and *joy* are found only in His presence,
and in communion with Him, therefore at the three great
festivals (Passover, Pentecost, and Tabernacles) Israel
had to come up from whatever distant place in the land

they might dwell, and appear before Jehovah their God in the courts of His sanctuary in Jerusalem, which is meant to teach us that we can only find the fulness of joy in His presence, and true pleasures at His right hand, and that the feast of rest and blessedness can only be enjoyed if we dwell in His pavilion, and abide in the secret place of His presence.

IV. Finally, on these solemn occasions of joy they were "not to appear before the Lord empty, but *every man shall give as he is able, according to the blessing of Jehovah thy God which He hath given thee*" (Deut. xvi. 16, 17)—for the exhortation, "Eat the fat, and drink the wine, and *send portions to them for whom nothing is prepared*" (Neh. viii. 10), applies not only to Tabernacles but also to all other feasts. Indeed, the Rabbis connect the *joyousness* of the feast more particularly with the freewill offerings that each brought, and which were afterwards shared with the poor, the desolate, and the Levite in the joyous meal which followed the public services in the Temple, for God wanted to teach His people that the way to get the greatest amount of good and blessing from the gifts which He bestows upon them is to dedicate them back to Himself, and to seek to share them with others. And in this grace of generous *liberality* for the cause of God, and unselfishness to the poor, the Church of Christ has much to learn from Israel; and if Christians were awakened to the duty and privilege of giving "as they are able *according* to the blessing which Jehovah their God has bestowed on them," they themselves would be more joyous and blessed, and a great deal more would be accomplished for the glory of Christ, and the extension of His kingdom.

How beautiful was the spectacle of Israel's pilgrim bands carrying their first-fruits and their freewill offerings, in addition to all their prescribed tithes and sacrifices, on the occasion of their coming up for these annual festivals to the House of God. "First went one who played the pipe; then followed a sacrificial bullock, destined for a peace-offering, his horns gilt and garlanded with olive branches; next came the multitude, some carrying the baskets with the first-fruits, others singing the Psalms, which many writers suppose to have been specially destined for that service, and hence to have been called 'the Songs of Ascent': in our Authorised Version 'the Psalms of Degrees.' The poorer brought their gifts in wicker baskets, which afterwards belonged to the officiating priests; the richer theirs in baskets of silver or gold, which were given to the Temple treasury. In each basket was arranged, with vine leaves between them, first the barley, then the wheat, then the olives; next the dates, then the pomegranates, then the figs; while above them all clustered in luscious beauty, the rich swelling grapes. . . . As they reached the Temple Mount, each one, whatever his rank or condition, took one of the baskets on his shoulder, and they ascended singing that appropriate hymn, 'Praise ye Jehovah! Praise God in His sanctuary: Praise Him in the firmament of His power,' &c. As they entered the court of the Temple itself, the Levites intoned Psa. xxx.: 'I will extol Thee, O Jehovah, for Thou hast lifted me up, and hast not made my foes to rejoice over me,' &c. Then the young pigeons and turtle doves which hung from the baskets were presented for burnt-offerings. After that each one as he presented his gifts repeated this solemn confession: 'I profess this day unto Jehovah my God, that I am come unto the country that Jehovah sware unto our fathers to give us.' At these words he took the basket from his shoulder, and the priest put his hands under it and waved it; the offerer continuing: 'A Syrian ready to perish was my father, and he went down into Egypt, and sojourned there with a few, and became there

a great nation—great, mighty, and populous.' Then, re-
citing, in the words of inspiration, the narrative of the
Lord's marvellous dealings, he closed with the dedicatory
language of ver. 10: 'And now, behold, I have brought
the first-fruits of the land, which Thou, O Jehovah, hast
given me.' So saying he placed the basket at the side of
the altar, cast himself on his face to worship, and de-
parted. The contents of the baskets belonged to the
officiating priests, and the offerers were to spend the
night at Jerusalem." [40]

And we, too, must learn that giving to the Lord for His
cause, of that which He has first given to us, is *a joyous
privilege and a solemn act of worship,* and must be done,
(*a*) not on mere impulse, or in response to this or that
sensational appeal, but *deliberately,* "as he purposeth in
his heart"; (*b*) not haphazard, or spasmodically, but
methodically and *regularly,* "upon the first day of the
week," or other regular definite occasions; (*c*) not "spar-
ingly," or "grudgingly," but *proportionately,* "as God hath
prospered him," and *"bountifully"* that he may also reap
bountifully, and *joyously,* because "God loveth a cheerful
giver" (2 Cor. ix. 6, 7).

Perhaps the richest promise in the Old Testament and
the greatest promise in the New Testament are associated
with, and are conditional on the joyous spontaneous obedience to God in this matter of giving to Him for His cause.
The first is in Mal. iii. 10: "Bring ye all the tithes into the
storehouse, that there be meat in Mine house, and prove
Me now herewith, saith Jehovah of hosts, *if I will not
open you the windows of heaven, and pour you out a
blessing, that there shall not be room enough to receive it."*
But in the Hebrew there are only three little words

---

[40] Edersheim.

"ad-beli-dai"—for the last ten in the English translation just quoted, and they literally mean "till there is not enough," or "sufficient" (in heaven)—that is, all the infinite resources of heaven, all the treasure of God, will be opened to you in return for your poor gifts to Him. And the second promise is in 2 Cor. ix., where, after exhorting believers in this matter of unselfish, generous Christian liberality, the Apostle continues: "And *God is able to make all grace to abound toward you;* that ye, *always having all sufficiency in all things,* may abound unto every good work." Therefore, O Christian, while you "keep the feast," and "eat the fat and drink the sweet," forget not to "send portions to them for whom nothing is prepared," for so thine own joy and blessing shall be multiplied.

II

SIN AND FORGIVENESS—A DOCTRINAL AND EXPERIMENTAL VIEW

PSALM XXXII

"Blessed is he whose transgression is forgiven, whose sin is
 covered.
Blessed is the man unto whom the Lord imputeth not iniquity,
And in whose spirit there is no guile.
When I kept silence, my bones waxed old
Through my roaring all the day long.
For day and night Thy hand was heavy upon me:
My moisture was changed as with the drought of summer. Selah.
I acknowledged my sin unto Thee, and mine iniquity have I not
 hid:
I said, I will confess my transgressions unto the Lord;
And Thou forgavest the iniquity of my sin. Selah.
For this let every one that is godly pray unto Thee in a time
 when Thou mayest be found:
Surely when the great waters overflow they shall not reach unto
 him.
Thou art my hiding place; Thou wilt preserve me from trouble;
Thou wilt compass me about with songs of deliverance. Selah.
I will instruct thee and teach thee in the way which thou shalt
 go:
I will counsel thee with Mine eye upon thee.
Be ye not as the horse, or as the mule, which have no under-
 standing:
Whose trappings must be bit and bridle to hold them in,
Else they will not come near unto thee.
Many sorrows shall be to the wicked:
But he that trusteth in the Lord, mercy shall compass him about.
Be glad in the Lord, and rejoice, ye righteous:
And shout for joy, all ye that are upright in heart."

II

SIN AND FORGIVENESS [1]

THIS is the second of the so-called Penitential Psalms,[2] and is didactic, or *teaching*, in its character, but the precious "instruction" concerning the blessedness of "the forgiveness of sins according to the riches of His grace" has David's own experience for its foreground. Indeed, this Psalm is a notable example of doctrine merging itself into experience—even as the experience of inspired Psalmists, Prophets, and Apostles, is sometimes recorded for doctrine.

We all know the black chapter in David's history—that terrible fall which "gave occasion to the enemies of God to blaspheme" (2 Sam. xii. 14); and which not only landed him in many sorrows, but kept his soul for a whole year in the blackness of spiritual darkness.

To this day, men who are not sufficiently awake to the plague of sin in their own hearts are very ready in condemning David, forgetting that if David's sin was great, his repentance was indeed most deep and sincere, the proof of which is that he not only publicly confessed his sin, but in a sense goes on through the ages confessing

---

[1] The exposition of the first two verses of this Psalm appeared as an article in *The Christian* in March, 1901, under the title "Sin and Forgiveness—An Old Testament View," and was subsequently embodied in the valuable series of essays by different writers, called "Foundation Truths of the Gospel," published by Messrs. Morgan & Scott, Ltd., in separate volume. The exposition of the whole of the thirty-second Psalm is now written out for the first time.

[2] The other six so-called Penitential Psalms are Psa. v.; xxxviii.; li.; cii.; cxxx.; and cxliii.

it with tears and anguish of spirit, *by the record which he himself has left us of it.*

But out of the abyss of spiritual darkness into which David had fallen by his sin, he emerged again with some precious treasures, for which the whole Church, from generation to generation, has had occasion to bless God.

One of these treasures is the fifty-first Psalm, which was written in the very midst of his penitential struggle, and expresses his anguish of soul, and his longing that the face of God, which was averted on account of his sin, may again be lifted upon him, and that the joy of God's salvation may be restored unto him.

"Cast me not away from Thy Presence:
And take not Thy Holy Spirit from me.
Restore unto me the joy of Thy salvation,
And uphold me by Thy free [or 'willing' or 'abundant'] Spirit.
Then will I teach transgressors Thy ways;
And sinners shall be converted unto Thee."

Now in this thirty-second Psalm, which is the first of the thirteen Psalms which bear the inscription of *Maschil, "for instruction"* or "to make wise," David fulfills the vow contained in the last two lines of the quotation from the fifty-first just made. It comes next in order, and though it goes back upon that terrible experience when the great transgression was still rankling in his conscience, and life itself became unbearable because day and night God's hand was heavy upon him, has for its chief aim the setting forth of the blessedness of deliverance when, having confessed his sin to the prophet, God commissioned Nathan to say, "The Lord hath put away thy sin; thou shalt not die" (2 Sam. xii. 13).

Our Psalm begins with a beatitude: *"Ash'rey"*—literally "Oh, the happinesses," or "the blessednesses," for the word is in the plural.

Even so did the first Psalm begin; but there the blessedness of the man is celebrated who has never strayed from the fountain of life, but has ever found his delight in Jehovah and in His holy law.

Alas! whatever David might have thought before, he knows now that the blessedness of the ideally perfect man cannot be realised by a child of Adam who is born in sin and "shapen in iniquity."

That path of absolute innocence was only trodden by the Messiah, the ideally righteous man of the Psalms, who has therefore the pre-eminence of blessedness by being "anointed with the oil of joy above His fellows." But by God's mercy there is still a way to blessedness open even to fallen and sinful men like David, namely, a new and living way, sprinkled by the blood of a Redeemer, and leading to spiritual blessings in heavenly places which even unfallen Adamic perfection could never have secured.

Sin and Atonement

The first two verses set forth the great facts of sin and atonement from an objective point of view.

First, let us look at the three words used to describe the terrible malady of sin. They are—

(a) *Pesha*—"*transgression*," rendered in the Septuagint by *anomia*, "lawlessness," and meaning literally *rebellion*—the breaking away from God, expressed by a defiance of His will and authority as revealed in His holy law.

(b) *Chataah*—"*sin*," which describes an erring from the mark, "a violation of the Eternal Rule of Right," a deviation from the path of well-pleasingness to God.

(c) *Avon*—"*iniquity*," describing the inward perversion of our nature; the depravity of our being manifesting itself in misdeed.

These three words are found in all the great Scriptures
dealing with the foundation doctrines of sin and atonement, and they are the three attributes of that deadly
moral plague the roots of which are in the heart of every
human being.

And the Scriptural doctrine of the universality of sin
is amply confirmed by experience. "Whether we look
north or south, east or west, without or within," admits
a rather broad Anglican theologian, "we see evil. If we
say, as some have foolishly said, that it is the growth of
civilisation, that it would not be found in man if he were
but in a state of nature; if we resolve to fly from civilised
society, and take the wings of the morning, and abide in
the uttermost parts of the savage wilderness, even there,
whatever and whoever we may see will bear the scar and
mark of evil, like the mark which was set upon Cain.
If, on the other hand, we fancy, as others have no less
foolishly fancied, that evil springs wholly from ignorance,
and that the laws of man, and the arts of man, and the
craft of man, will be able to overcome and get the better
of it, then we need only turn our eyes towards those
nations which have made the greatest advance in knowledge; and we shall find that, so far as that advance has
been made by man and by human means only, while men
have advanced in knowledge, they have also advanced in
wickedness, and gone on devising new vices and abominations before unheard of! How evil came into the world we
know not; but that it is there, we all of us know far too
well."

At first our conscience becomes awakened perhaps to
the guilt of some *act* of transgression, but as the terrible
question presses itself more and more upon our attention
we are finally landed in the painful conviction that behind
the isolated *acts* of transgression, and the *manifestations*

of sin, there is *"iniquity"*—the natural depravity of our being—"the taint of sin in our hearts, which runs through all our thoughts and feelings, through all our words and deeds."

"O wretched man that I am! who shall deliver me from the body of this death?"

And yet the Psalm begins with "Oh, the blessednesses!" for already David had experienced the grand doctrine propounded by the Apostle that "where sin abounded, *grace did over-abound.*"

As there are three words used, in the first two verses of our Psalm, to give us a complete view of sin, so there are also three terms used to describe God's method in forgiving sin, "according to the riches of His grace."

(*a*) *Nasa.*—This is the first of the three words used, and is rendered in the Authorised Version "forgiven," but which means "borne away."

(*b*) *Kasah.*—"To cover, to hide," as with a covering, "so that it becomes invisible to God, the Holy One, and is as though it had never taken place."

(*c*) *Lo-chashav.*—"Not reckoned, or not imputed," cancelling the account, because it has already been paid.

These three terms are full of significance, but they can only be properly understood in the light of the solemn transactions on the Day of Atonement, as described in Lev. xvi., *to which they all refer.*

Without entering on a description of the elaborate ceremonial of that great day in the Jewish year, we may just glance at that part of the ritual which was connected with the sin-offering.

There were two sin-offerings on that day.

First, after careful preparation by repeated bathing and washings, the High Priest, having exchanged his

garments of glory and beauty—in which he had offered
the usual morning sacrifice of a lamb—for the simple
linen robes prescribed for the occasion (Lev. xvi. 4),
came down into the inner court, where *his own sin-offering,* a young bullock, stood facing south, but his head
turned westward toward the Holy of Holies. Leaning
both his hands upon it, he made the following confession:
"Oh, Jehovah, I have committed iniquity; I have transgressed, I have sinned, I and my house. Oh, then, Jehovah, I entreat Thee, let there be atonement for the
iniquities, the transgressions, and the sins which I have
committed, transgressed and sinned before Thee, I and
my house, even as it is written in the law of Moses, Thy
servant: 'For on this day shall atonement be made for
you to cleanse you; from all your sins shall ye be clean
before the Lord.' "

Then the High Priest turned to *the people's* sin-offering
(Lev. xvi. 5-10).

This consisted of two kids of the goats. Placing himself by the north side of the altar, and in full view of the
throng of worshippers who attended in the outer court,
one of the goats was placed at his right hand, and the
other at his left hand. Two small tablets of gold were
cast into an urn, on one of which was engraven the word
"la-Yehovah" (for Jehovah), and on the other the mysterious word "la-Azazel" (for Azazel). The urn was
shaken, and the High Priest thrust both his hands in at
the same time, taking up one lot in each, and placing the
one in his right hand on the head of the goat at his right,
and the one in his left hand on the head of the goat at
his left.

In order to prevent the two goats from being exchanged,
a crimson band was tied round the head of the one on
which the lot fell for Azazel, and it was placed facing the

eastern gate, through which it was afterwards to be led forth in full view of the people.[8]

After the lot of the two goats had been thus fixed, the High Priest once more returned to his own sin-offering, and laying his hand a second time on the bullock, repeated the confession already recorded; only including in it this time, "the sons of Aaron the people of Thy holy things." He then killed the bullock and caught his blood in a basin, which he gave to one of the attending priests to keep stirring while he ascended the altar of burnt-offering and took a censer full of glowing coals (Lev. xvi. 11-14). Taking the censer in his right hand and sweet incense in his left, he reverently entered the Holy Place.

"Every eye was strained towards the sanctuary as slowly, bearing the censer and the incense, the figure of the white-robed High Priest was seen to disappear. After entering the Holy Place nothing further could be seen of his movements. The curtain of the Most Holy Place was folded back, and the High Priest stood alone and separated from all the people in the awful gloom of the Holiest of All, only lit up by the red glow of the coals in the priest's censer. He now most carefully emptied the incense into his hand and threw it on the coals of the censer, as far from himself as possible, and so waited till the smoke had filled the Most Holy Place." [4]

Then, retreating backwards, he uttered a short prayer outside the veil, the form of which, as used in the second Temple, is preserved in the Talmud.

---

[8] The ritual here described was that in practice in the second Temple, but in all its essential features, especially as far as the sin-offering was concerned, as described in Lev. xvi., the same order was doubtless observed in the ritual of the Tabernacle.

[4] Edersheim.

But he was not to prolong the prayer, lest his protracted absence should alarm the people and cause them to fear that he had been smitten before the Lord.

At last they saw him reappear from the Holy Place, and they knew that his service had been accepted.

Advancing rapidly, he took from the attendant the vessel with the blood of the bullock, and once more entered into the Most Holy Place, where he sprinkled it once upwards and seven times downwards, so that it fell upon and before the mercy-seat.

Leaving this basin with the blood before the veil, in the Holy Place, he emerged again and killed the goat of the people's sin-offering, upon which the lot fell "la-Yehovah," and did with its blood exactly as he did with the blood of the bullock. Then retreating from the Most Holy Place for the last time on this most solemn day, he deposited the basin with the blood of the goat, and took up that with the blood of the bullock, and sprinkled again once upward and seven times downward toward the veil, outside the Most Holy Place, in the same manner as he had done inside. Then putting down this vessel, he took up the one with the blood of the goat, and did the same. He then mixed the blood of the two sacrifices, pouring it repeatedly from one basin into the other, and with it he sprinkled each of the horns of the altar of incense, and seven times on the top of that altar.

The rest of the blood was poured out at the foot of the altar of burnt-offering.

Thus was "atonement" made. But we note that the Hebrew word *Kaphar*, which is rendered "to atone" in English, means properly *"to cover,"* and the essential idea connected with "atonement" as far as this word is concerned, is the *covering* or *hiding* of sin from the Holy One, who is otherwise "of purer eyes than to behold evil," without visiting it with death and judgment. To the question as to *how* alone sin can be effectually covered from the sight of the offended Majesty of the Holy God, the Book of Leviticus supplies the answer. There we read: "The life of the flesh is in the blood, and I have given it to you upon the altar to make a covering for your souls, *for it is the blood which with the life (that is in it) covereth*" (Lev. xvii. 11, Hebrew)—that is, life covereth life; the life of the innocent offering, in the blood poured out upon the altar, covereth the life forfeited by the guilty offerer. It is only in view of the altar, and what it signifies, that man can know "the blessedness of the one *whose sin is covered.*"

But, secondly, to return to the sixteenth of Leviticus, after "atonement" had been thus made with the blood of the goat on which the lot fell "for Jehovah," the High Priest came to the goat on which the lot fell "for Azazel," and "Aaron," we read, "shall lay both his hands upon the head of the live goat, and confess over him all the iniquities of the children of Israel, and all their transgressions, in all their sins, putting them upon the head of the goat, and shall send him away by a man that is in readiness into the wilderness. *And the goat shall bear upon him* all their iniquities unto a solitary land, and he shall let go the goat into the wilderness" (Lev. xvi. 20-22). The exact form of the confession as used by the High Priest in the time of the second Temple was as follows: "Oh, Jehovah! they have committed iniquity: they have sinned—Thy people, the house of Israel. Oh, Jehovah, atone for the iniquities, transgressions, and sins which Thy people, the house of Israel, have wickedly committed, transgressed, and sinned before Thee, as it is written in the law of Moses Thy servant: 'For on this day shall atonement be made for you to make you clean from all your sins, before Jehovah ye shall be clean.' "

Each time the name of Jehovah was mentioned by the High Priest in the course of his own confessions over the bullock, or in the confession for the people over the goat, the worshippers near him fell on their faces, while those farther off cried, "Blessed be the Name of the glory of His Kingdom for ever and ever!"

This last time, while the prostrate multitudes worshipped at the mention of the Name, the High Priest turned his face toward them as he uttered the last words, *"ye shall be clean"*—as if to "declare to them the absolution and remission of their sins."

It was most probably on the evening of the Day of Atonement, in full view of the solemn transaction he had just witnessed, that the sweet Psalmist of Israel, overwhelmed with awe and gratitude in thus realistically seeing, as it were, his own burden lifted from off him, was inspired to give utterance to the feeling of the worshipping multitude in the exclamation, "Oh, how blessed is the man whose transgression *is borne away* (as if he actually saw the sin-laden goat being led past him), *whose sin is covered"* (referring to the "covering" made by the shedding of the blood of the other goat [5]). "Oh, how blessed is the man unto whom Jehovah imputed not iniquity (because it has been 'put upon the head' of the sin-bearer, Lev. xvi. 21), and in whose spirit there is no guile"—who no longer "attempts to cloke his sins, or stifle conscience by sophistications," but has honestly faced "iniquity, transgression, and sin" in all their heinousness in the sight of the Holy God, and has found full forgiveness in His own appointed way.

Need I remind any one of my readers that the antitype of all the sacrifices is Christ, and that the true Day of Atonement was the day of Calvary?

---

[5] The words "Kaphar" and "Kasah" are cognate.

Oh, it is *in Him* that "we have redemption through His blood, the forgiveness of our sins according to the riches of His grace."

It is interesting to observe that the Messiah is regarded not only by the Apostles, but already by the Prophets in the Old Testament, as the One to whom the Levitical sacrifices and the Mosaic ordinances pointed.

The scripture in the Prophets parallel to the sixteenth of Leviticus is the fifty-third of Isaiah.

It, too, is a great atonement chapter, where "iniquity, transgression, and sin" stand out in all their horrid moral ugliness, and are being dealt with; only here Jehovah Himself takes, as it were, the place of the High Priest, and His righteous servant the Messiah, whose moral spotlessness is attested by the fact that "He had done no violence, neither was deceit found in His mouth," takes the place of the people's "sin-offering."

There are several allusions to the solemn transactions on the Atonement Day in the fifty-third of Isaiah, but in the twelfth verse there is a direct reference to the twofold aspect of atonement as set forth in the two goats.

"He," we read, "poured out His soul unto death, and was numbered [or 'reckoned'] with transgressors; and He bare the sin of many."

"He poured out His soul unto death," for, like the goat on which the lot fell "la-Yehovah," He was "led to the slaughter" and "cut off" by a violent death from the land of the living, in order by His precious blood to provide "a covering" for the sins of His people; but He also *"bare the sin of many,"* like the live goat in Lev. xvi. 22, whence the very word is taken, because, just as the High Priest put upon the head of that goat "the iniquities of the children of Israel and all their transgressions in all their sin," so "Jehovah laid upon Him the iniquity of us all," making Him, the Holy One, who knew no sin, to be sin

for us, and counting Him as a "transgressor," in order
that we might be made the righteousness of God in Him.

And the very figure is carried over from the pages of
the Old into the New Testament:

"Behold the Lamb of God *which beareth* the sin of the
world."

"Who His own self *bare* our sins in His body up to
the tree, that we, having died unto sin, might live unto
righteousness; by whose stripes we are healed."

The Doctrine Illustrated from David's Own Experience

But David proceeds next to illustrate the doctrine of
the forgiveness of sins, according to the riches of God's
grace, which he had set forth in the first two verses, from
his own personal experience. First he takes a step backward and tells us of the awful miseries which he endured
while the great transgression was lying heavily on his
conscience, and stood out as an iron wall of partition between him and his God:

> *"When I kept silence my bones waxed old ['wasted away' or*
> *'rotted'],*
> *Through my roaring all the day long.*
> *For day and night Thy hand was heavy upon me;*
> *My moisture was changed as with [or 'into'] the drought of*
> *summer. Selah."*

"For wickedness," says Isaiah, "burneth as the fire";
and here we get a glimpse of the terrors of a sin-burdened
conscience which can speak loud enough in self-condemna-
tion while the lips are constrained and "silent" before
God.

It has been well said that "he who will not speak his
sin to God has to groan. A dumb conscience often makes
a loud-voiced pain.

"This man's sin had indeed missed its aim; for it had brought about three things: rotting bones (which may be but a strong metaphor or may be a physical fact); the consciousness of God's displeasure dimly felt as if a great hand were pressing him down; and the drying up of the sap of his life as if the fierce heat of summer had burned the marrow in his bones.

"These were the fruits of pleasant sin, and by reason of them many a moan broke from his locked lips. Stolid indifference may delay remorse, but its serpent fang strikes sooner or later, and then strength and joy die." [6]

We can imagine David terrified by the thought of the terrible threatenings of Divine judgments against sinners as they occur in the law; and he had an example before him of the severity of God against sin and disobedience in the fall of Saul and of his family, but his greatest torments were doubtless occasioned by the hiding of God's face from him, for in spite of his awful sin and guilt he was God's servant, to whom the loss of His Presence and favour was as death itself.

This doleful experience is marked off by a *"Selah"* which in the ritual use of the Psalter in the Temple worship probably indicated not only that it marked a pause, but was intended to give the singers an opportunity to stop and meditate, while an interlude by those who accompanied with musical instruments gave solemn emphasis to the words just uttered. Here, as Delitzsch observes, the *"Selah"* indicates that while the singers pause "the music breaks in, and does what it can to represent the hell anguish of an awakened conscience *not* accompanied by a broken heart."

But the sweet Psalmist hastens on to instruct us out of his own experience that the only way out of this

---

[6] Dr. Alexander Maclaren.

anguish is by a sincere and unreserved confession of our sin to God:

> *"I acknowledged ['made known'] my sin unto Thee,*
> *And mine iniquity have I not hid.*
> *I said, I will confess my [or 'concerning my'] transgressions*
>   *unto Jehovah;*
> *And Thou forgavest the iniquity of my sin. Selah."*

"He that covereth his transgressions shall not prosper; but whoso confesseth and forsaketh them shall obtain mercy" (Prov. xxviii. 13).

"If we say that we have no sin [or if we 'hide' our sin], we deceive ourselves, and the truth is not in us; but if we confess our sins, He is faithful and just to forgive us our sins, and to cleanse us from all unrighteousness" (1 John i. 8, 9).

What an apparently simple process, yet what a wonderful and far-reaching transaction is recorded in these words! Blessed indeed is the point in the sinner's experience when he is brought to say, "I will confess," and to see the folly of trying to "hide" away his iniquity and shame from the all-seeing eye of God or his own conscience; but such a resolution presupposes faith in God as He has been pleased to reveal Himself, namely, a God full of compassion and gracious, slow to anger and plenteous in goodness and truth . . . *forgiving iniquity and transgression and sin,* and who, although "by no means clearing the guilty," has Himself devised a way by which sinners may return and live.

But it must have been infinitely more difficult, as Hengstenberg observes, "under the Old Testament dispensation, to rise to this confidence than it is now under the New, where we behold the compassion of God in Christ, and are taught to regard Christ's merits as the cause of our justification. If *we* hesitate to take refuge in the forgiving grace of God, we shall be much more guilty than David was before his confession."

And it is *"unto Thee,"* O Lord, that confession must be made, even as it is *"Thou, even Thou,"* who alone canst forgive my sin apart from all human mediators, or the intervention of so-called "saints" or angels; for Thou art accessible to every broken heart, and truly contrite spirit, and art a God ever ready to hear and to pardon. But when David speaks of a making known or confessing of his sin, it is obvious that it is not only of a confession with the lips or mouth that he speaks, but "of an *inward* confession such as is accompanied with painful repentance and sorrow, with begging of pardon for sin, and for the offence rendered to the Divine Majesty. Mary Magdalene did not utter one word; she wept and spoke with the heart." [7]

David, indeed, openly confessed to Nathan, saying, "I have sinned against Jehovah"; but, as has been well observed, "though Nathan's parable was the *occasion* of David's confession, yet it could not have produced its effect so instantaneously, had not David previously in his own mind arrived at the very threshold of repentance. Till this crisis was reached Nathan received no Divine commission to appeal to the King's conscience; but that appeal once made, the long pent-up feeling of contrition burst into unreserved confession." It is that which his heart had already uttered with painful contrition before God, that his mouth now spoke to God's prophet, who was sent to him on the special errand, and it is therefore that Nathan was instantaneously commissioned with the comforting assurance, "Jehovah also hath put away thy sin; thou shalt not die" (2 Sam. xii. 13).

---

[7] Johann Arndt, quoted by Hengstenberg.

It is interesting to note that in this verse we have again all the three great words for sin as in the first two verses, though in different order—"sin"—"transgression"—"iniquity."

There is also a threefold mention of the act of confession—"I acknowledged" ("made known")—"I will confess"—"I hid not"—corresponding to the threefold designation of forgiveness in those first verses, but all this is to show how completely his experience answers to the doctrine there set forth, and that if we *fully* confess God will *fully* pardon.

The word translated "hid" in this verse is also the same as rendered "covered" in the first verse, and shows the difference between man trying to "cover" his own sin— an attempt made already in the Garden of Eden (Gen. iii. 7, 8), but which has never "prospered" (Prov. xxviii. 13), and the Divine method of covering sin by atonement as already shown.

"Let God cover thy wounds," said Augustine; "do not thou. For if thou wish to cover them being ashamed, the Physician will not come. Let *Him* cover; for by the covering of the Physician the wound is healed; by the covering of the wounded man the wound is concealed. And from whom? From Him who knoweth all things." Or as another has said: "He only has his sins covered who does not himself cover them. Forgiveness of sin from God is in proportion to the confession of it to Him." [8]

Another *"Selah"* marks off this experience, and here it is "the antithesis of the one which stands at the end of verse 4." "There we have a shrill lament over the sinner who tortures himself in vain, here the clear tones of joy at the blessed experience of one who pours forth his soul

---

[8] Quoted by de Burgh.

to God—a musical Yea and Amen to the great truth of justifying grace." [9]

But forgiveness of sins brings with it a sense of security in God, and full assurance of deliverance from sin and trouble. And in this further truth—this higher step in the blessedness of a saved man—this *Maschil* Psalm proceeds to instruct us:

> *"For this* [*or 'because of this' or 'for this reason'*] *let every one that is godly pray unto Thee in a time when Thou mayest be found;*
> *Surely when the great waters rise* [*or 'when great floods come'*] *They shall not reach him."*

It is on the ground of his own experience of God as the gracious One who is ready to forgive that David bases his exhortation, for the words *al-zoth* mean not *"for* this," as expressing the contents of the petitions, but *"because* of this" or "for this reason"—*i. e.,* Let my experience just related in verse 5 serve as an example and encouragement to others to pray. And who is it that is here exhorted to seek from God the blessing of forgiveness? Not the godless or hardened, but the *chassid*—the godly one, or "one who is a recipient of God's favour, and tenderly loves God in return." Yes, even God's beloved or "favoured ones" have need to ask for forgiveness—for renewed pardon; for more strength against sin and temptation day by day, even though they may not have fallen into any such gross sin as David. Nor let it be thought that a dead sense to sin and to the evil bias in our nature is a true mark of holiness; on the contrary, the holiest of God's saints have been characterised by the keenest and deepest sense of sin, for the more we dwell in the full and unsullied light of His Presence, with whom

---

[9] Delitzsch.

"there is no darkness at all," the more do we see, not only His absolute purity and perfection, but the deep-seated corruption in our flesh which can only be kept down by His grace and the power of His indwelling Spirit. But let every "godly one" pray for forgiveness and power over sin, and he shall find his very prayer a means in God's hand of delivering him from it.

And let him pray *l'-eth-metso,* "in a time of finding," which as the phrase stands may be taken, as by some writers, to refer to the time of finding or discovering of the sin and the guilt in our hearts, but it is, I think, more satisfactory to regard it as an idiomatic equivalent to the expression "while He may be found." Every time of true seeking by prayer in the spirit is "a time of finding," but as has been observed, "the phrase implies *that there is a time of not finding,* and in its very graciousness is heavy with warning against delay." [10] "The time when God, according to the sure promise, may be found, is the time previous to the *infliction* of that punishment which invariably follows sin unless averted by forgiveness." The expression "at a time of finding" corresponds exactly to "ere the decree is executed," "ere the day of the wrath of the Lord comes upon you"—it is the space between the sin and the punishment, the day of grace which is designed to lead the sinner to repentance." [11]

But in a more general sense it stands for the day or dispensation of grace. Such was the former dispensation to Israel, as their prophet Isaiah says to them, chap. lv. 6, "Seek ye the Lord *while He may be found;* call ye upon Him while He is near." And such is the present more eminently—"an acceptable time" and "day of salvation," as the Apostle terms it (2 Cor. vi. 2)—when (as he there,

---

[10] Maclaren.
[11] Hengstenberg.

in the capacity of the ambassador of Heaven, announces), "God is in Christ reconciling the world to Himself, not imputing their trespasses unto them," and we see the grace and love of God revealed as did not David: so that if we refuse to be "reconciled to God," or "receive the grace of God in vain" so ministered to us, we shall be deserving of far greater condemnation than the unbelieving or impenitent of that day.[12]

And one who thus by prayer seeks and finds God, and experiences the blessedness of forgiveness, has no more need to fear the coming judgments—*"Surely when the great waters rise,"* or *"when the floods come"*—a figure for the overflowing of the Divine judgments which shall overspread the earth, in the day of judgment and perdition of ungodly men, as of old the deluge—*"they shall not come nigh unto him,"* for "the penitent, praying, pardoned man is set as on a rock islet in the midst of the flood, whether these be conceived of as temptation to sin, or as calamities." From the mental view of the overwhelming floods of God's judgments which will surely overtake all those who do not know experimentally the blessedness of transgression borne away and sin covered, the Psalmist, reminded of what he has been delivered from, expresses anew his confidence in Jehovah:

> *"Thou art my hiding place;*
> *Thou wilt preserve me from trouble;*
> *Thou wilt compass me about with songs of deliverance. Selah."*

This is a confirmation from David's own experience of the statement in the previous verse that a man who has made sure that his sins are forgiven "for His Name's sake" is at the same time delivered from danger and judgment.

------

[12] De Burgh.

"Thou art my hiding place," or, as he confidently sings in the twenty-seventh Psalm:

"For in the day of trouble He shall keep me secretly in His pavilion.
In the court [or 'secret place'] of His tabernacle shall He hide me.
He shall lift me up upon a rock."

"Thou art my hiding place," and in that great day of the Lord of hosts, when the proud and impenitent shall flee *from* Thee and seek to hide themselves in the dens and in the rocks of the mountains, saying to the mountains and rocks, "Fall on us and hide us from the face of Him that sitteth on the throne and from the wrath of the Lamb"—*Thou Thyself* wilt be the Refuge of Thy people; and because I have already confidence by Thy grace to approach Thee now, I will fly *to* Thee to hide myself in Thee, "until the indignation be overpast."

"Thou art *my* hiding place," or, as it is more forcefully expressed in the Hebrew, "Thou art a secret place of shelter *to me."* Need I remind you, dear reader, that there is all the difference in the world between knowing God as *a* hiding place and knowing Him as *our very own* hiding place? "Suppose a traveller upon a bleak and exposed heath to be alarmed by the approach of a storm. He looks out for shelter. But if his eye discern a place to hide him from the storm, does he stand still and say, 'I see there is a shelter, and therefore I may remain where I am'? Does he not betake himself to it? Does he not run, in order to escape the stormy wind and tempest? It was *a* 'hiding place' before; but it was *his* hiding place only when he ran into it and was safe."

"Thou shalt preserve me from trouble." The word *tzar* is frequently used of the "tribulation" at the time of the end, as, for instance, in Deut. iv. 30; Jer. xxx. 7; Psa. l. 15; cxviii. 5, &c. But though the seventh verse of the thirty-second Psalm anticipates that great "day," the expression here must be taken in the more general sense as applicable to God's people at all times. It is true we may not always be delivered *from* the trouble, but, blessed be God, there is such a thing as being delivered *in* it, and to receive for an answer, "My grace is sufficient for thee" (even with the thorn in thy flesh), "for My strength is made perfect in weakness." In view of the relation of the sufferings of this present time "to the glory which shall be revealed in us" by and by, we do not always know which is the greater deliverance—whether to have God specially near and present with us in the trouble (Psa. xci. 15), or to have it removed from us. But He knoweth our frame and remembers the weakness of our flesh, and graciously permits us to ask that, "if it be possible," the cup of suffering may pass from us, though, in the power of His Spirit, we too should ever be ready to add, "Oh, my Father, if this cup may not pass from me, Thy will be done." And He will deliver us, if not by removing the burden, by sending an angel from heaven to strengthen us to endure it, so that we shall be able all the more to glorify Him.

But whether delivered *from* the trouble or delivered *in* it, "Thou wilt compass me about with songs of deliverance," which songs, or literally "shouts," [13] of triumph

---

[13] *Ranei,* the plural *Ranan,* is of unusual formation, and only used in this one place. *Ranan* means to *"shout for joy,"* and occurs in ver. 11 and in Psa. xxxiii. 1. There is a peculiar play in the Hebrew on the three words rendered "from trouble," "Thou shalt preserve me," "songs," inasmuch as the consonants of each of the words (which stand in the order as here given) are a repetition of the last three letters of the preceding word, thus—me'*tzar*-te'-*tzr*einee-*ranei;* on which account some expositors have suggested the dropping of *ronai* as a scribal repetition of the last three letters of the preceding word; but there is no justification for this theory, as the assonance here has many other parallels in the Hebrew scriptures, and is not undesigned.

and victory are the echoes of His exceeding great and
precious promises which are as God's sweet music to us,
and enable us to rejoice whatever our outward circumstances might be.

Once again, and for the third time, a *"Selah"* marks
off this new experience, and while the music breaks in in
joyous strains to emphasise the blessedness of such a condition, "pause," my dear reader, and remember that the
man who here sings is the same one who, in the fourth
verse, could only "roar" in his anguish; and that the
same one who there felt the presence of God as an in-
supportable burden, is here nestling in His bosom, and
saying, *"Thou art my hiding place."*   Such is the transforming power of God's grace; such is the blessed fruit
of the assurance of transgression borne away, of sin
covered!

The next verse seems to break in as a kind of Divine
response to the confidence of the Psalmist just expressed:

> *"I will instruct thee and teach thee in the way which thou shalt*
>   *go;*
> *I will counsel thee with Mine eye upon thee."*

There is a great deal to be said in favour of the con-
tention that it is still David and not Jehovah who is the
speaker in this verse, in which case it would be the direct
fulfilment of his vow in Psa. li . 13: "Then will I teach
transgressors Thy ways: and sinners shall be converted
unto Thee"; and in keeping with the *Maschil* character
of the Psalm in which the writer announces already in
the title the purpose he has in this composition, namely,
"to give instruction."   But the last line of the verse does
not fit the lips of man, and can be true only of the "ever
Living and Seeing One."   But whether the speaker be
David or Jehovah, it is a precious Divine *promise* which

will be made true to all who make God their hiding place, and are willing to be instructed and led in His way.

> *"Show me Thy ways, O Jehovah;*
> *Teach me Thy paths.*
> *Guide me in Thy truth and teach me;*
> *For Thou art the God of my salvation;*
> *On Thee do I wait all the day"* (Psa. xxv. 4, 5)

is the prayer of every forgiven soul, for next to pardon and protection, guidance is our greatest need; and blessed be His Name, He will not, after all He has done for us in and through His Son, leave us to ourselves henceforth to stumble along in the way as best we can. No, "for *His own Name's sake He will* lead and guide us" (Psa. xxxi. 3), or in the words of the beautiful promise before us, "I will instruct thee" (or *"give thee understanding"* or *"insight"*—i. e., the ability to discern between good and evil— between what is of God and what is not of Him), "and I will teach thee" (or *"give thee light"*) "in the way" (or literally *"in the way—this one"*—i. e., the only way for the pardoned, justified man to walk in, viz., the way of truth and holiness in which alone God will walk with men), "and I will counsel thee with Mine eye upon thee" [14] (or "I will counsel thee, putting or fixing Mine eye upon thee"— i. e., "with sympathising love taking an interest in thee," as Delitzsch expresses it)—which has a precious promise

---

[14] The Chaldaic has, "I will place upon thee My eye for. good" (compare Jer. xxiv. 6, "I will set Mine eye upon them for good"). God's direction as to duty and protection in peril are both included in the promise. With His eye upon His servant, He will show him the way, and will keep him ever in sight as he travels on it. The beautiful meaning in the Authorised Version, that God guides with a glance those who dwell near enough to Him to see His look, is scarcely contained in the words, though it is true that the sense of pardon binds unto Him in such sweet bonds that they are eager to catch the faintest indications of His will, and "His looks command, His slightest words are spells."—*Alexander Maclaren.*

in it also of *protection* while we walk in His way, and do and live as He directs.

In contrast to the man with the peace of God in his heart, and God's light on his path, because he knows from his experience that real good and blessing lie not away from but only *in* God, who has now become his "hiding place," we have in the words of counsel and warning which follow the restless, wild impetuosity of the man with the unbroken heart and untamed spirit.

> *"Be ye not as the horse, or as the mule, without understanding;*
> *Whose harness [or whose 'trappings' or 'ornaments'] to hold*
>   *them in must be bit and bridle,*
> *Else they will not come near to thee."*

The meaning of which is that God expects from man, not constrained but *willing* obedience. But if necessary He knows how to tame and break the pride of the stubborn, even as men know how to make wild, irrational animals to carry out their wills by bit and bridle; or as Hengstenberg, quoting from an old annotated German Bible, puts it, "If we do not consent to serve God *willingly,* we *must* serve Him in the long run whether we will or not. He who runs away from God's willing service falls into His compulsory service. On this account the conscientious Stoic prayed, 'Lead me, O God, the way which Thou hast chosen; and if I *will* not, nothing is better than that I be compelled.' Recourse is not had to bit and bridle, unless we will not become wise by gentler means. God employs these for the purpose of delivering us from destroying ourselves. Let us, then, rather follow with good will, than be dragged along by compulsion. . . . The ungodly will make a cross of everything that has been sent them by God in punishment of their sins. But that is not worth the name. It is nothing more than a rod of punishment for an ass." Or, as Johann Arndt quaintly puts it, "You have received from God a reasonable soul; yea, you hear the friendly, pleasing voice of your Father and His dear Son. But if you will be as stupid as the horse or the mule, God, in that case, will act well in putting upon your neck a bridle, and a bit in your mouth, for the purpose of compelling and restraining you like a senseless brute. God, for example, put a bridle and bit into Nebuchadnezzar's mouth, and tamed the proud beast. God also put a bridle and bit into Manasseh's mouth: when he lay bound in iron chains he would gladly have bowed the knee before God, if his iron fetters would have permitted him. God brought down the proud Pharaoh by means of contemptible creatures—frogs, lice, and grasshoppers—and put a wonderful bridle into the mouth of this proud horse."

And the contrast in state and disposition between the righteous and the ungodly, between those who trust and those who fret and rush, leads the Psalmist to the consequent contrast of their experiences and destiny:

"Many sorrows [or 'pains'] shall be to the wicked;
But he that trusteth in Jehovah, mercy shall compass him about
[or 'with loving-kindness will He encompass him']."

The *rasha*, the "wicked" or "lawless" man, is here the antithesis to the one "that trusts in Jehovah," which is significant as "showing that faith is the true opposite of sinfulness." And this is the meaning of the terms "wicked" and "righteous" in the whole Book of Psalms. The "wicked" are not alone the morally depraved, but *the unbelieving*—the rebellious against the counsel of God; and the "righteous" are not those absolutely righteous, but those that trust in Him—those who, though sinful by nature, have been reconciled to God and brought into submission to His teaching and guidance.[15] And not less full of meaning is the sequence of trust, righteousness, and

---

[15] De Burgh.

uprightness of heart in ver. 10 and ver. 11. "Faith leads to righteousness; and they are upright, not who have never fallen, but who have been raised from their fall by pardon." [16]

And here is the sum of human experience as seen by the eye of faith. To the *rasha*, notwithstanding the fact that he often temporarily prospers, there shall be many "pains" and "sorrows" which, except they lead him by the mercy of God to repentance and faith, will not be limited to this life only, but shall extend to that awful eternity which awaits the ungodly and impenitent; but as to him that has learned to trust in Jehovah "mercy shall compass him about." He shall be *surrounded* with loving sunlight. "He shall find mercy and favour everywhere—at home and abroad; by day and by night; in society, in solitude, in sickness and health; in life and death; in time, in eternity; he shall walk amidst mercies; he shall die amidst mercies; he shall live in a better world in the midst of eternal mercies."

It is interesting to observe how these verses lead from the particular to the general.

In the seventh verse David thought and spoke of himself as compassed with shouts of deliverance, but here in the tenth verse "another circle is cast round him, and all who, with him, trust in Jehovah. A ring of mercies, like a fiery wall, surrounds the pardoned, faithful soul without a break through which a real evil can creep. Therefore the encompassing songs of deliverance are continuous as the mercies which they hymn, and in the centre of that double circle the soul sits secure and thankful." [17] The Psalm which begins with *ashrey*, "Oh, how happy," or "Oh,

---

[16] Dr. Maclaren.

[17] Maclaren.

the blessednesses," ends with a joyous summons to general joy on the part of the man whose experience is primarily described:

"Be glad in Jehovah,
And rejoice, ye righteous:
And shout for joy, all ye that are upright in heart"—

on which we shall have something to say in connection with the first line of the following Psalm to which these words form both a point of connection and transition. Here I will only add that in these last lines of the thirty-second Psalm we have a *gradation* of joy presented to us. For the word in the Hebrew for "be glad" signifies "an inward and hearty joy by the presence or hope at least of a thing desirable or good"; the word rendered "rejoice" is used to express joy by some outward gesture, and is used sometimes for dancing; while the last word means *"shout for joy."* "This gradation," observes an old writer, "teacheth us that this is the nature of spiritual joy—that it still increaseth in us by certain degrees, until it come to the perfection of all joy which is signified by the last word for joy in our Psalm, importing, as it were, *a triumph and shouting after victory."*

III

THE PRAISEWORTHINESS OF JEHOVAH AND THE BLESSEDNESS OF HIS PEOPLE

PSALM XXXIII

"Rejoice in the Lord, O ye righteous:
Praise is comely for the upright.
Give thanks unto the Lord with harp:
Sing praises unto Him with the psaltery of ten strings.
Sing unto Him a new song;
Play skilfully with a loud noise,
For the word of the Lord is right;
And all His work is done in faithfulness.
He loveth righteousness and judgment.
The earth is full of the lovingkindness of the Lord.
By the word of the Lord were the heavens made;
And all the host of them by the breath of His mouth.
He gathereth the waters of the sea together as an heap;
He layeth up the deeps in storehouses.
Let all the earth fear the Lord:
Let all the inhabitants of the world stand in awe of Him.
For He spake, and it was done;
He commanded, and it stood fast.
The Lord bringeth the counsel of the nations to nought;
He maketh the thoughts of the peoples of none effect.
The counsel of the Lord standeth fast for ever;
The thoughts of His heart to all generations.
Blessed is the nation whose God is the Lord:
The people whom He has chosen for His own inheritance.
The Lord looketh from heaven;
He beholdeth all the sons of men;
From the place of His habitation He looketh forth
Upon all the inhabitants of the earth;
He that fashioneth the hearts of them all,
That considereth all their works.
There is no king saved by the multitude of an host:
A mighty man is not delivered by great strength.
An horse is a vain thing for safety:
Neither shall he deliver any by his great power.
Behold, the eye of the Lord is upon them that fear Him,
Upon them that hope in His mercy;
To deliver their soul from death,
And to keep them alive in famine.
Our soul hath waited for the Lord:
He is our help and our shield.
For our heart shall rejoice in Him,
Because we have trusted in His holy Name.
Let Thy mercy, O Lord, be upon us,
According as we have hoped in Thee."

III

THE PRAISEWORTHINESS OF JEHOVAH AND THE BLESSEDNESS OF HIS PEOPLE

IN ITS fulness, this glorious Psalm of praise will be sung by redeemed Israel by and by, when, in the light of Christ, they shall enter into the full knowledge of God's character and ways; and shall be, as never before, "the nation," whose blessedness is celebrated in the middle line of this Psalm—the nation, namely, "whose God is Jehovah, and the people whom He has chosen for His own inheritance."

But inasmuch as in and through Christ it is already our blessedness to know Israel's God in all the various aspects of His character which are unfolded in this Psalm, and inasmuch as we anticipate Israel in all the spiritual blessings of the new covenant of grace, we too are called upon to join in this glorious song of joy and praise.

Psalms xxxii. and xxxiii. form a pair. Indeed, in a few ancient manuscripts they are written as one, by reason, probably, of the apparent continuity of subjects which was observed. Anyhow, it is no mere chance that the thirty-third Psalm begins with the same words with which the thirty-second closes.

The thirty-second Psalm may be regarded as the prelude and basis of the thirty-third. There the blessedness is described of the man whose transgression is borne away, whose sin is covered, whose iniquity is not imputed, and it leads on to fellowship with, and joy in the Lord.

Now the climax of the thirty-second Psalm forms the basis of the thirty-third. In structure this is one of the most symmetrical and beautiful in the whole collection.

There are twenty-two verses in it, just as many as there are letters in the Hebrew alphabet, though it is not one of the so-called alphabetical Psalms. Of these twenty-two verses, the first three (or the first six lines in Hebrew) are *the call,* or *invitation,* addressed to the righteous, to rejoice in Jehovah and to praise His Name.

To this call the last three verses (or six lines) of the Psalm are *the direct response,* but in between the invitation and the response we have sixteen verses, or eight short stanzas of four lines each, in which the subject matter of praise, or *the praiseworthiness of Jehovah,* is spread before us.

The Call or Invitation

"Rejoice in Jehovah, ye righteous."

The word translated "rejoice" expresses *exuberance,* or audible *demonstrative* joy. It is the same word which, in the last line of the thirty-second Psalm, is rendered by the expression *"shout for joy."* In that same sense, as expressive of a holy joy which cannot contain itself, but must utter itself in a song of gladness, it is used in many other places in Scripture. Thus we find it in that beautiful little millennial song to be used by converted Israel by and by: "Cry out *and shout for joy,* thou inhabitant of Zion, for great is the Holy One of Israel in the midst of Thee."

"In Jehovah"—all emphasis in this verse is thrown on the Holy Name as the great object of our joy.

God wants His people to be a *joyous people,* and the great cause and unfailing source of our joy is *Himself*—His eternal and unchangeable being; His glory and majesty; His holiness, wisdom, and power; His faithfulness and love—and all the wonderful attributes of His character summed up in the Holy Name *"Jehovah."*

The exhortation in another Psalm is *"Delight thyself in Jehovah,"* so that He Himself, the blessed God, and not merely His gifts and benefits, may be thine "exceeding joy." Indeed, the power to joy in God alone may be taken as the mark of a true Christian. Even worldly men can rejoice in God's outward gifts and benefits, but it takes a true believer to rejoice in *Himself*.

These, then, are the first words of this Psalm, *"Rejoice in Jehovah."* If it said, "Rejoice in yourself," some of us might well be sad; if it said, "Rejoice in your circumstances," many of us might well be gloomy; but to this call to "Rejoice in Jehovah" there is not one of His children, whatever their outward circumstances may be, who cannot respond.

Have all earthly sources of joy failed, you?—yea, do your very flesh and heart fail you? Then remember *God Himself* still remains the rock of your heart, and your portion for ever; and there is a river the streams whereof continue to make glad the city of God, and which can never fail, because it proceeds not from any earthly source, but "out of the throne of God and of the Lamb."

Therefore, fellow-Christian, "Rejoice in the Lord alway; and again I say, Rejoice."

"Ye righteous"—this describes those who are invited to this holy task. But who are the righteous?

Not those innately so, for there are none such among the sons of men, and the spiritual in Israel, more particularly, knew well that their own righteousness was but as "filthy rags," and that if they were to enter into the presence of God it must be in a righteousness provided by Himself.

The "righteous" in our Psalm, dear reader, are those who have learned the secret, and passed through the experience of the thirty-second Psalm, which describes "the blessedness of the man to whom the Lord *imputed* right-eousness apart from works," and know the truth of the promise in Isaiah that *"their righteousness shall be of Me, saith Jehovah."*

But, linked with it, as one of the first-fruits of our justification by faith through the blood and righteousness of our Saviour, is that *subjective* righteousness, showing itself in holiness of life, and this is brought out more particularly in the second line of our Psalm, where we read that *"praise is comely to the upright."*

The word translated "upright" describes those who walk in a straight course, and to such—that is, to all who avoid all moral crookedness, all that is of the darkness—in their mouths praise is "comely," or "meet," or "beauti-ful." There is harmony and appropriateness in the right-eous singing the praises of the thrice holy Jehovah. "But to the wicked God saith, What hast thou to do to declare My statutes [or 'to sing My praise'], or that thou shouldest take My covenant in thy mouth? seeing thou hatest in-struction, and castest My words behind thee."

But when a man's heart is full of the joy of the Lord, he not only wants a thousand tongues, but he tries to bring everything into requisition to help him to utter God's praise. "Praise Jehovah with the harp [or cithern], with the ten-stringed psaltery sing unto Him."

I suppose the origin of the use of instrumental music in the worship of God, was the feeling of inadequacy on the part of man to make the praises of God glorious enough with his unaided lips and tongue, so he invented himself the harp, the psaltery, stringed instruments and organs; but remember, whatever the instrument which you may call to your aid, the praise must be yours, and the sound of the dead harp or organ, however fine, must not be substituted for the living praises of your heart and soul.

But we proceed to the last two lines of the invitation addressed to the righteous: "Sing unto Him a *new song*."

The new song is the Redemption song, which only a saved man can sing. An instance of individual response to it is found in Psalm xl.: "I waited patiently [or, 'I waited and waited'—I continued waiting] for Jehovah, and He inclined unto me and heard my cry. He brought me up also out of an horrible pit, out of the miry clay, and set my feet upon a rock and established my goings. *And He hath put a new song in my mouth, even praise unto our God;* many shall see it, and fear, and shall trust in Jehovah."

I am aware that the speaker in that Psalm is the Messiah—the same who, farther on in the same Scripture, says of Himself: "Then said I, Lo, I come, in the scroll of the Book it is written of Me, I delight to do Thy will, O My God; yea, Thy law is within My heart"; and that it is primarily Messiah's sufferings, descent into the pit of death on our account, and glorious resurrection, which the verses quoted set forth. But these great objective facts, which are the ground and cause of all our life and salvation, find their subjective counterpart in the believer's experience, and therefore the song of deliverance which our Lord Jesus sang when He was raised from the dead becomes the "new song" of His redeemed people.

"A new man, a new Testament, a new song," said Augustine. "A new song belongeth not to men that are old. None learn it, but new men, renewed through grace from oldness, and belonging to the New Testament which is the Kingdom of Heaven."

But together with redemption, the song of which should ever be fresh in our mouths, the "new song" should include fresh praise, provoked by fresh impulses of gratitude to God for continually fresh mercies which are renewed from day to day.

The full melody and sweetness, however, of this new redemption song, will not be heard on earth till the millennial period, when, in a renewed earth, Israel shall walk in the light of Jehovah, and our Lord Jesus shall see of the travail of His soul and be satisfied. Then the cry will go forth, "Sing unto the Lord a new song, and His praise from the end of the earth; ye that go down to the sea, and all that is therein, the isles, and the inhabitants thereof. Let the wilderness and the cities thereof lift up their voice, the villages that Kedar doth inhabit; let the inhabitants of Sela sing, let them shout from the top of the mountains. Let them give glory unto Jehovah, and declare His praise in the islands" (Isa. xlii. 10-12, R.V.).

The last line of the invitation is *"Play skilfully with a loud noise,"* or more literally "Play merrily with a joyful noise." The Hebrew is, "Do well in playing," &c.—that is, put into this sacred service of praise to Jehovah your very best, your very highest powers. Do not do it carelessly, do not do it negligently; do not do it gloomily, but say with the Apostle: "I will sing with the spirit, and I will sing with the understanding also."

The Praiseworthiness of Jehovah.

So far the call or invitation to rejoice in Jehovah and to praise His Name.

To these first six lines the last six lines of the Psalm are, as already stated, the direct response, but in between we have eight short stanzas of four lines each, in which the *various causes* which the righteous have for their joy in the Lord are brought before us.

I. *The Praiseworthiness of Jehovah as the God of Revelation in the Kingdom of Grace.* This is the subject of the first of the eight short stanzas (vers. 4, 5).

"For the Word of Jehovah is right." Jehovah has spoken—astounding and blessed fact.

He has not left us to our own darkness and speculation in reference to our Maker, and the destiny which He has appointed for us; but "He has told thee, O man, what is good, and what the Lord requireth of thee." And His voice has not faded away with the sound of its first utterance, with the dim past, into infinite space, leaving man to speculate again as to what that Heavenly Revelation might have been, but is preserved to us in "the Word"—which is one of the names which the Psalmist uses for Holy Scripture, or as much of it as he then had. And this "Word is *right*," or, as the same word is more properly rendered in the first verse, "*upright*." The sense of this line is that Jehovah has spoken what He did *in good faith*. His Word is "upright" in intention; there is no double meaning in it; there is no possibility of any one being deceived by it.

It also, in spite of man's foolish doubts and quibblings, proves itself all through the ages to be "right." And, moreover, there is a day coming when *all* men, whether esteemed wise or foolish in this world, will discover that *they* have been rightly only in so far as they have brought their thoughts and words into subjection to it.

But not only is His Word right or upright, but "*All His work* [*or, 'His every act'*] *is done in faithfulness*"— in faithfulness, that is, to His word. There is never any inconsistency between His word and His work; but, as He says, so He does, whether it be in the sphere of mercy, in faithfulness to His promises, or of judgment, in faithfulness to His threatenings.

It was, for instance, in faithfulness to His word that He sent a Saviour and raised up for us a horn of salvation in the house of His servant David, "as He spake by the mouth of His holy prophets, which have been since the world began."

It is in faithfulness to His word, also, that poor Christless Israel is now scattered among the nations, and Jerusalem trodden down of the Gentiles; and it will be in faithfulness to His word, that He that is now scattering Israel will again gather him, and keep him as a shepherd doth his flock, so that He may "perform the truth to Jacob and the mercy to Abraham, which He has sworn to our fathers from the days of old."

But to proceed to the next verse, *"He loveth righteousness and judgment."* He Himself is the absolutely Righteous One, and "He loveth righteousness" as a principle manifesting itself in the conduct of His people—the difference between "Tsedakah" ("righteousness"), and "Mishpat" ("judgment"), being that the one describes *conduct* and the other a *rule* of judgment—a state or condition.

This line of the Psalm reminds us of Psalm xi. 7, which is not properly rendered in the Authorised Version. The Hebrew of that verse reads: "For righteous is Jehovah; He loveth righteousness; *the upright shall behold His countenance."* The doctrine is the same as in the First Epistle of John: *"If we walk in the light,* as He is in the light, we have fellowship one with another," but if we say we have fellowship with Him and walk in the darkness, we lie, and do not the truth; "for righteous is our God," and without holiness of character, and righteousness of life, no man shall see the Lord.

And this is true of beholding God's face by faith now, and of that blessed, glorious, and glorifying actual sight of His countenance on the resurrection morn hereafter. "As for me," says David, in another Psalm, *"I shall behold Thy face in righteousness;* I shall be satisfied when I awake with Thy likeness."

The last line of the stanza reads, *"The earth is full of the goodness* [literally, 'the grace,' or 'mercy'] of Jehovah."

This refers not only to the general beneficence of our God, which might be seen in Nature, but to His special goodness *in grace.* It is the word used for His "loving-kindness, which is better than life."

Already this is partially true, for wherever there is a sinner saved the world over, there is a monument to the grace of God. But this Psalm looks on to the time when the glory and knowledge of Jehovah shall *cover* the earth as the waters cover the sea; when Israel shall walk in the light of Jehovah, and when through the mercy which shall fill "the land" (which is perhaps the more proper rendering here of the word translated "earth") all the ends of the world shall see the salvation of our God.

II. The next two short stanzas (vers. 6-9) set forth the praiseworthiness of Jehovah as *the God of Creation in the Kingdom of Nature.*

"By the word of Jehovah were the heavens made."

How gloriously sublime is this simple announcement of Scripture! The only parallel to it is found in that majestic statement on the very first page of the Bible, where we read that "In the beginning God created the heaven and the earth"; and, by this one sentence alone, Scripture stands removed from all the other so-called sacred books of the nations, with their grotesque cosmogonies and fabulous accounts of the universe, as far as the heavens are above the earth.

Philosophers have puzzled their heads, from age to age, about the origin of the material system, and have elaborated a great many contradictory theories, leaving mankind, for the most part, in a labyrinth of fancies and speculations; but the merest child who has learned these sublime and confident declarations of Scripture, and the most illiterate believer who has experimental knowledge of a personal Creator, is wiser than they all; for *"by faith* we understand that the worlds were framed by the Word of God, so that things seen were not made of things which do appear." [1]

It is not without design that in these eight short strophes of our Psalm in which the praises of the wonderful ways of Jehovah in creation, redemption, and providence are celebrated, revelation stands first; for it is *through His Word* that we arrive at the truest views, even as regards the material universe.[2] Some of you, my dear readers, may have neither the time nor the necessary knowledge to follow the many treatises on geology and astronomy, and the scientific and philosophic speculations on this great and comprehensive subject, which are within the reach of the learned and men of leisure, but I can tell you with confidence that if you hold fast to these simple declarations of Scripture, in spite of the various theories and hypotheses

---

[1] "Reason *cannot* ascend from nature to nature's God. The most comprehensive observation of things seen (that is, phenomena) of which we can take cognisance, and the most minute analysis of things to the most remote and simple elements, leave the question of creation or the origin of things perfectly untouched and un-approached. The step from matter to mind, from things which appear to that which is the cause, spring, origin of all, is one which reason cannot take. God reveals it; we believe.

"Ancient mythologies and philosophy, as well as modern science and speculation, cannot rise to the conception of the original, free and infinite cause of all things. It cannot get beyond some primeval substratum of elementary atoms, and by tracing developments from a lower to a higher form of existence, only removes by millions and billions of years the question which lies dormant in every child's mind: Who made all things?

"Scripture announces in sublime simplicity: 'In the beginning God created the heaven and the earth.' Every house is built by some one; but He that built all things is God."—*Adolph Saphir.*

[2] "Nur Gottes Worte werfen das rechte Licht auf Gottes Werke." —*Hasenkamp.*

which preclude or exclude the doctrine of a personal Creator, you will land in eternity, not only with the best theology, but also with the best science. Neither science nor philosophy will ever be able of themselves to inform us aright about the *origin and the destiny of things.*

It is the Bible which tells us that "of Him, and for Him, and to Him, are all things"; and through its pages we see the door opened in heaven, and behold the vision of the representatives of the Church and of redeemed creation, falling down and worshipping Him that sitteth on the throne, and that liveth for ever and ever, saying, "Worthy art Thou, O Lord, our God, to receive the glory and the honour and the power, *for Thou didst create all things, and because of Thy will they are, and were created.*"

But to return to our Psalm. Not only were the heavens made "by the Word of Jehovah," but *"all the host of them"*—all those myriads of stars and systems with which the heavens are studded—*"by the Breath of His mouth."*

"Jehovah," "His Word," and "His Breath" (or "Spirit"). There is a possible reference in this verse to the blessed Trinity of Persons in the One Godhead, as co-operating in the work of creation, which we know from other Scriptures to have been the case. Thus, "In the beginning GOD created the heaven and the earth," yet we are told of the divine Logos, or "Word," that "all things were made by (or through) Him; and without Him was not anything made that hath been made"; and as to the blessed "Breath," or Spirit, we read of Him already in the second verse of the Bible, that in the beginning He "moved" or "brooded over the face of the waters." Even so, Father, Son, and Holy Spirit co-operate in the still more glorious work of the new creation, which is the fruit of redemption.

Then having pointed us to the heavens above, the inspired writer directs our attention next to the waters beneath, as another miracle of God's creative power:

> "He gathereth the waters of the sea together as an heap;
> He layeth up the depths in storehouses."

That which seems especially to strike psalmists and prophets in connection with the waters, and calls forth their wonder and admiration, is the fact of His having confined them within fixed bounds, and that He continues to keep them within the same, all through the ages.

Once and again God Himself points to this fact as a proof of His power and majesty. Thus He says in Jer. v. 22, "Fear ye not Me? saith Jehovah: will ye not tremble at My presence, which hath placed the sand for the bound of the sea for a perpetual decree that it cannot pass it? and though the waves thereof toss themselves, yet can they not prevail; though they roar, yet can they not pass over it"; and Himself addressing Job, He asks:

> "Where wast thou when I . . . shut up the sea with doors,
> When it brake forth as if it had issued out of the womb?
> When I made the cloud the garment thereof;
> And thick darkness a swaddling band for it;
> And prescribed for it My decree; and set bars and doors; and
>   said, Hitherto shalt thou come, but no farther;
> And here shall thy proud waves be stayed?"
>
> (Job xxxviii. 1-11).

And not only does He gather the waters of the sea together as an heap, but "He layeth up the depths in storehouses"—that is, in the beds of the seas and rivers which are prepared for His storehouses (or "treasuries," as the word literally means), and into which the foaming oceans and mighty waters are, so to say, stored and kept by His power, and prevented from flooding the earth.

In view of these displays of His infinite power, wisdom, and beneficence, the Psalmist exclaims:

"Let all the earth fear Jehovah;
Let all the inhabitants of the world stand in awe of Him";

which is to be understood not only in the sense of a prayer or command, but as a *prophecy,* for the day is assuredly coming when all the earth *shall* fear Jehovah: when all the inhabitants of the world *shall stand* in awe of Him, because He alone, the God of Israel, shall be known as the true and the *living* God, the Everlasting King, "who hath made the earth by His power, who hath established the world by His wisdom, and who by His understanding hath stretched out the heavens."

This section of our Psalm devoted to God's ways in creation ends with the words:

"For He spake, and it was done;
He commanded, and it stood fast."

The first of these two lines is almost bodily taken from the first chapter of Genesis, and it is a pity that the words are not rendered in the same way. Literally it reads: *"For He said, and it was."* "He said," for instance, "Let there be light; and *there was* light"; and so with every other created object.

Oh how wonderful is our Omnipotent God! "He need only speak the word, and that which He wills comes into being out of nothing." He need only utter His creative "Let there be," and that which He commands "stands fast," or literally *"stands forth,* like an obedient servant that appears in all haste at the call of his Lord." [3] And this infinite Almighty Creator—the God who quickeneth the dead and calleth things that are not as though they

---

[3] Delitzsch.

were—is *our* God, the Redeemer and Shepherd of His people. Therefore "Rejoice in Jehovah, O ye righteous, for praise is comely for the upright."

III. The next, or fourth, short stanza of four lines sets forth the praiseworthiness of Jehovah as the great Ruler among the nations, or as *the God of Providence in the sphere of history:*

> "Jehovah bringeth the counsel of the nations to nought;
> He maketh the thoughts of the peoples to be of none effect.
> The counsel of Jehovah standeth for ever;
> The thoughts of His heart to all generations."

It is perhaps necessary to explain that when it is stated that Jehovah bringeth the counsel of the nations to nought, and frustrates the thoughts of the peoples, that it refers to the *wicked* counsel of men when it is opposed to the set purpose of God. All history, if properly known and rightly understood, would supply an exemplification of this truth, but I shall content myself with bringing before you two striking illustrations—first, the counsel of the nations in relation to our Lord Jesus Christ, brought to nought by the counsel of God; and, secondly, the thoughts of the peoples in relation to Israel, made of none effect by the "thoughts of His heart."

(*a*) What is the counsel of the nations in relation to Christ? It is expressed in many Scriptures, but particularly in the second Psalm:

> "Why do the nations rage,
> And the peoples imagine a vain thing?
> The kings of the earth set themselves,
> And the rulers take counsel together
> Against Jehovah and against His anointed [Christ], saying,
> Let us break their bands asunder,
> And cast away their cords from us."

This has been their "counsel," and these have been their thoughts all along.

Herod was the representative of world-power in Jerusalem when the infant Christ was born in Bethlehem; and already Joseph had to be warned by the angel of the Lord, who said, "Arise, and take the young child and His mother and flee, . . . for Herod will seek the young child to destroy Him." Ultimately, "the princes of this world" did crucify the Lord of Glory (1 Cor. ii. 8), urged on by Satan and "the world-rulers of this darkness"; and when the Church of this dispensation was born with His resurrection, the counsel of the nations and their rulers was to strangle it in its infancy, and so blot the very memory of Christ out of existence.

Already in the fourth of Acts we find the disciples quoting the second Psalm, and saying, "For of a truth in this city against Thy holy servant Jesus, whom Thou didst anoint, both Herod and Pontius Pilate, with the Gentiles and the people of Israel, are gathered together."

And this hatred to God and His Christ on the part of the nations is as strong today as it was at the beginning, and throughout the ages, and it will reach a climax at the time of the end, in the great confederacy of the apostate nations under Antichrist.

Then the drama of the second Psalm will be fully enacted, and nations and peoples, kings and rulers, shall take counsel together, and make a final desperate effort to break loose from God, and to defy the authority of His anointed.

But Jehovah bringeth the counsel of the nations to nought. He maketh the thoughts of the people of none effect; for—

> "He that sitteth in the heavens shall laugh;
> The Lord shall have them in derision.
> Then shall He speak unto them in His wrath,
> And vex them in His sore displeasure";

and in spite of the wicked "counsel" of men and devils,

Christ's throne shall be established, and God will set His King upon Zion, the hill of His holiness.

For "thus saith Jehovah, the Redeemer of Israel, and His Holy One, to Him whom man despiseth, to Him whom the nation abhorreth, to a servant of rulers: Kings shall see and arise; princes, and they shall worship; because of Jehovah that is faithful, even the Holy One of Israel who hath chosen Thee" (Isa. xlix. 7).

(b) The "counsel of the nations" in relation to our Lord Jesus Christ finds its parallel in the thoughts of the peoples in relation to Israel. The Jewish nation, too, has been hated and in danger from its infancy.

"Many a time [or 'O, how greatly!'] have they afflicted me from
        my youth up.
Let Israel now say:
O, how greatly have they afflicted me from my youth up!
Yet they have not prevailed against me" (Psa. cxxix. 1, 2).

Not only do the Jewish people live, but they are more numerous today than they have been at any previous period of their history.

And when the sorrows of Israel shall yet reach a climax, in the cry of the confederate nations under the leadership of Antichrist: "Come, let us destroy them from being a nation, that the name of Israel be no more in remembrance"—let us make one final effort to exterminate this nation from the face of the earth—the answer of God will be: "Associate yourselves [or 'make an uproar'], O ye peoples, and ye shall be broken in pieces; and give ear, O ye of far countries. Gird yourselves, and ye shall be broken in pieces; gird yourselves, and ye shall be broken in pieces. *Take counsel together, and it shall come to nought; speak the word, and it shall not stand: for* Immanu-El—God is with us" (Isa. viii. 9, 10.)[4]

―――――――

[4] See the exposition of Psa. cxxix. in the chapter "Songs of Ascents," pp. 289-306.

And not only does Jehovah bring the counsel of the nations to nought, and make the thoughts of the peoples of none effect, but—

"The counsel of Jehovah standeth for ever;
The thoughts of His heart to all generations."

What *is* this counsel of Jehovah?
What *are* these thoughts of His heart?
I cannot give a more satifactory answer to this question than in words of Paul, who speaks of *the counsel of His own will* in the salvation of His people; *"His good pleasure which He hath purposed in Himself,"* that in the dispensation of the fulness of the times "He might sum up all things in Christ, both the things in the heavens and the things upon the earth," and that "in the ages to come He might show the exceeding richness of His grace in kindness towards us in Christ Jesus." This, the establishment of His kingdom, the manifestation of His glory in the blessedness of His people—not only His earthly people Israel in the millennial age, but of His Church through all eternity—is "the ultimate motive of everything," the central thought in His government of the world. Toward this great good all things are made to "work together," and everything that is opposed to it shall assuredly be frustrated and broken to pieces.

Individually, my dear fellow-believers, you may read your eternal safety in this counsel of Jehovah, which is "the counsel of peace," and in these thoughts of His heart, "which are thoughts of salvation."

He has purposed from eternity to bless you, and to conform you to the image of His Son; He has chosen you in Him before the foundation of the world, that you should be holy, and without blame before Him in love, and in the end "to set you before the presence of His glory in exceeding joy," and in that good pleasure He shall never be frustrated.   It is true that there are "those who are against us"; and in our pilgrimage to our final blessed destiny there is many a hard fight to be fought, and we are often only too conscious that "we wrestle not merely against flesh and blood, but against principalities, against powers, against the world-rulers of this darkness, against wicked spirits in high places," but greater and more is He who is for us than all who can be against us; and our God bringeth not only the counsel of the nations to nought, but of Satan, and of all the powers of darkness, and therefore we can triumphantly sing: "For I am persuaded that neither death, nor life, nor angels, nor principalities, nor powers, nor things present, nor things to come, nor height, nor depth, nor any other creature, shall be able to separate us from the love of God which is in Christ Jesus our Lord."

Oh glorious counsel of Jehovah, which shall stand fast for ever!

Oh blessed thoughts of His heart which shall abide to all generations!

The Blessedness of God's People.

In the last four of the eight short stanzas which form the body of our Psalm, the original call to the righteous to rejoice in Jehovah and to praise His name (vers. 1-3) is supported by the setting forth of *what God is to His people, and the blessedness which His people find in Him.*

These sixteen lines (vers. 12-19) are almost a paraphrase of the beatitude which Moses pronounced upon Israel at the conclusion of his prophetic benedictions on the twelve tribes in Deut. xxxiii.:

> "Happy art thou, O Israel (he exclaims):
> Who is like unto thee, a people saved by Jehovah,
> The shield of thy help;
> And that is the sword of thy excellency!
> And thine enemies shall submit themselves unto thee;
> And thou shalt tread upon their high places."

Now in the verses of our Psalm which we are about
to consider, each point of this Mosaic blessing is enlarged
upon and turned into a subject of praise. But let us re-
sume the exposition.

"Blessed is the nation whose God is Jehovah."

This is the central thought and middle line of the whole
Psalm, and is designedly put in this commanding position.
Even all that we are told about God in the sixteen preceding lines, where His glory is made to pass before us as
the God of Revelation, Creation, and Providence, is with
a view to illustrate the truth of this verse, and to enhance
the blessedness of His people, who are thus highly favoured in having Him as their portion.

The word translated "blessed" is the same as that used
by Moses in the passage quoted, and rendered "happy."
It is really in the plural form, and may be translated, "Oh,
the blessednesses [or 'happiness'] of the nation whose
God is Jehovah!"

The nation, as we have seen in the original passage in
Deuteronomy, of which this part of the Psalm is an inspired paraphrase, is *Israel;* and oh, who can describe
the blessedness which Jehovah intended to be the lot of the
nation, which He has chosen from among all other nations,
to be His own peculiar possession!

And let it be remembered that Israel remains the one
people to whom, *as a nation,* this peculiar position belongs,
and that it is not only "the ancient nation" in the sense
of being the people of the past, now superseded by the
Church, but the *"everlasting* nation," the people of the
present, and pre-eminently of the future; for the gifts and
the calling of God in relation to Israel are without "repentance" (or "without a change of mind" on God's part).
But while this is true, and I cannot emphasie it too
strongly, that it is primarily the blessedness of Israel, and

especially the *future blessedness* of that nation, which this verse celebrates, it is also a blessed fact that now, "in Christ," it includes us too, and all believers of this present dispensation. You, my dear believing brethren and sisters from among the Gentiles, were, in times past, not a people, "but now are a people of God." "Ye are a chosen generation, a royal priesthood, *an holy nation.*" This word "nation" (ἔθνος), as used of the Church, is very significant.

Apart from being chosen and separate unto God, let us see what were the chief elements which constituted Jewish nationality. They were these:

(*a*) A common origin.

To this day wherever a Jew is found the world over, when referring to Abraham he always uses the word "Abhinu"—Abraham, "our father."

(*b*) One land.

(*c*) One language.

(*d*) One hope of a common destiny.

Now all these essentials of nationality are to be found in their truest and deepest sense in the Church.

(1) We, too, have a common origin—born again, not of corruptible seed, but of incorruptible, by the word of God which "liveth and abideth for ever." *"For as many as are led by the Spirit of God these are the sons of God"*; and we have received not the spirit of bondage again to fear, but the spirit of sonship, whereby we cry, Abba, Father. And not only are we all the children of God by faith in Christ Jesus, but we, too, can all claim Abraham for our father, "for if ye are Christ's then are ye Abraham's seed, heirs according to promise" (Gal. iii. 29).

(2) We, too, have one land—our heavenly fatherland. On earth we are like Israel during the dispersion, pilgrims and strangers; and ours is an inheritance incorruptible, undefiled, and which fadeth not away.

(3) We, too, have one language—the language of the spirit which now can only express itself for the most part in groanings which cannot be uttered, but which, by and by, will burst forth into fulness of praise.

(4) And we, too, have one hope of a common destiny, even "that blessed hope" of seeing Christ and being for ever with Him.

Yes, we are a "holy nation," a new and blessed brotherhood, animated by the same spirit; and ours, too, is the blessedness of having Jehovah, the God of Abraham, Isaac, and Jacob, as *our God*.

The second line of this verse brings before us another aspect of this blessedness—

"The people whom He hath chosen for His own inheritance."

Not only is God the portion and everlasting inheritance of His people, but the converse is also true, that God's special inheritance is His people—and this, of the two, is perhaps the greater mystery. That we, as His creatures, should find all our blessedness in God is wonderful, but that He, the infinite Creator of heaven and earth, should find His special joy in fellowship with those who have been redeemed by the blood of His Son, is still more wonderful.

Primarily the reference in the second line of this verse is also to Israel, and the basis of it is again the words of Moses in Deuteronomy,

> "Jehovah's portion is His people;
> Jacob is the lot of His inheritance"—

words which are echoed again and again in the prophetic Scriptures.

But while this is true, and Israel naturally remains God's everlasting inheritance from among the nations, the Church is His spiritual inheritance from among men.

This is one of those blessed mysteries in connection with our high calling in Christ which the Apostle prays that all Christians may comprehend: "Having the eyes of your heart enlightened, that ye may know what is the hope of His calling, what the riches of the glory of *His inheritance in the saints*" (Eph. i. 18).

The theme of the twelfth verse (the blessedness of God's people) is proved in the next six lines by the fact that this Jehovah, who is the very portion of His people, is the Omniscient, Omnipresent Creator and Ruler, and that without His knowledge nothing can be undertaken either secretly or openly; hence His people need not fear the plots or machinations of their enemies.

> "The Lord looketh from heaven;
> He beholdeth all the sons of men;
> From the place of His habitation He looketh forth
> Upon all the inhabitants of the earth;
> He that fashioneth the hearts of them all,
> That considereth all their works."

In these lines it is the omniscience of God *as viewed in relation to the safety of His own people which is brought before us.*

"Jehovah looketh"—not with a passing superficial glance, but with intentness—*narrowly.*

"From the place of His habitation [or 'dwelling'] He looketh forth."

This second word for "looking" conveys the sense of controlling power, and is the word to this day in use among the Jews to express God's providence.

And nothing which the enemies of God's people may plan can be hid from Him, for "He fashioneth the hearts of them all," He considereth (or "understandeth") all their works.

Before passing on, it may be well, in connection with these lines, to pause for a brief glance at what the Scriptures say on the subject of God's omniscience.

To the Christian there is no more comforting truth in the whole range of the Bible than that expressed in the words, "Thou God seest me"; while to the ungodly it is a terrible thought, and they therefore try vainly to persuade themselves that it cannot be so, and that even if there be a God, it cannot be that He knows and observes them so closely.

What the wicked think in reference to God's omniscience is well expressed in Job xxii. 12-14:

"Is not God in the height of heaven?
And behold the height of the stars how high they are,
And thou sayest, What doth God know?
Can He judge through the thick darkness?
Thick clouds are a covering to Him that He seeth not,
And He walketh in the circuit of heaven."

These words were wrongly applied by Eliphaz in his address to Job, for Job was not a godless man; but at the same time they do describe the thoughts of the wicked in reference to this subject.

In Ezekiel the Lord twice complains to the prophet concerning the wickedness of the godless majority in Israel, saying, "Son of man, hast thou seen what the elders of the House of Israel do in the dark, every man in his chambers of imagery? *For they say, Jehovah seeth us not; Jehovah hath forsaken the earth.*"

The answer of God to this blasphemy is found in Psa. xciv. Here again we read "they" (namely, "the wicked") "say, Jehovah shall not see, neither shall the God of Jacob consider," but the answer is—

"Consider, ye brutish among the people:
And ye fools, when will ye be wise?
He that planteth the ear, shall He not hear?
He that formed the eye, shall He not see?
Jehovah knoweth the thoughts of men that they are vanity"—

and in spite of the fool endeavouring to persuade himself that God doth not see, Jehovah remains "the Living One and the Seeing One."

But *how* does God see?

I. *God's look is an all-embracing one.*

This is brought out strikingly in the lines of the Psalm we are considering:

> "Jehovah looketh from heaven,
> He beholdeth *all the sons of men;*
> From the place of His habitation He looketh forth
> Upon *all the inhabitants of the earth."*

And in Prov. xv. 3 we read:

> "The eyes of the Lord are in every place,
> Beholding ['watching'] the evil and the good."

II. God's look is not only an all-comprehending one, *it is also an all-searching one.*

He seeth not as man seeth, "for man looketh on the outward appearance, but Jehovah looketh on the heart," and "there is no creature that is not manifest in His sight, but all things are naked and laid open before the eyes of Him with whom we have to do."

There are many Scriptures which might be quoted in connection with this point, but Psa. xi. 4 is especially striking:

> "Jehovah is in His holy temple;
> Jehovah, His throne is in heaven;
> His eyes behold, His eyelids try the children of men—
> Jehovah trieth the righteous."

III. I have spoken of the comprehensiveness and of the depth of God's look, let me also remind you *of the minuteness* with which He sees.

He beholds not only men in general, but man individually; not only *all* men, but *each* man; not only things in mass, but things in detail: "Doth not He see *my* ways and number all *my* steps?" (Job xxxi. 4).

"O Lord, Thou hast searched me and known me;
Thou knowest my downsitting and mine uprising;
Thou understandest my thought afar off;
Thou searchest out my path and my lying down,
And art acquainted with all my ways.
For there is not a word in my tongue,
But, lo, O Lord, Thou knowest it altogether.
Thou hast beset me behind and before,
And laid Thine hand upon me.
Such knowledge is too wonderful for me;
It is high—I cannot attain unto it."

But this has been partly a digression from the continuity of thought unfolded in this Psalm.

In the next two short stanzas (vers. 16-19) the theme of verse 12—*i.e.*, the blessedness of God's people—is proved by the fact that in this omniscient and omnipresent God His people have a defence greater, and more certain, than the greatest world-power or human might could guarantee them.

In verses 16 and 17 the Psalmist shows the impotency of all human physical strength and valour and material resources; even as in verses 10 and 11 he showed the impotency of all human intellect when opposing itself to God and His people:

"There is no king saved by the multitude of an host."

How contrary is this statement to the maxims of the world! The world says numbers, physical valour, large armies, or, in modern times, sufficient armaments, the most approved weapons, &c., will win the day. Have you not read in the press of even this "Christian" England the blasphemy first uttered by Frederick the Great, that "God is always on the side of the largest battalions"?

But this is not only a blasphemy but an historical falsehood. In wars among nations equally estranged from God, and given over by Him to work out their mutual destruction, this may sometimes be the case, though not always; for there are remarkable instances in profane history when a comparative handful have put mighty armies to flight. At the battle of Arbela in 331 B. C., for instance, Alexander with his 50,000 utterly overthrew the mighty Persian army of 1,000,000 men; and there are many other like cases which might be cited.

But this is not the point here at all.

In our Psalm "the multitude of an host" is not regarded in relation to itself, or as matched with another "host." It is not a question of man against man, or of material resources as brought into conflict with physical strength and valour, but of human might and material force *when brought into opposition with the power of God exercised in the defence of His own people and His own cause.*

Do you know the history of Israel and of the wars of the Lord? Then you know the truth of this part of the Psalm, and of the words of Asa, that "it is nothing with Jehovah to save with many or with them that have no might."

When Israel sinned against God He was sometimes pleased to afflict them with the rod of men, and permitted the "multitudes" of the Gentile hosts to overthrow them, but so long as He was in their midst all the forces in the world could not prevail against them.

Pharaoh had "a great host," but immediately he brought it into conflict with the "Keeper of Israel" it was overthrown, and he himself was not "saved" by it.

Sennacherib brought against Israel a mighty host which he thought irresistible. In the words of the poem, which

is worthy of having been penned by a holier hand than
the one which wrote it:

"The Assyrian came down like the wolf on the fold,
And his cohorts were gleaming in purple and gold;
And the sheen of their spears was like stars on the sea,
When the blue wave rolls nightly on deep Galilee.

"Like the leaves of the forest when summer is green,
That host with their banners at sunset were seen;
Like the leaves of the forest when autumn hath blown,
That host on the morrow lay withered and strewn.

"For the Angel of Death spread his wings on the blast,
And breathed in the face of the foe as he passed;
And the eyes of the sleepers waxed deadly and chill,
And their hearts but once heaved, and for ever grew still.

"And there lay the steed with his nostril all wide,
But through it there rolled not the breath of his pride;
And the foam of his gasping lay white on the turf,
And cold as the spray of the rock-beating surf.

"And there lay the rider distorted and pale,
With the dew on his brow, and the rust on his mail;
And the tents were all silent, the banners alone,
The lances unlifted, the trumpet unblown.

"And the widows of Ashur are loud in their wail,
And the idols are broke in the temple of Baal;
And the might of the Gentile, unsmote by the sword,
Hath melted like snow in the glance of the Lord!"

And this great truth shall yet receive a final and striking demonstration at the time of the end, when the last
great king of Gentile power shall marshal his confederate
Gentile hosts against Israel and Jerusalem. But his
armies shall melt away into destruction, and he himself
shall be smitten by the breath of the Holy One. "And
the multitude of all the nations that fight against Ariel,

even all that fight against her and her stronghold, and that distress her, shall be as a dream, a vision of the night. And it shall be as when an hungry man dreameth, and, behold, he eateth; but he awaketh, and his soul is empty: or as when a thirsty man dreameth, and, behold, he drinketh; but he awaketh, and, behold, he is faint, and his soul hath appetite; so shall the multitude of all the nations be that fight against Mount Zion" (Isa. xxix. 7, 8).

And not only is no king saved by the multitude of an host when brought into conflict with God, but—

"A mighty man [the single warrior] is not delivered by great
    strength."

Goliath supplies a striking illustration of such a mighty man boasting in his own strength: "I defy the armies of Israel this day: give me a man that we may fight together," was his confident cry; but there came the stripling David and said to this proud Philistine: "Thou camest to me with a sword and with a spear and with a shield, but I come to thee in the name of Jehovah of Hosts, the God of the armies of Israel whom thou hast defied. . . . So David prevailed over the Philistine with a sling, and with a stone, and smote the Philistine and slew him"; and demonstrated once again the principle in God's kingdom that "by strength shall no man prevail."

And as with man's individual prowess and collective strength, so with his material resources. The horse is the symbol of strength and swiftness, and was, by the ancients especially, much relied on in time of war; but when found in opposition to God and His people—

"An horse is a vain thing for safety:
*   Neither shall he deliver any by his great strength."*

Israel had to learn this by experience.

"For thus said the Lord God, the Holy One of Israel, In returning and rest ye shall be saved; in quietness and confidence shall be your strength"; but they said, "No, for we will flee upon horses: and we will ride upon the swift." But that which they counted for strength proved weakness; and because they had broken away from reliance upon God, "one thousand fled at the rebuke of one," and at the rebuke of five the whole multitude fled, that they might learn that it is "not by might nor by power," but "that Jehovah is a God of Judgment; and blessed are all they that wait for Him" (Isa. xxx. 15-18).

And this still remains true, my dear reader. Even in the pursuit of earthly things the race is not always to the swift, "nor the battle to the strong, neither yet bread to the wise, nor yet riches to men of understanding, nor yet favour to men of skill"; and if this be so with the things "under the sun," and in the race between man and man, it is still more true of the things which are eternal, and of man's relations with his Maker. Here our only chance is by laying hold of His strength, and so be at peace with Him, for "Hast thou not known? hast thou not heard? the everlasting God, the Lord, the Creator of the ends of the earth, fainteth not, neither is weary; there is no searching of His understanding. *He giveth power to the faint; and to him that hath no might He increaseth strength.* Even the youths shall faint and be weary, and the young men shall utterly fall: but they that wait upon the Lord shall renew their strength; they shall mount up with wings as eagles; they shall run, and not be weary; they shall walk, and not faint" (Isa. xl. 28-31).

In contrast to the "multitude of an host," and mere physical strength and material resources, all of which are "a vain thing for safety," we are, in the last of the eight stanzas which make up the body of our Psalm, pointed to the real source of strength and blessedness.

"Behold, the eye of Jehovah is upon them that fear Him;
Upon them that hope in [or 'wait for'] His mercy,
To deliver their soul from death,
And to keep them alive in famine."

"Behold"—this is God's way of calling particular attention, and the great fact to which our thoughts are thus directed is *His special providence* over them that fear Him. There is a general providence of God over all His creatures, as we have seen, and the eyes of the Lord are *in every place,* beholding, or "watching," the evil and the good; but *there is also a special* providence of God over His own people, and "the eyes of Jehovah run to and fro throughout the whole earth, *to prove Himself strong in the behalf of them whose heart is perfect toward Him*" (2 Chron. xvi. 9).

I love the simple characterisation of God's people in these lines as *"those that fear Him,"* and who "wait for" (or depend on) "His mercy"; this description takes in the weakest and simplest believer, even as it includes the most "advanced."

Do you fear God, with a filial fear not only of awe, but of loving veneration, which is the outcome of His self-manifestation as the God of Grace?

Have you renounced all confidence in the flesh, and are you depending only on the mercy of God in Christ Jesus your Lord? then you are one upon whom His eye especially rests for *protection*—to deliver your soul from death; for *provision*—"to keep you alive in famine"; and for *direction*—"to instruct and teach you in the way in which you should go; to guide you with His eye."

THE RESPONSE

But to come to the last six lines which form the direct response to the call, or invitation, addressed to the righteous in the first six lines of our Psalm. After the praise-worthiness of our God and the blessedness of His people have been thus unfolded to us in the preceding sixteen verses, what shall we say? How shall we reply?

This we shall say:

"Our soul waiteth for Jehovah;
He is our help and our shield.
For our heart shall rejoice in Him,
Because we have trusted in His holy Name."

"Our *soul*"—with all the energies of our being. "*Our* soul"—for we being many are yet one, united for ever in one common life and destiny, and are to be henceforth one in faith, hope, and service. "*Waiteth*"—a fervent word this, used in only one other place in the Psalms, and describing a yearning, clinging faith, mixed with the strongest confidence. "*For Jehovah*"—this infinite, glorious God, whose wonderful character and ways in creation, redemption, and providence have been spread before us. "*He*"—all the emphasis of this passage resting upon this august personal pronoun—"He," not "the multitude of an host," not our own strength, not material resources—"*is our help and shield*," and therefore "*our hearts shall rejoice in Him*," even as we are invited to do in the very first line of the Psalm. "*In Him*," not in ourselves; "in Him," not in circumstances; "in Him," beyond all things in heaven above or in earth beneath, for He alone is "the unlimited sphere, the inexhaustible matter, and the perennial spring of our joy." Yes, "in Him" our heart shall rejoice, "*because we have trusted in His holy Name*," or in the words of the 20th Psalm: "Some trust in chariots, and some in horses, but we will make mention of the Name of Jehovah our God"—that "holy Name" which is itself the most precious message to weak and sinful man, and forms the ground of the Church's faith, hope, and love, as well as the "strong tower" into which the righteous can run and be safe—that blessed "Name" which in Scripture stands for *"God manifest"*—God no longer silent, as in nature, but revealing Himself in words of covenant and promise, and in acts of redemption—in that "Name" now fully "made known" to us by our Lord Jesus Christ, who was Himself the fullest manifestation of it (John xvii. 21, 26)—we have trusted, and by His grace shall continue to trust for ever.

The whole Psalm ends with a prayer which has in it the confident tone of expectancy—"Let Thy mercy, O Jehovah, be upon us, according as our hope is in Thee."

The word translated "according as," ought, perhaps, to be understood in the sense of *"inasmuch as"*—inasmuch as Thou hast already given us the grace to hope in Thee, it is surely not like Thee to suffer our hope to be put to shame. Let Thy mercy then, O Jehovah, still be upon us, for we depend on it alone, and Thy mercy is our only hope, especially after it has been shown us in the preceding verses that nothing else can avail either for our safety or blessedness.

And once again, "Blessed be His Name for ever," for the assurance that His mercy shall still be upon us, because He is faithful that promised, and His mercy, like Himself, "endureth for ever."

"For the mountains shall depart and the hills be removed; but My kindness shall not depart from thee, neither shall the covenant of thy peace be removed, saith Jehovah that hath mercy on thee." Amen!

IV

THE GLORIOUS KING AND BRIDEGROOM

PSALM XLV

L'm'natse'ach, al-Shoshannim, l'benai Korah, Maschil. Shir
Yedidoth

"My heart overfloweth with a goodly matter:
I speak the things which I have made touching the King:
My tongue is the pen of a ready writer.   '
Thou art fairer than the children of men;
Grace is poured into Thy lips:
Therefore God has blessed Thee for ever.
Gird Thy sword upon Thy thigh, O Mighty One,
Thy glory and Thy majesty.
And in Thy majesty ride on prosperously,
Because of truth and meekness and righteousness:
And Thy right hand shall teach Thee terrible things.
Thine arrows are sharp;
The peoples fall under Thee;
They are in the heart of the King's enemies.
Thy throne, O God, is for ever and ever:
A sceptre of righteousness is the sceptre of Thy kingdom.
Thou hast loved righteousness and hated wickedness:
Therefore God, Thy God, hath anointed Thee
With the oil of gladness above Thy fellows."

IV

THE GLORIOUS KING AND BRIDEGROOM

IN APPROACHING this most beautiful Psalm, which, in its very style and language, surpasses any mere human composition, even as the Glorious Person of whom it sings is "fairer than the children of men," the first question to be settled is, of whom does the Psalmist speak?

The writer of the Epistle to the Hebrews had no doubt on the subject, but proceeds on the assumption that it is the future Christ, the Son of God. In this assumption he is supported by a tradition of the ancient synagogue, in accordance with which the Targum renders verse 2: "Thy beauty, *O King Messiah,* is greater than that of the children of men." [1]

This Messianic interpretation, as it has been well observed, must be even a good deal more ancient than the Targum and the Epistle to the Hebrews, for it is most probable that just as Ezek. xxi. 27 ("until He come whose right it is") refers back to the promise of "Shiloh" [2] in Gen. xlix. 10, so El-Gibbor ("the Mighty God"), among Messiah's titles in Isa. ix. 6, refers back, in a similar manner, to Psa. xlv. Modern commentators, however, who for the most part seem nervously afraid to discover any too direct reference in the pages of the Old Testament Scriptures to the Person and work of the

---

[1] Most of the ancient Jewish commentators, including Kimchi and Ibn Ezra, also interpret this Psalm of "King Messiah."

[2] One rendering—and perhaps the most probable one—of this word is "to whom [or 'whose'] it is."

Messiah, labour hard, either to eliminate, or to explain away, the Messianic reference, and land in consequence in great confusion, and in contradiction with one another. The older and most generally received opinion is, that Solomon is the subject of this Psalm, and his marriage with Pharaoh's daughter is, according to these writers, the occasion which prompted its composition; but the language of this Psalm is altogether inapplicable to Solomon, for the inspired writer celebrates the deeds of a warrior "who girds on his sword" for conquest, and subdues his enemies with his sharp arrows (vers. 3-5); while the special characteristic of Solomon was that he was "a man of rest," a prince of peace. Besides, it would be very strange if this were a nuptial song in celebration of Solomon's marriage to Pharaoh's daughter, that there should be no mention in it of Egypt, while Tyre and other peoples are alluded to.

One German commentator, on the ground of a misinterpretation of verse 12, makes Ahab the subject of this Psalm because Jezebel his wife was the daughter of a king of the Zidonians, and because he had an "ivory house."

"But it is hard to believe that that wedded pair of evil memory are the originals of the lovely portraits in this Psalm, or that a Psalmist would recognise the (northern) kingdom of Israel as divinely established, and to be eternally upheld. Besides, the attributes of the king and the promises for his descendants cannot be extended without incongruity beyond the Davidic line." [3] But even Delitzsch, who shows forcibly enough the inapplicability of the Psalm to Solomon, and rejects Hitzig's application of it to the marriage of Ahab with Jezebel, on the ground that "the poet idealises the person celebrated, as foreshadowing the Messiah in a way that can only be justified in connec-

---

[3] Maclaren.

tion with a *Davidic* King," himself proceeds to unfold a
theory which is equally untenable—namely, that it was
composed in connection with the marriage of Joram of
Judah with Athaliah. His chief reasons for choosing
Joram are: because he is the son of Jehoshaphat, the
second Solomon of the Israelitish history; he became king
during his pious father's lifetime, under whom the Solo-
monic prosperity of Israel was revived; he was also
married to Athaliah, a Tyrian by origin, which, according
to the learned Professor, "makes it intelligible why the
homage of Tyre in particular, and only of Tyre, is mentioned; moreover, Jehoshaphat, his father, turned his attention to foreign wares, more especially Indian gold; he
even prepared a fleet for the purpose of going to Ophir,"
which fleet, as we know, was wrecked ere it started at
Ezion Geber, but which is supposed to account for the
allusions in the Psalm to "gold of Ophir" and "ivory."
But these, as has been well observed, are slender grounds
of identification, to say nothing of the miserable contrast
which Jehoram's reign—"a dreary record of apostasy and
defeat, culminating in a tragic death and a dishonoured
grave (2 Chron. xxi.)—would present to the Psalm."
Some commentators, hopeless of finding any one among
the kings of Israel answering to the inspired portraiture
drawn in this Psalm, have gone to the Gentiles in search
of the right person, and have found the occasion of its composition in the marriage of some Persian king; while the
English Canon Cheyne has perhaps gone to the lowest
depths in degrading this sublime Scripture by suggesting
its application to Ptolemy Philadelphus, whose "hands
were red with blood," and who married his own sister!

"All these conjectures show the hopelessness of identi-
fying the person addressed in the Psalm. It is said that
a knowledge of the historical allusions in the Psalter is
indispensable to enjoying it. They would often be helpful

if they could be settled, but that is no reason for elevating conjecture to the place of knowledge.

"One reason for the failure of attempts at identification is that the language is a world too wide for the best and greatest of Jewish kings. Much in the Psalm applies to an historical occasion, the marriage of some monarch; but there is much that as obviously goes beyond it.

"Either, then, the Psalm is hyperbole, outstripping even poetical licence, or there appear in it characteristics of the ideal monarch whom the Psalmist knew to be promised to Israel. Every king of Judah by descent and office was a living prophecy. The singer sees the Messiah shining, as it were, through the shadowy form of the earthly King, whose limitations and defects, no less than His excellencies and glories, pointed onwards to a greater than Solomon, in whom the 'sure mercies' promised to David should be facts at last." [4]   In brief, even if some historical occasion could be found for its composition, and there was strong reason to suppose that it were an Epithalamium in celebration of the marriage of a beloved king and hero in Israel, the Messianic character of the Psalm would still be apparent, "for if he was a king belonging to David's family (and no other can possibly be supposed), then he was the possessor of a kingship to which were attached, according to 2 Sam. vii., great promises extending into the unlimited future, and on which consequently hung all the prospects of the future prosperity and glory of Israel; and the poet is therefore fully warranted in regarding him in the light of the Messianic idea, and the Church is also fully warranted in referring the song which took its rise in some passing occasion, as a song for all ages, to the great King of the future, the goal of its hope." [5]   But my

---

[4] Maclaren.

[5] Delitzsch.

own judgment and sympathies go with the remarks of an English annotator [6] that "even if the New Testament furnished no intimation of its true meaning, yet so striking is the Psalm in many of its leading points, that every unprejudiced and humble inquirer after truth must, in contemplating this composition, be irresistibly led to the sense which the inspired writer intended. But when we have the Epistle to the Hebrews for a guide, and find in it the Psalm cited and used as an argument to prove the divinity of the Messiah, all doubt as to the real interpretation vanishes, and we at once acquiesce in the apostolic explication." Or, as the great English preacher has quaintly summarised it: "Some see in this Psalm only Solomon and Pharaoh's daughter—they are short-sighted; others see in it both Solomon and Christ—they are cross-eyed; well-focused spiritual eyes see here *Jesus only,* or if Solomon (or any one else) be present at all, it must be like those hazy shadows of passers-by which cross the face of the camera, and therefore are dimly traceable on a photographic landscape. The King—the God whose throne is for ever and ever—is no mere mortal, and His everlasting dominion is not bounded by Lebanon and Egypt's river. This is no wedding song of earthly nuptials, but an Epithalamium for the heavenly Bridegroom and His elect spouse." [7] No, as it has been well observed, this sacred song, like the holy ointment to which it refers in verses 7 and 8, was not made for the use of any man. "As for the

---

[6] Phillips.

[7] *Spurgeon.* "In such a state of matters," observes Hengstenberg, "we can only ascribe it to the power which a prejudice, having once obtained a firm footing for itself at the beginning of rationalism, even now exerts over the minds of men when a more impartial view of things is wont to be taken, that the Messianic exposition still finds so little favour. We see at least that the dislike to it appears without foundation."

perfume which thou shalt make, ye shall not make for
yourself, according to the composition thereof—it shall be
unto thee holy for Jehovah. Whosoever shall make like
unto the smell thereto, shall even be cut off from his people" (Exod. xxx. 37, 38).[8]

The Title

There can be no doubt that, in some cases at least, the
titles of the Psalms—which in many instances are as old
as the compositions to which they are attached, and were
inscribed by the same hand—are enigmatic, and, if properly
understood, would supply us with valuable hints as to the
contents and meaning of these sacred songs. This seems
to me to be particularly the case with the title of the beautiful Psalm we are about to consider. But the meaning of
the words in the original is not easy to fix, and the translations and interpretations which have been given by
Jewish and Christian commentators are for the most part
conjectural.

The first of the eight Hebrew words which make up
the title—*L'm'natse'ach*—is usually rendered "to the chief
musician." This word, which occurs as the first word in
fifty-five Psalms (of which thirty-nine at least are David's,
and nine of the Korahites, and five of Asaph),[9] is a participle noun of *netsach*, a verb, "the primary notion of
which is that of shining, and, in fact, of the purest and
most dazzling brightness: this, then, passes over to the
notion of shining over, or outshining, and, in fact, both of
uninterrupted continuance and of excellence and super-
iority. Thus, therefore, *m'natse'ach* is one who shows
eminent ability in any department, and then it gains the

---

[8] W. Kay, D.D.

[9] It is also found at the end of the Book of Habakkuk.

general signification of master, director, or chief overseer. At the head of the Psalms it is commonly understood of the director of the Temple music." But, as Delitzsch proceeds to point out, this translation cannot be the correct one, for: (1) "Even the Psalms of Asaph have this *L'm'natse'ach* at the beginning, and he himself a director of the Temple music, and, in fact, the chief director (1 Chron. xvi. 5), or at any rate he was one of the three (Heman, Asaph, Ethan) to whom the twenty-four classes of the 4000 Levite singers under the Davidico-Solomonic sanctuary were subordinate." (2) "The passage of the chronicler (1 Chron. xv. 17-21) which is most prominent in reference to this question does not accord with this explanation," [10] and he therefore understands it to mean "the Master of Song."

But *netsach* has not only the notion of *"shining"* and *"excelling,"* it means also strength, victory, stability, faithfulness, then the strong, the mighty, the faithful (unchangeable) One; and in 1 Sam. xv. 29 it is the name of the "Strength of Israel"—*"Netsach Israel"*—who lies not, nor repents; "for He is not a man that He should repent," and personally I see no reason why *L'm'natse'ach* should

---

[10] "According to this passage the three directors of the Temple music managed the cymbals, '*to sound aloud,*' eight other musicians of high rank, the *nablas,* and six others the *citherns,* 'to lead.' This expression cannot mean 'to direct,' for the direction belonged to the three, and the cymbals were also better adapted to it than the citherns. It means 'to take the lead in the playing'—the cymbals directed, and the citherns, better adapted to take the lead in the playing, were related to them, somewhat as the violins to the clarionets nowadays. Hence *m'natse'ach* is not the director of the Temple music, but in general the master of song, and *L'm'natse'ach* addresses the Psalm to him, whose duty it is to arrange it, and to train the Levite choristers; it therefore defines the Psalm as belonging to the songs of the Temple worship that require musical accompaniment. The translation of the Targum (Luther) also corresponds to this general sense of the expression."—*Delitzsch.*

not be regarded *as the dedication* of the particular composition on the part of the Psalmist to the "Strong," or
"Ever Abiding," or "Victorious One." This would be
specially applicable as a dedication to this Psalm, which
goes on to sing of Him who goes forth "conquering and to
conquer, and whose throne is for ever and ever."

The next two words, "al-Shoshannim," literally mean
"upon [or 'concerning'] *the Lilies.*" It has been suggested, but without any shadow of historical ground, that
there probably existed a well-known popular song which
began with the word "Lilies," and that this Psalm was
set to be sung after the same melody; but I am inclined,
with Hengstenberg and others of the older writers, to see a
symbolical reference in these words *to the theme of the
Psalm,* or, in the words of Bugenhagen and Joh. Gerhard,
"The heavenly Bridegroom and the Spiritual bride, they
are the lilies that are discoursed in this Psalm."

It is a disputed question whether "L'benai-Korah"
should be understood as *"by* the sons of Korah," in which
case they would, according to the inscription, be the
authors of the Psalm; or *"for* the sons of Korah," that is,
compositions handed over by the sweet Psalmist of Israel
to this Levitical family who, as we know from 1 Chron. vi.,
were appointed by David to be leaders of the service of
song in the House of the Lord.

There are two series of Psalms bearing the inscription
"To the sons of Korah," viz.: Psalms xlii. to xlix., and
also lxxxiv., lxxxv., lxxxvii., and lxxxviii.—eleven altogether; and they are all not only pervaded by a strong
prophetic element, but they have this in common that
"they delight in the praise of the God of Israel *as the
King* who sits enthroned in Jerusalem, and express a
delight in the services of His temple, with the tenderest
and most genuine emotion." Some of these "Korahitic"

Psalms bear a strong Davidic impress on their style and contents; but it is quite probable that "God was pleased to endow these sons of Korah with the inspiration of His Spirit, so that they used those poetic talents which their connection with the kindred art of music has led them to cultivate, in the production of compositions like those of their king and patron."

But whether or no the sons of Korah were the authors, or only those to whom these sacred prophetic songs were handed over to be set to appropriate music for liturgic use in the House of God, the mention of the "sons of Korah" reminds us of God's grace in sparing them from wrath and destruction, in which they were involved through the rebellion of their father, "so that the children of Korah died not" (Num. xxvi. 11), and the family became notable in Israel for their devotion to God and His service, and was, perhaps, brought into special relation with David through Samuel, who was himself "a son of Korah" (compare 1 Chron. vi. 33, 34 with 1 Sam. i. 1).

Our Psalm also bears the inscription of *"Maschil,"* which we find on twelve other Psalms, and describes *the object of the sacred composition.* According to Delitzsch, "the word means just *pia meditatio*—a devout meditation, and nothing more"; but his explanation does not seem to me satisfactory. It is the Hiphil participle used as a noun of the verb *sakhal,* "to understand," and in this voice "to make to understand," and, therefore, it would seem, must be taken to mean *"for instruction, i. e., a didactic poem."* A very decisive circumstance in favour of this interpretation of *Maschil* is (as pointed out by Hengstenberg), the occurrence of *Askil'kha* ("I will instruct thee") in verse 8 of Psa. xxxii.—the same verb, in the same voice, as *Maschil,* which is found as an inscription, for the first time, in that very Psalm. *Maschil,* then, signifies that the Psalm contains some deep teaching in which it is designed to instruct us, and which we could not otherwise acquire; and the subject in which we are to be instructed is disclosed in the last two words, which tell us that it is a *Shir Yedidoth*—"a song of that which is beloved," *i. e.*, lovely or lovable; and the very words which the writer is led by the spirit of inspiration to use mark the sacred character of the song and the *holiness* of the love of which it sings.[11]

No, this is no "mere ballad or romancing idle lay"; nor does it speak of mere human or sentimental love; but it celebrates the holy love and the tender spiritual affection subsisting between the glorious heavenly Bridegroom and His elect bride. It is "a song," but like unto that which Moses sang, which is described by the same word; it is a song like unto "the Song of Songs, which is Solomon's,"[12] of which, indeed, the germ is to be found in this Psalm.

It is indeed an Epithalamium, but in celebration of the marriage of Jehovah to His beloved Israel and of Christ and His Church.

---

[11] "It is things that are loved, because exciting love, therefore lovely, most pleasing things, which, as *Shir Yedidoth* says, form the contents of the song. Shir Yedidoth does not signify a marriage song; this would be *Shir chathûnnah*. Nor does it signify a secular erotic song—instead of which the expression *Shir anabhim* (Ezek. xxxiii. 32), or even *Shir dodim*, after Ezek. xvi. 8, and other passages would have been used. *Yodid is a noble word, and used of holy love.*"—*Delitzsch.*

In Jer. xii. 7 *Yedidoth* is used as a term of Israel.

[12] "The two in a way go together, and if there is a doubt as to whether the Song of Songs refers to Jehovah and His covenant relation to His people, then it must also be doubtful as to whether Psa. xlv. refers to the Divine Man and Heavenly Bridegroom—and if not, the question arises, How did it get into the Canon?" —*A. Saphir.*

Its Relation to Psalm xliv

The connection of this Psalm with the preceding one is very apparent. In the 44th, which is a litany of the remnant of Israel in the midst of the final tribulation at the time of the end, we hear the appeal of those who for His sake "are killed all the day long, and accounted as sheep for the slaughter." The last verses of that Psalm form one long, piteous cry for God's help and interposition:

"Awake, why sleepest Thou, O Lord?
Arise, cast us not off for ever.
Wherefore hidest Thou Thy face,
And forgettest our affliction and our oppression?
For our soul is bowed down to the dust;
Our belly cleaveth unto the earth.
Arise for our help, and redeem us for Thy mercies' sake."

To this cry the 45th Psalm is the answer.

Here we see Israel's Shepherd starting forth, at the voice of the cry of His slaughtered sheep, for their help and deliverance.

His long-suffering is at an end; "the day of vengeance" against the apostate anti-Christian nations "is in His heart," and "the year of His redeemed" is at last come (Isa. lxiii. 4); and the Psalmist beholds in his vision the Omnipotent champion of right arraying Himself in His armour, girding His sword on His thigh, and setting forth as the Vindicator of righteousness, meekness, and truth.

He sees Him not only setting out, but follows Him in spirit as He rides on prosperously, conquering and to conquer, and having caught a glimpse of Him, he is so ravished with His beauty, that before he can speak of the progress of His march, and the accomplishment of His mighty work, he must needs stop and describe the glory of His Person.

Unlike the artificial flatteries of court poets who may have no real interest in, or admiration for, the subject of their compositions, the Psalmist tells us that his whole heart and soul are centered on his delightful task. "My heart overfloweth"—literally "boils," or "bubbles over." [13] It is out of the overflowing abundance of his heart that his mouth speaketh. There is within him a well—a fountain which must overflow, and which he cannot suppress even if he would.

That which so fills his heart to overflowing he calls a *dabhar tob*, "a good word," or "a good matter that finds utterance and is put into the form of words."

"I say to myself, My work ['my composition'] is for [or 'touching'] the King"; [14] therefore it must be "good," for something of the beauty and majesty of this most glorious King must be reflected in the very language which is used to set Him forth.

It is from the object that the goodness of the "word" or "matter" is derived, and it is the thought that the theme to which he is to address himself is so glorious that causes his heart to boil within him, and which inspires him not only with the desire but with a certain *enabling* to be eloquent, so that his tongue is "the pen of a ready writer," in the sense of being not only fluent but skilful (Ezra vii. 6).

But it would almost seem from the words which he employs as if the Psalmist were astonished at himself, and

---

[13] The figure is from the water of a fountain bursting forth, or from a seething pot or cauldron boiling over.

[14] "It does not *all* concern the ,King immediately, for much of it concerns the Queen, and about one-half is directly addressed to her. But it relates to Him inasmuch as it relates to His family. Christ ever identifies Himself with His people; so that whatever is done to them is done to Himself. Their interests are His."—*George Harpur*.

at the multitude of the thoughts which he feels are within him, but not of him.

His tongue is but the "pen"—the real writer which gives it such readiness and skill to set forth the glories of the Person, and exploits in battle of this Hero-King, is Another, and One greater than any of the sons of Asaph, or than the sweet Psalmist of Israel himself. *We* know whence these beautiful thoughts and words came which sometimes filled the prophets themselves with surprise, and the import of which they themselves often did not understand, when the Spirit who was in them testified beforehand of the sufferings of the Christ, and of the glories which should follow (1 Pet. i. 10, 11). The specific nature of inspiration must for ever remain a mystery to all of us who are not prophets; but this we know—that prophecy hath its source not on earth in the finite thoughts of man, but in heaven, in the infinite thoughts and purposes of the Infinite and Omniscient God, and that these "holy men of God," who told us so much about the King long before His advent, spoke not merely out of their own hearts, but as they were moved, or "borne along," by the Holy Ghost (2 Pet. i. 21).

"The King in His Beauty"

How the Psalmist's own soul is ravished with the King's beauty is expressed in the second verse:

> "More beautiful art Thou than the sons of men;
> Grace is poured on Thy lips:
> Therefore God hath blessed Thee for ever."

This begins the address to the glorious King and Bridegroom, which extends to the end of the ninth verse, after which it is the royal Bride who is addressed.

The Hebrew word *yafyafitha,* "More beautiful art Thou" (or "Thou art fairer," as in the Authorised and Revised

Versions), is of remarkable formation, and there is no parallel to it in the Old Testament. Some have supposed that it is formed by a reduplication of the first two radicals of the verb *yafa,* in which case the sense might be given by the repetition, "Beautiful, beautiful art Thou"; but as this has no analogy in the Hebrew Scriptures, Hengstenberg and Ewald have suggested that it might be a contraction of the two words *yafa-yafeetha:* "Beauty! Thou art beautiful—*i. e., Thou art perfectly beautiful.*" Delitzsch renders it in the passive sense, and says the meaning is, "Thou art beyond compare beautifully fashioned, or endowed with beauty beyond the children of men." Yes, so fair and altogether beautiful is our glorious King, that even inspired psalmists have to coin words of sufficient intensity in order to give us at all an adequate idea; but even then they seem at a loss how fully to show forth His praise or to utter all His glory.

That it is not of mere physical beauty that the Psalmist speaks is evident from the whole context, though some have supposed that the physical beauty of the King is here dwelt on "as the indication of a fair nature which moulds the fair form":

> "For of the soul the body form doth take:
> For soul is form, and doth the body make."

How beyond compare beautifully fashioned, even physically, must He have been who is the true King, because He was in every way the true and perfect Man, whose outward form was not spoiled and disfigured by the distemper of innate sin as is the case with the rest of the "sons of men," until He who knew no sin was made sin for us, and Jehovah laid upon Him the iniquity of us all— when gradually, through His vicarious sorrows and sufferings, His visage became more marred than that of any man, and His form more than that of the sons of men (Isa. lii. 14).

No wonder that in the early Church one party, in opposition to the repulsive representations of another tendency, pictured our Lord's physical appearance "as fair as that of a woman and majestic as that of a hero." "The Heavenly Father," says Chrysostom, "poured out on Him in full streams that personal beauty which is distilled only drop by drop upon mortal man"; and Augustine says that "He was beautiful in His mother's bosom, beautiful in the arms of His parents, beautiful on the cross, and beautiful in the sepulchre"; while in the fifteenth century the Romish historian Nicephorus ventures on a fuller sketch of the outward appearance of our Lord "as handed down from antiquity" in the following words: "He was very beautiful; His height was fully seven spans; His hair bright auburn, and not too thick, and was inclined to wave in soft curls. His eyebrows were black and arched, and His eyes seemed to shed from them a gentle, golden light. They were very beautiful. His nose was prominent; His beard lovely, but not very long. He wore His hair, on the contrary, very long, for no scissors had ever touched it, nor any human hand, except that of His mother, when she played with it in His childhood. He stooped a little, but His body was well formed. His complexion was that of the ripe brown wheat, and his face like His mother's rather oval than round, with only a little red in it, but through it there shone dignity, intelligence of soul, gentleness, and a calmness of spirit never disturbed." But all these mere beautiful guesses and fictitious descriptions of our Lord's physical appearance, which rather jar against our sense of reverence, are beside the mark. It is one of the marks of the inspiration of the Gospels that they are altogether silent about the bodily appearance of our Lord, even as it is a work of God's providence, that neither authentic description, nor any likeness of Christ has been handed down to man, for it is not after the flesh, but after the Spirit, that we must learn to know Him, and it is to the *moral* beauty of our Saviour that the Spirit of God would direct our souls.

In spiritual beauty our Lord Jesus is truly peerless among the sons of men, although there have been some men of great moral excellence.

We think of men like Abraham, "the friend of God"; of Joseph, of Moses, of David, of Daniel, of John the beloved, and Paul; but their beauty was but a drop derived from His infinite fulness, for the beauty of the most beautiful of the saints is but the perfection of His comeliness which is put upon them (Ezek. xvi. 14), while His is innate.

Even unbelievers who have refused to bow their knees in homage to Him as the Son of God have had to confess that for moral beauty Christ is the King of men. And He is *only* beautiful. Others, however beautiful, have still had some flaw, but in Him there never was any spot nor blemish, and the record of His life in the Gospel is absolutely unique, even as the wonderful Personality, of which it must of necessity be a truthful portrayal, stands removed, and high above every other life that has ever been lived on earth.[15]

---

[15] Since these notes on Psa. xlv. were first printed in the "Scattered Nation," I have been struck, in reading "The Fact of Christ," by P. Carnegie Simpson, M.A., with the following passage, which I have much pleasure in quoting: "This aloneness of Jesus appears in two ways, or, rather, has two degrees. First, His whole manner betrays that His moral experience and that of other men were not parallel. He who so searchingly told others of the evil within their hearts made no confession for Himself. He who gave the despairing sinner every other token of brotherhood never spoke as if He Himself had been in the same case. He who was so morally sensitive that He has become the supreme conscience of mankind, yet challenged men to convict Him of sin. All this reveals a singularness by which He is not only separate from sinners, but is also distinct from the saints. The saints among men all tell us how they reached sanctity, if at all, only from below, having toiled with

He who taught His disciples to pray "Forgive us our
trespasses," and preached repentance as an essential qualification for entering into the kingdom, never Himself
asked for forgiveness, or felt any need of repentance, but
• could in the fullest self-consciousness face His enemies
with the question, "Which of you convinceth Me of sin?"

Let us imagine an assembly of all the morally "fair"
and beautiful of the sons of men in all ages, including
prophets, psalmists, and apostles, and Jesus Himself in
their midst; and what would their attitude to Him be?
Would they not all fall down before Him and kiss the
hem of His garment, and confess that they were not
worthy to unloose the latchet of His shoes?

"O fair sun and fair moon and fair stars and fair flowers
and fair roses and fair lilies!" exclaims Samuel Ruther-
ford, "but O ten thousand times fairer Lord Jesus! Alas!
I have wronged Him in making the comparison. O black
sun and moon, but O fair Lord Jesus! O black flowers
and black lilies and roses, but O fair, fair, ever fair Lord
Jesus! O black heavens, but O fair Christ! O black
angels, but O surpassingly fair Lord Jesus!" While another old divine exclaims, "In Thee, O Christ, we can
contemplate and must confess all the beauty and loveliness
both of heaven and earth; the beauty of heaven is God,

---

tears and prayers up the bitter path of repentance to a newness of
life. The Psalms tell us that, and the *Confessions,* and the *De
Imitatione;* the whole company of holy and humble men of heart
tell us that. But Jesus never tells us that. And this is not all.
There is a second thing about this strange moral aloneness of
Jesus—something not negative, but positive. Not only did Jesus
never betray a sense of any moral imperfection or moral need, but,
further, He regarded Himself as the sufferer of all others' needs.
. . . Others are lost sheep; He is not only not lost, but is the
shepherd. Others are sick; He is not only in health, but is the
physician. Others' lives are forfeit; He is not only His own, but
is the ransom. Others—all others—are sinners; He not only is
not a sinner, but is a Saviour."

the beauty of earth is man: the beauty of heaven and earth together art Thou, O Thou God-Man."

But whatever the attitude of men on earth, in heaven the redeemed family, even when perfected in glory, will ever cast their crowns at His feet and cry, "Thou alone art worthy! For Thou art not only the chiefest among ten thousand, but *altogether* lovely; and if there is any moral beauty in us, it is because we have gazed upon Thy glory, and have been transformed into Thine image!"

One feature of beauty is especially singled out by the Psalmist, and that is expressed in the words—

"Grace is poured on Thy lips"

The utterance of the lips may in a special manner be taken as an index of moral character, for it is out of the abundance of the heart that the mouth speaketh. But here it is perhaps not so much the words that proceed from His lips as the lips themselves, which the inspired singer stops to admire. Their very form, the heavenly smile resting upon them, and each of their movements, are graceful and lovely, and the sight of them is enough to awaken love and trust. No wonder that from these beautiful lips, on which grace was poured without measure, there poured forth such wonderful and beautiful words. Only those blessed lips *could* have uttered them, and as we read the words of Christ in the Gospels, and are compelled to join in the exclamation, "Never man spake like this Man"; or, as with the men at Nazareth, we marvel at the gracious words which proceed out of His mouth (Luke iv. 22)—we once again pause and echo the words of our Psalm:

"Grace is poured on Thy lips,
Therefore God hath blessed Thee for ever,"—

for Thou art the rightful Heir, and fit Inheritor of the

Messianic promises made to the Fathers, as when God spoke to Abraham saying, "I will bless thee, . . . and be Thou a blessing; . . . and in Thee shall all the families of the earth be blessed" (Gen. xii. 2, 3) ; and because in Thy blessing of universal dominion is bound up the blessing of all nations, "therefore shall peoples praise Thee for ever and ever" (ver. 17).

But the ideal King is not only All-glorious—He is also All-mighty. In Him strength and beauty are mingled, and this combination of gentleness and warrior strength— "a union which has been often realised in heroic figures, and which is needful for the highest type of either, is perfectly fulfilled only in the Lamb of God, who is also the Lion of the tribe of Judah." [16]

"Gird Thy sword on Thy thigh, O Mighty One;
 Thy glory and Thy majesty.
And in Thy majesty ride on prosperously [literally 'prosper—
     ride forth'] ;
In behalf of truth and meekness, righteousness [or 'in behalf of
     truth and the oppression' or 'affliction of righteousness'] ;
And Thy right hand shall teach Thee terrible things."

The sword is the symbol of war and of punitive justice. For long centuries the flag of truce has been, so to say, hung out by God, and the message has gone forth, "Peace, peace!" but men have taken no heed; they have despised the long-suffering of God, which was exercised with a view to lead them to repentance, and the whole of this dispensation of grace is a commentary on the words that "though favour be shown to the wicked, yet will he not learn righteousness."

Therefore at last the challenge of war which has been declared by man against God and His Anointed will be

---

[16] Maclaren.

taken up by Messiah, and wicked men and devils will then learn what it is to provoke the wrath of the Almighty.

The name by which the blessed champion of truth and righteousness is addressed, *Gibbor* ("O Mighty One"), is a well-known Messianic title. In Psa. xxiv. 8 it is twice used of "the King of Glory," before whom alone "the gates lift up their heads," and "the everlasting doors" open, on His return from the conquest of His enemies, having proved Himself "the Lord strong and mighty, the Lord mighty in battle"; and in Isa. ix. 6 (which, as I have said in the introduction, probably refers back to Psa. xlv.), we find it in what is perhaps the richest constellation of Messianic titles to be found in the Old Testament:

> "Unto us a Child is born,
> Unto us a Son is given:

and the government shall be upon His shoulder: and His name shall be called Wonderful, Counsellor, Mighty God [*El-Gibbor*—'God-hero' or 'God-mighty Man,' as it might be rendered], Everlasting Father, Prince of Peace" —a most glorious prophecy of the same Son of David and Son of God, and in which we mark the same wonderful blending of the human and the Divine in the One Person as in Psa. xlv. And not only is this Mighty One to gird His sword on His thigh, but He is to clothe Himself in His "glory and majesty," and it is important to note that these two words, *hod* and *hadar,* when so united, are the common designation of the brilliancy of the Divine glory. Thus we read of Jehovah in Psa. xcvi. 6 that "honour and majesty—*hod ve-hadar*—are before Him: strength and beauty are in His sanctuary," though it is true that they sometimes describe also the *reflection* of the Divine glory on the Davidic or theocratic kings of Israel.

Oh, what a contrast to His first coming! Then there was the *veiling* of His glory, and the *hiding* of His power, but now the time has come for the display of His power and the manifestation of His glory.

And thus arrayed "in this *Thy Majesty*" (showing that in His case it is His own glory, and no mere reflection), the voice of the Father and of the Spirit, as well as of the oppressed Church, which utters itself through the soul of the Psalmist, is "Prosper"—for this word stands first in the Hebrew after "Thy glory," and constitutes, so to say, the Divine benediction on the mission on which He is about to start.

Yes, "Prosper," O Thou Glorious One, for it is a good cause on behalf of which Thy power is to be exercised— "ride forth" in Thine irresistible strength, for it is "because" in behalf of, or on the business of [17]truth and meekness and righteousness; or, as already suggested, on behalf of truth and the "oppression" or "affliction of righteousness." Long has truth been held bound, and where it has asserted itself, it has been persecuted and trampled upon. It is so now, alas! not only in the world, but in the "Church"; it will be so yet to a degree unknown before, and at the time of the end, when the "blasphemer and reproacher" will succeed in causing all men, except the very elect, to believe a lie. The favourite motto, *"Magna est veritas, et praevalebit,"* shall indeed be true in the end, but not in this age; for this dispensation, according to the Divine forecast of Christ Himself and of His inspired apostles, ends in the temporary triumph not of good, but of evil; not of righteousness, but of wickedness—apostasy and wickedness which will reach to such an unprecedented height that men will believe that Antichrist is Christ and that Satan is God.

---

[17] So the Chaldaic renders the Hebrew—*al-debhar.*

A graphic picture of the condition of things at the time of the end is to be found in the confession and prayer of the godly remnant in Isa. lix.:

"For our transgressions are with us;
And as for our iniquities we know them;
In transgressing and denying Jehovah
And turning away from following our God,
Speaking transgression and revolt;
Conceiving and uttering from the heart words of falsehood.
And judgment is turned away backward,
And righteousness standeth afar off,
For truth is fallen in the street;
And uprightness cannot enter;
Yea, truth is lacking;
And he that departeth from evil maketh himself a prey."

In this prophecy also, as in Psa. xlv., it is the oppression and suppression of truth and the affliction of righteousness, or of those who exemplify these virtues, which is the final cause of the interposition in judgment of the King of Righteousness:

"And Jehovah saw it, and it displeased Him that there was no judgment.
And He saw that there was no intercessor;
Therefore His own arm brought salvation unto Him,
And His righteousness it upheld Him;
And He put on righteousness as a coat of mail,
And an helmet of salvation upon His head.
And He put on garments of vengeance for clothing,
And was clad with zeal as a cloke.
According to their deeds accordingly He will repay,
Fury to His adversaries,
Recompense to His enemies;
To the islands He will repay recompense;
So [by means of these judgments] shall they fear the name of Jehovah from the west,
And His glory from the rising of the sun,
For the adversary [or 'affliction' or 'tribulation'] shall come like a rushing stream;
The Spirit of Jehovah driveth him [or 'driven on by the Spirit of Jehovah']."

It is to be noted also that in this prophecy as in the Psalm the glorious King is *alone* in His mighty exploits; for even as when He came to accomplish our salvation it was *"His own Self"* that did it all, and it was alone that He trod the path of humiliation and suffering, culminating in His vicarious death on the cross, so also in the final overthrow of evil it is *"His own arm"* that brings salvation unto Him, and when He shall tread down nations in His anger, and trample them in His fury, He shall be "alone" in His work of venegance, and of the peoples there "shall be no man" with Him (Isa. lxiii. 1-6). This is particularly emphasised in the last line of the fourth verse: *"And Thy right hand shall teach Thee terrible things"*—it alone, without any outside aid, without any guide or counsellor, "shall teach Thee" or "make Thee witness awe-striking deeds," as the words may be rendered. The word translated "terrible things" is the same as used in Psa. lxv. 5, where we read that:

"By terrible things Thou wilt answer us in righteousness,
O God of our Salvation:
Thou that art the confidence of all the ends of the earth,
And of them that are afar off upon the sea."

And what these "terrible things" or "awe-striking" deeds are by which the knowledge of Jehovah shall become universal, and God shall finally become "the confidence of all the ends of the earth," we have described for us in many of the Psalms and prophecies, but especially in chapters vi. and xix. of the Book of Revelation. They are the awful signs and judgments which will accompany the Second Advent of the Great King, in consequence of which "the kings of the earth and the princes, and the chief captains, and the rich and the strong, and every bondman and every freeman, shall hide themselves in the caves and the rocks of the mountains; and shall say to the mountains and to the rocks, Fall on us and hide us from the face of Him that sitteth on the throne, and from the wrath of the Lamb; for the great day of their wrath is come, and who is able to stand?" (Rev. vi. 15-17).

In the next verse the Psalmist sees the Great Hero in actual conflict. The tense and style is that of vision. The order of the words in the Hebrew is:

> "Thine arrows are sharp;
> Peoples fall under Thee—
> In the heart of the King's enemies."

He *has* ridden forth; His sword is on His thigh; His bow is bent; His arrows, which are terribly sharp, are let loose; they go forth with irresistible force; they do not miss their aim; they pierce the very heart of His enemies, and the result is that peoples fall under Him.

"The King's enemies," as has been well observed, is not simply an expression for "Thy enemies," as some think, but rather implies that *Christ's Kingship* is the ground of their enmity; just as in the second Psalm their cry is, "Let us break their bands asunder." It is against those who have defied the Lord's Anointed, and are found ranged under the banner of the Antichrist, that His special anger is kindled.

> "See now that I, even I, am He,
> And there is no God with Me:
> I kill, and I make alive;
> I have wounded, and I heal;
> And there is none that can deliver out of My hand.
> For I lift up My hand to heaven,
> And say, As I live for ever,
> If I whet My glittering sword,
> And Mine hand take hold on judgment;
> I will render vengeance to Mine adversaries,
> And will recompense them that hate Me.
> I will make Mine arrows drunk with blood.
> And my sword shall devour flesh;

With the blood of the slain and the captives,
From the head of the leaders of the enemy"
(Deut. xxxii. 39-42).[18]

But in view of the general misinterpretation of these
solemn Scriptures, it is well, perhaps, once again to re-
vert to the question as to *the time* and nature of the judgments described in our Psalm and in the other connected
prophecies which have been quoted:

"Most modern expositors interpret the conquest in these verses
of the triumphs of Christianity: 'The Messiah' (in the words of

---

[18] It was this prophetic description of Messiah's future exploits
against His enemies, given in Psa. xlv. and other prophecies, which
supplied Milton with images for his lofty and spirited strains in
describing the victory of the Son of God over Satan and his angels:

"So spake the Son, and in terror changed
His count'nance, too severe to be beheld,
And full of wrath bent on His enemies.
At once the Four spread out their starry wings
With dreadful shade contiguous, and the orbs
Of His fierce chariot roll'd, as with the sound
Of torrent floods, or of a numerous host.
He on His impious foes right onward drove,
Gloomy as night; under His burning wheels
The steadfast empyrean shook throughout,
All but the throne itself of God. Full soon
Among them He arrived; in His right hand
Grasping ten thousand thunders, which He sent
Before Him, such as in their souls infixed
Plagues: they, astonished, all resistance lost,
All courage; down their idle weapons dropp'd;
O'er shields, and helms, and helmèd heads He rode
Of thrones and mighty seraphim prostrate,
That wish'd the mountains now might be again
Thrown on them as a shelter from His ire.
Nor less on either side tempestuous fell
His arrows, from the fourfold-visaged Four,
Distinct with eyes, and from the living wheels
Distinct alike with multitude of eyes;
One spirit in them ruled, and every eye
Glared lightning, and shot forth pernicious fire
Among the accurst, that wither'd all their strength,
And of their wonted vigour left them drained,
Exhausted, spiritless, afflicted, fall'n."

Bishop Horne) 'is magnificently described as, by the irresistible might of His power, subduing idolatry and iniquity to the faith and temper of the Gospel'; the 'sword' with which He is girded being 'the Word of God,' to which this emblem is applied (Heb. iv. 12, and Eph. vi. 17). And so even Bishop Horsley, who, to suit this view, proposes, instead of the 'terrible things' which the Conqueror's right hand should show Him (ver. 4), to read 'wonderful things,' which, he says, 'I take to be the overthrow of the Pagan superstition in the Roman Empire, and the other great kingdoms of the world, by the mere preaching of the Gospel, seconded by the exemplary lives and the miracles of the first preachers, and their patient endurance of imprisonment, torture, and death for the sake of Christ.' And again: 'The subjugation of nations by the prosecution of this war is the triumph of the Church over idolatry, which first took place in the reign of Constantine the Great, when the Christian religion was established in the Roman Empire, and idolatry put down by that emperor's authority.' And truly this was a 'wonderful' thing, as he proceeds eloquently to show in review of all the circumstances; but, independent of the meaning of this word, which is always found in the sense of 'terrible,' 'dreadful,' or 'fearful' (as it is variously rendered in the English version). The whole passage evidently pictures a work of judgment, not of grace; and the parallel is rather Rev. xix. 15, where, of the Lord Jesus coming in power, it is said—'And out of His mouth goeth a sharp sword, that with it He should smite the nations' (the Antichristian confederacy, xvii. 14): 'And He shall rule them with a rod of iron; and He treadeth the wine-press of the fierceness and wrath of Almighty God': the 'sword' here, too, is His 'word,' but pronouncing the doom of the rebellious, and thus the suitable accompaniment of the 'sharp arrows in the heart of the King's enemies' (ver. 5): identical with 'the rod of His mouth' in another parallel prophecy (Isa. xi. 4)—'He shall smite the earth with the rod of His mouth, and with the breath of His lips He shall slay the wicked' (Heb., 'the Wicked One')—'that Wicked One . . . whom the Lord shall consume with the spirit [breath] of His mouth, and shall destroy with the brightness of His coming' (2 Thess. ii. 8).

"The time is thus determined to be the Second Advent of the Messiah, and the war which He wages is 'in tthe cause of truth, meekness, and righteousness'—for their vindication against deceit, oppression, and injustice; as also stated in Isa. xi. 4, just quoted, in connection with His 'slaying the Wicked One.' 'With righteousness shall He judge [vindicate] the poor, and reprove with equity for the meek of the earth'; and, Psa. lxxii. 4, also relating to the same period—'He shall judge the poor of the people; He shall save the children of the needy, and shall break in pieces the oppressor'" (De Burgh).[19]

The conflict is at an end; His enemies are made His footstool, and the Mighty Victor is set on His throne, where He is thus addressed:

"Thy throne, O God, is for ever and ever;
A sceptre of uprightness ['equity'] is the sceptre of Thy kingdom;
Thou hast loved righteousness, and hated wickedness;
Therefore God, Thy God, hath anointed Thee
With the oil of joy above Thy fellows."

Here we have the prophetic realisation of the theocratic ideal. Here at last is the Kingdom of our God and the Power of His Christ. It is the reign of the true Man, for He that sits on that throne is the promised Son of David, yet it is a Man in whom dwelleth the fulness of the Godhead bodily, so that He can be addressed in the truest and divinest sense as Elohim. There is no doubt that this is one of the most striking passages in the Old Testament in reference to the Divine character of Messiah. Jews, Unitarians, and Rationalists may twist and wrest this Scripture as they will, and even "Orthodox" commentators may nervously shrink at finding such a direct

---

[19] The passage which, perhaps, has influenced commentators to decide for the First Advent, against the natural sense of the text, supported by these parallel prophecies, is Rev. vi. 2, where, on the opening of the first seal, we read: "And I saw, and behold a white horse; and He that sat on him had a bow; and a crown was given unto Him; and He went forth conquering and to conquer": a parallel, it is admitted, to vers. 4, 5 of the Psalm—"And in Thy majesty ride prosperously. . . . Thine arrows are sharp in the heart of the King's enemies." But it is assumed that in this seal Christ is described in the character of His first appearing and acting in grace; whereas, nothing is more evident than that the Apocalypse throughout (as well as the seals following) is a prophecy of judgment, and "The Revelation of Jesus Christ" in the day of His power—not of His humiliation.

statement about the Divinity of Messiah in the Old Testament—and, try to explain it away as they may, *no other sense can be* brought out of it than that the King, who in ver. 4 is addressed as *Gibbor*—"O most mighty"—and exhorted to clothe Himself in His Divine Glory and Majesty, is here directly addressed as God.

Various explanations have been attempted with a view to evade and to weaken the testimony of this prophecy to the Divine character of the Messiah. They may be summarised in the words of Professor Delitzsch, who writes as follows:

"In order to avoid addressing the King with the word *Elohim*, ver. 6 has been interpreted (1) 'Thy throne of God is for ever and ever . . .'; (2) 'Thy throne is God (=Divine) for ever and ever'; but it cannot possibly be so expressed after the analogy of 'the altar of wood = wooden,' or 'the time is showers of rain = rainy' (Ezra x. 13), since God is neither the substance of the throne, nor can the throne itself be regarded as a representation or figure of God; in this case the predicative *Elohim* would require to be taken as a genitive for the throne of Elohim, which, however, cannot possibly be supported in Hebrew by our Syntax. . . . Accordingly one might adopt the first mode of interpretation ('Thy throne of God is for ever and ever'), which is also commended by the fact that the earthly throne of the Theocratic King is actually called 'the throne of Jehovah' (1 Chron. xxix, 23).

"But the sentence, 'Thy throne of God is an everlasting one,' sounds tautological, inasmuch as that which the predicate asserts is already implied in the subject; and we have still first of all to try whether Elohim cannot, with the LXX., O θρονος σου, ο θεος, εις αιωνα αιωνος, be taken as a vocative. Now, since before everything else God's throne is eternal (Psa. x. 16; Lam. v. 19), and a love of righteousness and a hatred of evil is also found elsewhere as a description of Divine holiness (Psa. v. 4; Isa. lxi. 8), Elohim would be obliged to be regarded as addressed to God, if language addressed to the King did not follow with 'therefore.' But might Elohim by any possibility be even addressed to the king who is here celebrated? It is certainly true that the custom with the Elohim-Psalms of using Elohim as of equal dignity with Jahve is not favourable to this supposition; but the following surpassing of the Elohim by Elohim Eloekha (' God, Thy God') renders it possible. And since elsewhere earthly authorities are also called Elohim (Exod. xxi. 6, xxii. 8 *seq.;* Psa. lxxxii., *cf.* cxxxviii. 1) because they are God's representatives and the bearers of His image upon earth, so the King who is celebrated in this Psalm may be all the more readily styled Elohim, when in His heavenly beauty, His irresistible doxa or glory, and His Divine holiness, He seems to the Psalmist to be the perfected realisation of the close relationship in which had God set David and his seed to Himself. He calls him *Elohim* just as Isaiah calls the exalted royal child whom he exultingly salutes in chap. ix. 1-6 *El-Gibbor*. He gives him this name because in the transparent exterior of his fair humanity he sees the glory and holiness of God as having attained a salutary or merciful conspicuousness among men. At the same time, however, he guards this calling of the king by the name Elohim against being misapprehended by immediately distinguishing the God, who stands above him, from the Divine King by the words 'Elohim, thy God,' which, in the Korahitic Psalms, and in the Elohimic Psalms in general, is equivalent to 'Jahve, thy God' (xliii. 4; xlviii. 14; l. 7)."

The chief value of this critical disquisition is to show that the first line of the sixth verse must be rendered in the vocative as it is done in the English versions, and all the old translations, as well as by the writer of the Epistle to the Hebrews, who quotes it in this sense as addressed to the Messiah (Heb. i. 8), and that, in the words of Hengstenberg, the non-Messianic interpreters of this Psalm "have not been able to bring forward any other rendering which is grammatically tenable."   As to the suggestion that the king is so addressed not because He is Divine in character, but in the sense in which judges and rulers are sometimes called *Elohim,* on the ground, as our Lord puts it in John x. 35, that "unto them the word of God came," and that in their official and executive capacity they *represented* God, it is sufficient to answer that the direct ascription to the Messiah of the Divine Name is coupled with a throne *of eternal duration,* which distinguishes Him from all others "called Gods"— the kings and judges of the earth, who are so called only as His types, and whose dominion is *finite.*

But, I repeat, what we see here is but the realisation of the theocratic ideal and the fulfilment of the promises to

the House of David, and if we want to know what is
meant by a "theocracy," we find it expressed in one short
verse of the Prophet Isaiah, when, speaking of a future
time when it shall be fully realised, he says, "For Jehovah
is our Judge, Jehovah is our Law-giver, Jehovah is our
King; and He will bring us salvation," or "He also will
be our Saviour" (Isa. xxxiii. 22). What was God's original purpose in the establishment of the Davidic house as
a royal family in Israel? Was it not that from that family
there should ultimately spring One in whom the theocratic
ideal would be fully realised; One who, "although of
their brethren," and "from the midst of them" (Deut.
xviii. 15-18), should yet be Jehovah-Tsidkenu—"the
mighty God"—whose reign would be the reign of God, and
whose kingdom would be "the kingdom of heaven" on
earth? In the interval the mere human kings of the
house of David were regarded as types and God's representatives. Thus we read that when Solomon commenced
his rule "he sat on the throne of Jehovah as king instead
of David his father" (1 Chron. xxix. 23). The throne
was Jehovah's, and Solomon and his successors only occupied it until the real King, Jehovah's true representative,
should appear. Hence it is that even when Israel had
kings they were always pointed onward to another king:
"Behold, a King shall reign in righteousness, and princes
shall rule in judgment"; or, in the words of Jeremiah,
"Behold the days come, saith the Lord, that I will raise
unto David a righteous branch, and a king shall reign
and prosper." Did they not have kings at the time these
prophecies were uttered? Yes, but those kings were
mere shadows, filling up the gap for a time until the true
King should be manifested—"He who is the blessed and
only Potentate, King of kings and Lord of lords." This
also is the reason why in the Old Testament the coming
of the Messiah is often spoken of as the advent of God:

"Sing and rejoice, O daughter of Zion, for lo, I come, and I will dwell in the midst of thee, saith Jehovah"; and yet He who was thus to come is the Sent One, "the man whose name is the Branch."

In the fulness of time One in whom this ideal was fully realised did appear, and before His birth the following announcement was made to His mother: "Behold thou shalt conceive in thy womb, and bring forth a Son, and shall call His name Jesus." What can be more human? But it goes on: "He shall be great, and shall be called the Son of the Highest, and the Lord God shall give unto Him the throne of His father David, and He shall reign over the house of Jacob for ever; and of His kingdom there shall be no end." Here is that One for whose manifestation the ages were waiting, the "Immanuel," God in man—"He whose right it is," not merely because through His mother He is the true Son of David, but because He is the Son of the Highest; the irradiated brightness of His glory, the exact representation of the very Being of God, who is the true King of Israel.[20]

But Israel did not recognise the King when He appeared in the lowly form of the Man of Nazareth, and in the Divine purpose the mystery of the incarnation had to unfold itself into the mysteries of Gethsemane and of Calvary. A true and everlasting basis for the grace of God which has appeared with the offer of salvation to all men, as well as for His future righteous rule, had to be laid in His sufferings. He who is to be exalted, and extolled, and be very high, "was despised and rejected of men." He was "lifted up," not on a throne but on the cross; "He died for our sins according to the Scriptures," but that death was the greatest victory earth or heaven had ever witnessed; "for there at the foot of the cross lie

---

[20] From "The Ancient Scriptures and the Modern Jew."

death, slain with its own dart, and hell vanquished at its very gate." The very symbol of His humiliation and suffering has become the symbol of glory and victory, and, though invisible, it is a fact that the Cross exercises mightier power than all the thrones of earthly potentates. But the Prince of Life could not long be holden by the pangs and powers of death. He rose again the third day, and ascended to the right hand of the Father, where He now sitteth as the Great High Priest of His people, but "waiting" till the appointed hour, when the acceptable year of Jehovah shall have run its course; when the number of God's elect in this dispensation shall be fully accomplished; when the mystery of iniquity shall be fully developed in the man of sin—and then He shall be revealed from heaven with the angels of His power in flaming fire, rendering vengeance to them that know not God, and to them that obey not the Gospel of our Lord Jesus. Then, when all His enemies are made the footstool for His feet, shall He sit down on His throne and commence the long-promised reign of God on this earth.

But to return to ver. 6 of our Psalm.

In the words "for ever and ever" we have a direct echo of the promised perpetuity of the Davidic throne and kingdom, in such Scriptures as 2 Sam. vii. 13, where God says, *"I will establish the throne of His kingdom for ever"*; and Psa. lxxxix. 35-37, where we read:

> "Once have I sworn by My holiness
> I will not lie unto David;
> His seed shall endure for ever,
> And His throne as the sun before Me—
> It shall be established for ever as the moon,
> And as the faithful witness in the sky."

In the next lines we are taken from the perpetuity of His kingdom, and the stability of His throne, to the righteous and beneficent *character* of His rule; and here, again, in reading of the sceptre of uprightness (or "equity") as the sceptre of His kingdom,[21] we are reminded of other great Messianic prophecies—such as Isa. ix. 6, 7, where we read of Him whose Name is "Wonderful," that "of the increase of His government and of peace there shall be no end; upon the throne of David, and upon His kingdom, to establish it and to uphold it with *judgment and righteousness* from henceforth and for ever"; and of Psa. lxxii., where also the perpetuity of the King's throne is guaranteed, not only by His theocratic appointment by God, but by the righteousness of His rule; for

"He shall judge thy people with righteousness,
And thy poor with judgment."

And in both points—in reference to its perpetuity and in its righteous character—the throne of Messiah presents a contrast to all other thrones.

(*a*) All other thrones, however great and widespread their dominion, are temporal and transitory. Sooner or later, usually at the very point of attaining to the zenith of their power and greatness, they begin to decline and crumble, because they carry the seeds of decay and corruption within them; and at the best only mortal men, whose days are as a shadow, occupy them, but, as we have already shown, Messiah's throne "shall be established for ever," and of the increase of His government there shall be no end, because He Himself "shall endure for ever,

---

[21] "The straight sceptre," or wand—emblematic of impartial and undeviating justice—is the ensign of all governments, but in strictness belongs only to this King, as though it were said, "The sceptre of *Thy* kingdom is indeed a straight sceptre," because of Thee it is true as of none other that ever swayed sceptre, that "Thou lovest righteousness and hatest wickedness"; which 'righteousness' is His title to His throne.—*De Burgh*.

and His Name shall be continued as long as the sun" (Psa. lxxii. 17); and the kingdom which He shall establish after Gentile rule shall have run its evil course "shall never be destroyed, nor shall the sovereignty thereof be left to another people; but it shall break in pieces and consume all these kingdoms and it shall stand for ever" (Dan. ii. 44).

(b) Mere human rule has always been characterised by more or less of injustice and cruelty. At this very hour how many are the groanings of the oppressed and the sighs of innocent prisoners! How awful are the barbarities and the scenes of bloodshed and carnage which go on even under the ægis of organised "government"!

Truly well does the Word of God speak of the rule of Gentile world-power as the rule of untamed savage beasts (Dan. vii.).

And this cruelty and injustice has yet to reach a climax in the final great anti-Christian persecution at the time of the end, when Gentile rules shall be summed up in its great apostate head, who without mercy shall devour, break in pieces, and stamp the residue of God's people with his feet.

But of Messiah's rule we read·

"Behold, a King shall reign in righteousness,
  And princes shall rule in judgment" (Isa. xxxii. 1).
"For He shall deliver the needy when he crieth;
  And the poor that hath no helper.
He shall have pity on the poor and needy;
  And the souls of the needy He shall save.
He shall redeem their soul from oppression and violence;
  And precious shall their blood be in His sight"
      (Psa. lxxii. 12-14).

And the principles on which His throne will be built are derived from His own character.

This is more particularly brought out in the seventh verse, which forms the transition or connecting link between the first and second parts of this Psalm—between the enthronement of the King and the marriage-feast of the Bridegroom.

The special features of His character, as here stated, are "Thou lovest righteousness and hatest wickedness"; no wonder, therefore, that the sceptre of His Kingdom is a sceptre of righteousnes or equity, for, as *He is,* so will His blessed rule be.

And how does He love righteousness and hate wickedness? With no mere *passive* love or hatred. No; His devotion to righteousness went to the extent of His willingness to lay down His life for it; and as to wickedness, which is the antithesis to righteousness, He has such an irreconcilable hatred to it, that He has sworn to crush it out of existence. Oh, what a different condition of things we might witness in the world even now, if all who profess to be His followers were characterised by the same feeling and attitude to good and evil, instead of the spirit of temporising and of compromise which prevails amongst us!

The "therefore" in the seventh verse reminds us of the "wherefore" in Phil. ii. 9. *Because* He loveth righteousness, and because it was His love of righteousness and hatred of iniquity which led Him by way of Calvary, so that He humbled Himself and became obedient unto death—even the death of the cross—"Wherefore also God highly exalted Him, and gave unto Him the Name which is above every name: that in the Name of Jesus every knee shall bow; of things in heaven, and things on earth, and things under the earth, and that every tongue should confess that Jesus Christ is Lord to the glory of God the Father." But Psa. xlv. speaks of the time when the kingdoms of *the world* shall become the kingdom of our

God and of His Christ, and when, having by His might overthrown all sin and iniquity, every knee shall bow before Him *on this still rebellious earth,* even as every knee already bows before Him in heaven. Then alone— when the full results of His humiliation and death shall be manifested in the completion, and in His everlasting union with the Church which is His Bride; in the restoration and conversion of Israel; and in the renewal of creation— shall our Lord Jesus see of the travail of His soul, and "shall be satisfied."

Most of the versions and commentators render Elohim in the seventh verse in the nominative ("therefore God, Thy God," &c.), and, grammatically, there is nothing opposed to it; but, as Hengstenberg points out, "If we compare it with ver. 6, where Elohim is in the vocative, we must so construe it here also," viz., "Therefore, O God, Thy God," &c.—the more so, as Elohim, at the beginning of the second part corresponds with visible intention to the Elohim at the close of the first; and without pressing the point I may suggest that there is a probable reference in this verse to the blessed Trinity, "Therefore, O God [the King Messiah], Thy God [the Father] hath anointed Thee" (with the Spirit). It is from this verb translated "anointed" that the substantive *Mashiach*— Messiah—the Christ, is formed, and we are reminded of passages like Isa. lxi. 1, where we read, "The Spirit of the Lord God is upon Me, because He hath anointed Me to preach glad tidings unto the meek."

There were three offices in Israel which were consecrated by the solemn rite of anointing, namely, the Prophet, the High Priest, and the King; and the Lord Messiah is called pre-eminently *The Anointed,* because He combines and fulfils in His One Person in the fullest and most glorious sense all these offices.

And He is anointed with the oil of joy *"above His fellows,"* for in all things our Lord Jesus must have the pre-eminence. Among men He is *"the Man";* in the congregation of the saints He is "the Holy One"—the Head; among prophets He is *the* Prophet; compared with the High Priest, He is *the Great* High Priest; and among kings He is King of kings and Lord of lords.

But the anointing which the Psalmist has here before his prophetic vision has reference to a yet great *future* day, of which the whole Psalm speaks. "It was customary to anoint with oil on joyful occasions; hence to anoint any one with oil is to impart joy to him." In a sense joy characterised our Saviour, even during the period of His humiliation and suffering. "True, He was the Man of Sorrows," but beneath His sorrow He had a deep well of abiding joy which He bequeathed to us (John xv. 11; xvii. 13), with the assurance that to possess it would make our joy full. "His pure manhood was ever in touch with God, and lived in conscious righteousness, and therefore there was ever light within, though there was darkness around. He, the saddest, was likewise the gladdest of men, and anointed with the oil of joy above His fellows." [22] But, I repeat, the anointing here looks on to a yet future day, and the joy which shall then fill His heart above His fellows, will be the joy of seeing the *full results* of His sufferings and atoning death realised in relation to the Church, and to Israel, and to the whole earth. So long as the Church still remains in its present marred, imperfect, and incomplete condition; so long as His beloved Israel is still estranged from Him in a condition of darkness and unbelief, and the whole creation is still groaning and travailing in pain together—His joy is not yet full.

---

[22] Maclaren.

But in the day when "He shall be anointed with the oil of joy above His fellows," every trace of sadness shall have vanished from that blessed face, which for our salvation was once "marred more than that of any man," and both in relation to the Redeemer and of the redeemed it shall be true that all "sorrow and sighing" shall have fled away—for it is the day when He shall at last take unto Himself His kingdom and reign, and the joy shall be the joy of the King, the greater than Solomon, "in the day of His espousals, in the day of the gladness of His heart" (Cant. iii. 11).[23]

---

[23] The continuation of the exposition of this Psalm will be found in the next chapter.

V

THE KING'S MARRIAGE FEAST

PSALM XLV. 8-17

"All Thy garments smell of myrrh and aloes and cassia;
Out of ivory palaces stringed instruments have made Thee glad
Kings' daughters are among Thy honourable women:
At Thy right hand doth stand the queen in gold of Ophir.
Hearken O daughter and consider and incline thine ear;
Forget also thine own people and thy father's house;
So shall the King greatly desire thy beauty:
For He is thy Lord; and worship thou Him.
And the daughter of Tyre shall be there with a gift;
Even the rich among the people shall intreat Thy favour.
The King's daughter within the palace is all glorious:
Her clothing is wrought with gold.
She shall be led unto the King in broidered work:
The virgins her companions that follow her
Shall be brought unto Thee.
With gladness and rejoicing shall they be led:
They shall enter into the King's palace.
Instead of thy fathers shall be thy children,
Whom thou shalt make princes in all the earth.
I will make Thy name to be remembered in all generations
Therefore shall the peoples give Thee thanks for ever and **ever.**"

V

THE KING'S MARRIAGE FEAST

WE·come now to consider the second part of this Psalm, which sings of the grace and beauty of the Bridegroom, and of His marriage union with His chosen Bride, and it may serve to confirm our faith in the prophetic character of this wonderful Scripture, and in its Messianic application, if we observe that the sequence of thought unfolded in this ancient Hebrew Scripture corresponds exactly with the order of future events as foretold not only in other prophecies of the Old Testament, but with prophetic forecasts in the New Testament.

Just as in Revelation xix., which may be said to be the climax and summary of all previous prophecy on these solemn subjects, no sooner is the voice of the great multitude, and of the four-and-twenty elders, and of the four living creatures, raised in praises to God because of His true and righteous judgments, "for He hath judged the great harlot which did corrupt the earth with her fornication, and He hath avenged the blood of His servants at her hand"—no sooner does the cry go forth, "Hallelujah; for the Lord our God the Almighty reigneth," than it is followed by the proclamation: "Let us rejoice and be exceeding glad, and let us give glory unto Him; *for the marriage of the Lamb is come, and His wife hath made herself ready"*—so it is in our Psalm.

First, by means of awful judgments, and the terrible deeds of His right hand (ver. 4), the peoples are made to fall under Him, and His enemies are made the footstool of His feet; but no sooner is His throne firmly established in righteousness than the scene immediately changes from the battlefield to the wedding-hall, and from the shout of war to the sweet strains of nuptial music.

It is to the second half that the *Shir Yedidoth* of the inscription specially points, for it is here that the song of loves reaches its climax. But to proceed with the exposition. In consequence of His anointing, of which we read in ver. 7, which forms the point of transition from the mighty exploits of the King to the beauty of the Bridegroom, all His garments are so thoroughly scented that they seem to be altogether *woven* out of costly spices, for the Hebrew of the first line in ver. 8 literally reads, "Myrrh and aloes and cassia *are* all Thy garments"—a hint, surely, of the innate and absolute perfections and preciousness of this glorious Bridegroom, whose outer coverings are wrought of the same pure and fragrant substance as His character, which in all its manifestations sent up a sweet-smelling savour.

The garments of those who by the grace of the King are brought into relationship with Him as His companions or "fellows" (ver. 7) may be *sprinkled* with scent, but His are *made* out of it, as becomes Him who in all things must have the pre-eminence. Thus arrayed in His Bridegroom attire, all sweet, all precious, all beautiful, He comes for His Bride, and the occasion is one of festive joy.

"Out of ivory palaces [the music of] stringed instruments [1] make Thee glad."

"Out of the inner recesses of halls inlaid within with ivory, and consequently resplendent with the most dazzling

---

[1] *Minni* is rendered in the Authorised Version "whereby" (the LXX. version, ἐξ ὧν, "out of which"), on the supposition that it is an emphatic repetition of the preposition *min* used just before and translated "out of." But as there are anyhow critical difficulties in

whiteness, the Bridegroom going to fetch His Bride is met by the sounds of festive music. Viewed in the light of the New Testament, it is that music of citherns or harps, which the seer (Rev. xiv. 2) heard like the voice of many waters and of mighty thunder resounding from heaven." [2] And the music and joy then will pervade both heaven and earth, and will fill not only the earthly palaces of Israel and the nations, but the very dwelling of God, the many mansions of our Father's everlasting House; for if there be joy in heaven even now over one sinner who repents, what will be the joy when not only the whole nation of Israel is again joined to the Lord in bonds which will never more be broken, but when the spiritual Bride, too, is complete; and when the glorious Bridegroom, who purchased her with His own blood, shall at last present her to Himself a glorious Church, not having spot, or wrinkle, or any such thing, but that she should be holy and without blemish!

In the next verse the Psalmist's vision seems to rest on the consummating act in that blessed day when the mar-

---

connection with this rendering, modern scholars now generally understand it as the equivalent of *minnim,* which in Psa. cl. 4 stands for stringed instruments. Some, however, have suggested that it is the name of the territory called *"minni"* in Jer. li. 27, as contiguous to Ararat and Ashkenaz, *i.e.,* a district of *Armenia,* and have rendered the sentence, "Out of the ivory palaces of Armenia they make Thee glad," a rendering which derives some support from the Chaldaic, which reads, *"from the land of Minni."* "Out of palaces of ivory," *i.e.,* chambers or halls inlaid or ornamented with ivory, which seem often to have been the case in the dwellings of kings and great men.

Thus we read of Ahab that he made an "ivory house" (1 Kings xxii. 39), and in Amos iii. 15 the prophet announces that the "houses of ivory shall perish."

In Cant. vii. 4 the neck of the Bride herself is called a "tower of ivory."

[2] Delitzsch.

riage relationship between the glorious Bridegroom and the elect Bride shall be completed.

"The Queen," [3] arrayed in pure gold of Ophir, "doth stand" (or "hath placed herself") "at the King's right hand," the place of honour and power, ready for the nuptial procession, and in attendance, ready to do the Bride and Bridegroom any service, are a throng of "precious" [4] or "honourable" ones—those whom we should style "bridesmaids," among whom are to be found even "kings' daughters." Who are those daughters of kings the lustre of whose beauty adorns the great Monarch's court? and who is this Queen standing in close relationship to the King? The great German expositor, whom I have already quoted, aptly answers: "The kings' daughters are the heathen nations converted to Christ, and the Queen is Israel, which is remarried to God in Christ after the fulness of the heathen is come in. It is only when Israel is won to Him, after the fulness of the Gentiles is come in (Rom. xi. 25), that the morning of the great day will dawn which this Psalm, as a song of the Church, celebrates." [5] And with an even deeper spiritual insight into this great

---

[3] Instead of the Hebrew terms *Malcha* or *Gevirah*, we have here *Shégal,* a designation commonly used of Chaldean and Persian queens. In Neh. ii. 6 it is used for the queen of Artaxerxes, and in Dan. v. it is employed as a designation for the wives of Belshazzar in distinction from his concubines. Hengstenberg asserts that *Shégal* "is a rare and unusual designation of a consort of the first rank, which, as being such, poetry peculiarly appropriates to itself."

[4] The Hebrew word rendered in the "Authorised" and "Revised" Versions by the phrase "among thy honourable women" should be translated literally "among thy precious [or 'glorious'] ones." The word *women* is not represented in the Hebrew, and the term stands for anything precious and costly, and is highly prized and loved for its costliness, but from the mention of "kings' daughters" as of the number, the company of those in attendance on the queen, and who are also "precious" to the King, is doubtless meant.

[5] Delitzsch.

prophetic vision, Bishop Horsley says, in the fourth of his
series of sermons on this Psalm, "Kings' daughters, in the
general language of Holy Writ, are the kingdoms and
peoples which they govern, of which, in common speech,
they (the kings) are called 'fathers.' The expression may
be so taken here, and then the sense will be that the greatest kingdoms and empires of the world, converted to the
faith of Christ, and shining in the beauty of good works
and of true holiness, will be united, at the season of the
wedding, to Messiah's Kingdom." And in reference to
"the Queen," he says: "Some expositors have imagined
that the Consort is an emblem of the Church Catholic in
her totality, the 'kings' daughters' being typical of the
several particular Churches of which that one universal is
composed. But the Queen-Consort here is unquestionably
the Hebrew Church—the Church of the natural Israel—
reunited, by her conversion, to her Husband, and advanced
to the high prerogative of the Mother Church of Christendom. The restoration of the Hebrew Church to the rights
of a wife—to the situation of Queen-Consort in Messiah's
Kingdom upon earth—is the constant strain of prophecy.
To prove this by citing all the passages to that purpose
would be to transcribe whole chapters of some of the
prophets, and innumerable detached passages from almost
all. In addition to those which I have already cited in my
former discourses upon this subject, I shall produce only
the latter part of the second chapter of Hosea. In that
chapter, Jehovah, after discarding the incontinent wife
and threatening terrible severity of punishment, adds that,
nevertheless, the time should come when she should again
address her offended Lord by the endearing name of
Husband. 'And I will betroth thee to Myself for ever.
Yes; I will betroth thee to Myself with justice, and with
righteousness, and with exuberant kindness, and with
tender love. Yes, with faithfulness to Myself I will be-

troth thee.' These promises are made to the woman that had been discarded, and cannot be understood of mercies to be extended to any other. The Prophet Isaiah speaks to the same effect, and describes the Gentile converts as becoming, upon the reunion, children of the pardoned wife (see chaps. liv. 5 and lxii. 5).

"And I must not omit to mention that St. Paul, in his Epistle to the Romans, to clear up the mystery of God's dealing with the Jews, tells us that 'blindness is in part only happened unto Israel, till the fulness of the Gentiles be come in; and then all Israel shall be saved'; for the gifts and calling of God are without repentance (*i. e.*, 'change of mind' on His part). To expound these predictions of the ancient prophets, and this declaration of the Apostle—of anything but the restoration of the natural Israel—is to introduce ambiguity and equivocation into the plainest oracles of God." "To which it is only necessary to add"—to quote yet another writer [6]—"that it is to be borne in mind that the theme of this Psalm is the Kingdom of Christ on earth, and in its earthly polity, according to the original covenant with Abraham, renewed to David, and yet to be fulfilled at the Second Advent—which always recognises the distinction between the people Israel and the other nations, as well as the pre-eminence of the former, owing to Jerusalem being then the centre and seat of government. But in the heavenly glory—for, as 'the kingdom of heaven' upon earth, the kingdom will unite both glories, the celestial and terrestrial—there is no such distinction in the Church of the resurrection, which reigns with Christ; as also in the Church of the present dispensation, which is called to that glory; in which 'there is neither Jew nor Gentile,' but 'all are one in Christ Jesus,' and the whole, collectively, forms the Bride in the

---

[6] De Burgh.

distinctive New Testament application of the emblem (as
in Eph. v. 25-27, &c.)."

Yet, while in this 45th Psalm it is doubtless Israel who
is the Queen-Consort of Messiah in His reign over the
nations, and while the prophecies are full of references
and allusions to the elect nation under the figure of the
Bride and wife of Jehovah, we have to remember that
there is also a spiritual or heavenly [7] Bride, consisting of
the Church which He hath purchased with His own blood;
and that on the day when Israel is married to Jehovah
and reinstated as Queen for the long-promised millennial
day in His earthly palace in Jerusalem, there will also be
heard the voice of the redeemed Church in the heavenly
Jerusalem, "as it were the voice of a great multitude, and
as the voice of many waters, and as the voice of many
thunderings, saying Hallelujah, . . . let us be glad and
rejoice and give honour to Him; for the marriage of the
Lamb is come, and His wife hath made herself ready."
And if the earthly glory of Israel during the millennium
will be great, how much greater shall then be the spiritual
glory of the heavenly Bride, who shall then have been

---

[7] Or should it not rather be regarded as the One Bride, though
a portion of it will during the millennium be enjoying fellowship
with Messiah on earth, while the "firstborn one" will in a perfected
condition be already with Him in the heavenly Jerusalem? For my
own part, I verily believe that in the Eternal Day which is to
succeed the Millennium Dawn—when Israel's mission in relation
to the nations shall have been accomplished; when earth shall be
as heaven, and heaven as earth—all dispensational distinctions in
the One Redeemed Family shall cease, and there will be but One
Spiritual Temple for the eternal habitation of God through the
Spirit; One Bride of the Lamb consisting of all the Israel of God;
One Church of the Living God, "which is His Body, the fulness of
Him that filleth all in all;" "according to His good pleasure which
He purposed in Himself that in the dispensation of the fulness of
the times to sum up [or 'to bring under one headship'] all things
in Christ, the things in the heavens and the things upon the earth"
(Eph. i. 9-11).

presented to Himself without spot or wrinkle or any such thing, for ever to shine in a beauty which is perfect through His comeliness which is put upon her? "Then," indeed, to use another figure, "shall the righteous shine forth as the sun in the kingdom of their Father."

Before the nuptial procession actually starts, the Queen must listen to an address, which consists in a solemn charge to leave the things which are behind; to forget her past life, and even her very dearest associations, so as to give herself over entirely to her glorious Bridegroom, for only so can she expect the full flow of His affections toward her.

"Hearken, O daughter, and consider [or 'see'], and incline thine
     ear;
Forget also thine own people and thy father's house;
So shall the King desire thy beauty;
For He is thy Lord; and worship thou Him."

The one who thus addresses the royal Bride is the inspired Psalmist, and the forms of speech by which the exhortation is introduced are very significant, though simple. By the word ("hearken" literally *hear*") he implores for himself a hearing; by his appeal to her to "consider" (or "see") he directs her eye towards the new relationship into which she is just entering; by "incline thine ears" he bespeaks her special attention to the exhortation that follows; and by addressing her as "daughter" he puts himself in a position in relation to her similar to that which the teacher and preacher occupies who addresses the bridal pair at the altar. The exhortation is that she is to forget her people and her father's house—"to sever her natural inherited and customary relationships of life, both as regards outward form and inward affections; and should the King desire her beauty, to which He has a right—for He, as being her husband (1 Pet. iii. 6), and more especially as being King, is her Lord—she is to show towards Him her profoundest, reverent devotion." [8]

But the exhortation is of peculiar significance if we bear in mind that the royal Bride thus addressed is the Jewish nation, which is here viewed as in the very act of being remarried to Jehovah in and through Christ, for the words of exhortation which she is to consider, and lay to heart, are an inspired echo and application of the word of the Lord to Abraham: "Get thee out of thy country, and from thy kindred, and from thy father's house; . . . and I will make of thee a great nation, and I will bless thee and make thy name great, and thou shalt be a blessing" (Gen. xii. 1-3) ; and shows us that before Abraham's seed, the daughter of Zion can enter into full union with her heavenly Lord, and bear fruit to His praise in the earth, she must pass through spiritually the same experience as her father, who, for the sake of the God of Glory who appeared to woo him to Himself, was willing to part with earthly things and natural ties, "looking for a city which hath foundations whose Builder and Maker is God."

But there is something special which Israel, as the Bride of Jehovah, has to "forget" and unlearn.

"If a princess from a distant land, taken in marriage by a great king," says Bishop Horsley in the sermon already quoted, "were admonished to forget her own people and her father's house, the purport of the advice would easily be understood to be that she should divest herself of all attachment to the customs of her native country and to the style of her father's court, and learn to speak the language, and assume the dress, the manners, and the taste of her husband's people. The 'father's house' and 'own people' which the Psalmist advises the Queen-Con-

---

[8] Delitzsch.

sort to forget is the ancient Jewish religion in its external form. Not that she is to forget God's gracious promises to Abraham, nor the covenant with her forefathers (the benefit of which she will enjoy to the very end of time), nor the many wonderful deliverances that were wrought for them. Nor is she to forget the history of her nation, preserved in the Scriptures of the Old Testament; nor the predictions of Moses and her prophets, the full accomplishment of which she will at this time experience; and historically, she is never to forget the ceremonial law, for the Levitical rites were nothing less than the Gospel itself in hieroglyphics, and, rightly understood, they afford the most complete demonstration of the coherence of Revelation with itself in all its different stages, and the best evidence of its truth, showing that it has been the same in substance in all ages, differing only in external form in the rites of worship and in manner of teaching. But, practically, the rites of their ancient worship are to be forgotten—that is, laid aside; for they never were of any other importance than in reference to the Gospel, as the shadow is of no value but as it resembles the substance. Practically, therefore, the restored Hebrew Church is to abandon her ancient Jewish rites, and become merely and purely Christian; and thus she will secure the conjugal affections of her Husband, and render the beauty of her person perfect in His eyes. And this she is bound to do, for her royal Husband is indeed her 'Lord.' Moses was no more than His servant, and the prophets after Moses were servants in a lower rank than he. But the authority of Christ, the Husband, is paramount over all. He is entitled to her unreserved obedience; He is indeed her God, entitled to her adoration."

But having shown the true sense of the exhortation in its relation to Israel, I am prepared to admit also its practical application to Christians, and to see in the words addressed to the Bride "a shadowing forth of the duties of a soul wedded to Christ," for which most commentators contend, who, for the most part, are confused and uncertain as far as the sublime *prophetic* import of this Psalm is concerned. "Every true marriage," says Dr. Alexander Maclaren, "is in the same fashion a type of the union of the soul with Jesus the lover of all, the Bridegroom of the Church. . . . If a heart is really influenced by love to Him, that love will make self-surrender blessed. A child gladly drops toys when it stretches out its little hand for better gifts. If we are joined to Jesus, we shall not be unwilling to 'count all things but loss for the excellency of the knowledge' of Him. Have the terms of wedded life changed since this Psalm was written? Have the terms of Christian living altered since it was said, 'Whosoever he be of you that forsaketh not all that he hath, he cannot be My disciple'? The law still remains, 'Daughter, forget thine own people and thy father's house.' The exhortation is followed by a promise: 'So shall the King desire thy beauty.' The application of these words to the relations of Christ and His people carries with it a striking thought that He is affected by the completeness of our self-surrender and dependence. He pours love on the unworthy, but that is a different thing from the love with which He responds to such abandonment of self and other loves. Holy, noble living will bring a smile into His face and draw Him nearer to us. But whilst there is all this sweet commerce of love and giving, the Bride is reminded that the King is her Lord, and is to be reverenced as well as loved. There is here, no doubt, the influence of an archaic mode of thought regarding marriage and the wife's position. But it still is true that no woman finds all that her heart needs in her husband, unless she can bring her reverence where she has brought her love, and that love will not long remain if reverence departs. Nor is the warning less needed in the higher region of the wedlock of the soul with the Saviour. Some types of emotional religion have more to say about love than about obedience. They are full of half-wholesome apostrophes to a 'dear Lord,' and are apt to forget the last word in the emphasis which they put on the first. The beggar-maid married to a king was full of reverence as well as love; and the souls whom Jesus stoops to love, and wash, and wed, are never to forget to blend adoration with approach, and obedience with love."

It would, however, almost seem as if the words "For He is thy Lord, and worship thou Him," indicate that the Divine glory of the Bridegroom and the devout exercise of bowing in worship before Him will then be a new revelation and a new experience to the Jewish people. But Israel will learn then that it is "her *Maker* who is her husband," and when her eyes are opened to His true glory, she will not only henceforth love Him with a fervent love, but, like Thomas, she will fall down in worship before Him, crying "My Lord and my God."

And her reward for this willing submission and devotion of herself to her Kingly Bridegroom will be the universal homage of the nations:

"And the daughter of Tyre shall be there with a gift;
  Even the rich among the people shall entreat thy favour."

Or more literally:

"And the daughter of Tyre—with gifts shall they entreat thy
    favour [9]—
Even the richest among peoples."

---

[9] The words literally signify "to smooth or soften the countenance," to entreat so beseechingly that the one entreated cannot reject the suppliant and cannot show himself hard—a Hebrew

"Him that honoureth Me will I honour"; or, as Luther observes on this verse, 'Hold thy Bridegroom in honour, and thou shalt be in honour among all peoples, for He is so very powerful."

The daughter of Tyre stands doubtless for a personification of the people or kingdom of Tyre, even as "the kings' daughters" stands for the kingdoms and peoples, who at the time of Israel's re-marriage to the Lord shall be united to Messiah's Kingdom.

But while proud, opulent Tyre [10] is especially named, it is only by way of example, for the next line tells us that "the richest among the peoples" of the earth in general will come to her with presents in token of submission, and to obtain her favour.

And this is in keeping with many other prophecies which speak of the future glory and pre-eminence of restored and converted Israel.

"Whereas thou hast been forsaken and hated,
So that no man passed through thee.
I will make thee an eternal excellency;
A joy of many generations.
Thou shalt also suck the milk of the nations,
And shalt suck the breast of kings.

---

idiom for conciliating, used often in the Old Testament, of entreaty to God.

Hengstenberg remarks on this verse that "the Church of God exercises a drawing power toward those that are without in exact proportion to her own internal connection with the Lord."

[10] "Wonderful indeed it will be," observes one writer, "to see the proudest of the nations—in the spirit of the woman of Canaan from the coast of Tyre and Sidon, so highly commended by the Lord—deferring to the counsel of God which assigns to Israel the pre-eminence among the nations in the theocratical dispensation of Messiah's Kingdom, but in thus humbling themselves they shall be truly exalted: by submitting to this, the order of blessing to the world in that day, the nations shall be blessed."

And thou shalt know that I, Jehovah, am thy Saviour, and thy
Redeemer, the Mighty One of Jacob . . .
And the sons of them that afflicted thee shall come bending unto
    thee;
And all they that despised thee shall bow themselves down at the
    soles of thy feet;
And they shall call thee
The City of Jehovah,
The Zion of the Holy One of Israel" (Isa. lx. 14-16).

It is interesting to observe that similar language to what
is here used of Messiah's people is, in other Scriptures,
used of Messiah Himself. Thus we read in Psa. lxxii.:

"The kings of Tarshish and of the isles shall bring presents,
The Kings of Sheba and Seba shall offer gifts;
Yea, all kings shall fall down before *Him,*
All nations shall call Him blessed."

But this only shows how completely the favoured Bride
shares in the glory and reign of her heavenly Bridegroom,
and that it is on account of her union with Him who has
exalted her to be "Queen" among kings' daughters, that
even rulers, and the richest among peoples, are zealous
to express to her their loving and joyful recognition.

The address to the Queen, which in that day will doubtless find a full and joyous response in her heart, is ended,
and the Psalmist accompanies in the spirit the actual procession of the bridal party as the Queen, according to
Eastern custom, leaves her father's house, and, gloriously
arrayed, and with a numerous train in attendance, is led to
the King and makes her entry into His palace.

"All glorious is the King's daughter within [or, 'in the inner
    palace'].[11]

---

[11] *Penimah*—literally means "toward the inside," then also "in
the inside." It is used of the inside of the Holy Place (Lev. x.
18); of the interior cedar lining of the Holy Place (1 Kings vi.
18); and of the gold lining of the oracle or Holy of Holies (1
Kings vi. 21).

Of gold-woven texture [12] is her clothing.
In embroidered [variegated] garments is she led to the King.
Virgins follow her—her companions are brought unto Thee;
They are brought with joy and exultation;
They enter into the King's palace."

In this Psalm, which sets forth so beautifully the strength and beauty of the King, it is pleasant to get also glimpses of the future glory of the Queen. It is ideal, it is prophetic, it is anticipative, but its contemplation in contrast to the marred, mixed condition of the Church now, is sufficient to refresh our drooping spirits. We first get a glimpse of her in her own chamber, where she is all splendour (or "glorious"). Her clothing is gold interwoven textures (*i. e.,* "such as are interwoven with threads of ogld, or woven in squares or diamond paterns, and adorned with gold in addition"),[13] which not only correspond to her rank, and the dignity which the King has put upon her, but denote her glory, just as the shining white linen (byssus), in which the heavenly Bride of the Lamb, in the nineteenth chapter of Revelation, is seen to array herself for the marriage, denotes her righteousness and purity.

Thus, all glorious and all beautiful, she is led in to the King, for evermore to dwell in His presence and to continue in His love. But, though first in rank and in order of precedence, there are other "daughters"—those who are represented here by the "virgins her companions"—who

---

[12] *Mishbatzoth*—wrought gold or chequered work of gold. The only other connections in which this word is used are (1) of the gold "ouches" on the shoulder-pieces of the High Priest's ephod, in which were set the two onyx stones, on each of which were inscribed the names of six of the tribes (Exod. xxviii. 11, 13, 14, 25; xxxix. 1, 13); and (2) of the gold settings of the twelve precious stones in the High Priest's breastplate (Exod. xxxix. 1, 13).

[13] Delitzsch.

are none other than the "kings' daughters," and other
precious ones," to whom we have been already introduced
in ver. 9, who enter into the King's palace to share in His
love at the same time as the Queen; and this fact supplies
one of the strongest proofs (if more proof were needed)
of the Messianic and spiritual character of this *Shir Yedidoth,* for in the lower sphere of naturel relations the
introduction of more brides than one at the same time
would be immoral; and though it is true that some of
Israel's Kings practised polygamy, contrary to what was
evidently the will and purpose of God, often bringing
thereby sorrow upon themselves and their families, yet the
mere suggestion of such a state of things, in the natural
sense in relation to the ideal King, who is morally altogether beautiful, and whose chief characteristics are that
He loveth righteousness and hateth iniquity, would be in-
congruous and out of the question. But what would be
unsuitable—and here in the light of the whole context
impossible—in the lower relations of earthly love, is in
the figurative and spiritual sense in accordance with what
we know to be the truth, for Jesus is the Lover and
Bridegroom equally of each soul that loves Him, as well
as of the Church as a whole, and in that glorious day of
the re-marrying of Israel to her Messiah King "the virgins, her companions"—who, though inferior to her in
rank, are yet to be equally united with Him in spiritual
love—will be, as already explained, the heathen nations
who will share in the blessings of the Messianic kingdom.
This is in accord with the plainly declared purposes of
God, and the uniform testimony of prophets and psalmists.

From the very beginning, when God went to claim
Israel for Himself out of the hands of Pharaoh, He said:
"Israel is My son, My firstborn" (Exod. iv. 22)—a desig-
nation which contains in itself a prophecy that though
Israel was to have a certain precedence, and to be invested

with privileges and responsibilities which attach to the
birthright, the other nations, too, would be born unto Him
as sons in His kingdom in due time; and so in this Psalm
also, apart from the figurue of the Bride, Israel is singled
out as "the daughter" in a special sense; but, though she
is first in order, rank, and dignity, she is not the only
one, for there are other "daughters" (vers. 9-12) who are
His "precious ones" who also

> "Are brought with joy and exultation;
> They enter into the King's palace."

The scene moves to its close, and there remains only
the last four lines, of which the first two contain a prophecy of a numerous and mighty offspring from this spiritual
union—

> "Instead of thy fathers shall be thy sons;
> Thou shalt make them as princes in all the earth."

It was customary to express to the wedded pair some
such compliments as were addressed to Rebekah by her
relations: "Be thou mother of thousands of millions, and
let thy seed possess the gate of those that hate them",
or like that uttered to Boaz and Ruth in chap. iv. 11, 12,
of that beautiful idyll: but here, instead of a compliment,
we have a definite prediction. It is not absolutely clear
to whom these two lines are addressed—whether to the
king or the queen—for, although the Masoretic punctua-
tion of the pronoun is masculine, the Hebrew text suits
either. "If addressed to the queen," says one writer, they
are most appropriate, for they promise her, who had been
exhorted to "forget her father's house" (at ver. 10), that
she shall have children who shall eclipse them in glory—
to the restored Israel they say, "Thy glorious forefathers,
David, Solomon, and their sucessors, shall be cast into

the shade by thy still more glorious sons, and retire into the background before them." Instead of the patriarchs, of whom you have boasted, shall be the twelve apostles, sitting upon thrones, judging (governing) the twelve tribes of Israel, and others, in subordinate places of rule in the kingdom under the King Messiah (compare Rev. v. 10).

But it is, perhaps, preferable with most commentators to apply them to the King. The sense, however, is the same in either application. The second line of the sixteenth verse probably finds its historic foreshadowing in the histories of David and Solomon, and some of their successors on the thrones of Israel and Judah; and may be understood that, "just as the kings of Judah and of Israel allowed their sons to share in their dominion (2 Sam. viii. 18; 1 Kings v. 7; 2 Chron. xi. 23; 1 Kings xx. 15), so out of the loving relationship of the daughter of Zion, and of the virgins of her train to the King Messiah, there spring up children to whom the regal glory of the house of David, which culminated in Him, is transferred—a royal race, among whom He divides the dominion of the world (Psa. cxlix.); for He makes His own people kings and priests, and they shall reign on the earth" (Rev. v. 10).

In the last two lines the Psalmist discloses again his design in this inspired and sublime composition, viz., to perpetuate the fame and to show forth the praiseworthiness of the all-glorious King, with the Divine beauty of whose Person and mighty exploits as the champion of truth, righteousness, and meekness, his heart was "bubbling over" and his soul was enraptured on starting (ver. 1).

"I will make Thy Name to be remembered in all generations:
Therefore shall the peoples praise Thee for ever and ever [or 'through generation after generation']."

"By inditing this marriage song," says Bishop Horsley, in the sermon from which I have already quoted largely, "he hoped to be the means of celebrating the Redeemer's Name from age to age, and of inciting the nations of the world to join in His praise. The event has not disap-. pointed the holy prophet's expectation. His composition has been the delight of the congregations of the faithful for little less than three thousand years. For one thousand and forty it was a means of keeping alive in the synagogue the hope of the Redeemer to come; for eighteen hundred since, it has been the means of perpetuating in Christian congregations the grateful remembrance of what has been done—anxious attention to what is doing—and the cheerful hope of the second coming of our Lord, who surely cometh to turn away ungodliness from Jacob, and to set up a standard to the nations which yet sit in darkness and the shadow of death. 'He that witnesseth these things saith, Behold, I come quickly. And the Spirit saith Come! and the Bride saith Come! and let every one that heareth say Amen! Even so, come, Lord Jesus!' "

And now, before laying down my pen after this unworthy and inadequate exposition of this glorious Messianic prophetic song, let me, too, add my feeble note of praise by repeating the last prophecy and prayer of David the son of Jesse:

> "His Name shall endure for ever;
> His Name shall be continued as long as the sun;
> And men shall be blessed in Him;
> All nations shall call Him happy.
> Blessed be the Lord God, the God of Israel,
> Who only doeth wondrous things;
> And blessed be His glorious Name for ever.
> And let the whole earth be filled with His glory.
> Amen, and Amen."

VI

A WILDERNESS SONG

PSALM LXIII

"O God, Thou art my God; early will I seek Thee.
My soul thirsteth for Thee, my flesh longeth for Thee,
In a dry and weary land, where no water is.
So have I looked upon Thee in the sanctuary,
To see Thy power and Thy glory.
For thy lovingkindness is better than life;
My lips shall praise Thee.
So will I bless Thee while I live;
I will lift up my hands in Thy name.
My soul shall be satisfied as with marrow and fatness;
And my mouth shall praise Thee with joyful lips;
When I remember Thee upon my bed,
And meditate on Thee in the night watches.
For Thou hast been my help,
And in the shadow of Thy wings will I rejoice.
My soul followeth hard after Thee:
Thy right hand upholdeth me.
But those that seek my soul, to destroy it,
Shall go into the lower parts of the earth.
They shall be given over to the power of the sword:
They shall be a portion for foxes.
But the king shall rejoice in God:
Every one that sweareth by him shall glory;
For the mouth of them that speak lies shall be stopped."

VI

A WILDERNESS SONG

THIS beautiful song has made sweet music in the hearts of God's people at all times, even transforming to some the weary desert of life's present condition into a very Eden of the Lord.

According to one of the early Church fathers,[1] this Psalm formed part of the daily worship in the assemblies of the primitive Church, while Delitzsch, on the authority of Athanasius and Eusebius, calls it "the morning Psalm of the ancient Church, with which the singing of the Psalms was always introduced at the Sunday service."[2] The reason why the early Church loved to dwell on it, and why it is still such a favourite among the little flock of Christ's true sheep, is, I believe, partly found in the title, which shows its special application to our present state.

It is "a psalm of David when he was in *the wilderness of Judah,*" and this is where, spiritually, the Church of God still is; this is where we now are, for paint "this present evil world" as you like, it still remains a moral wilderness, a vale of tears, the valley of the shadow of death, a land of hunger and thirst, of toil and weariness, of pain and death. Before long we shall exchange the wilderness experiences of the present for the blessed state described in the Book of Revelation, when "we shall

---

[1] Chrysostom.

[2] "It was the favourite Psalm of M. Schade, the famous preacher in Berlin, which he daily prayed with such earnestness and appropriation to himself that it was impossible to hear it without emotion."—*Hengstenberg.*

hunger no more, neither thirst any more, neither shall the sun hurt us, nor any heat; for the Lamb which is in the midst of the throne shall lead us unto living fountains of waters, and God shall wipe away all tears from our eyes."

In course of time, when the Church became worldly, and when, because ungodly emperors and world power began to smile on her, she deluded herself with the thought that she had already reached the millennium, she ceased to sing this wilderness song, but by ceasing to recognise her heavenly calling, and her present wilderness condition, she ceased to be the pure Church that she had been, and degenerated into Christendom; and then those that were the called, and chosen, and faithful, Christ's true flock, who knew that they were not of this world, had to go forth from amongst her, often into literal deserts, or to hide in dens and caves of the earth, and there continue to worship God in the spirit.

A wilderness song! What a strange, unlikely place for a song to proceed from! but it is perhaps the special characteristic of God's people that they *can* sing in the wilderness.   The children of the world have also their wildernesses, but they cannot sing there; they can sing only amid flowers and sunshine, but flowers and sunshine do not last for ever, and then, when the flowers of outward prosperity fade, and the world's sun begins to set, their music ceases.   But the song of God's people is not dependent upon outward circumstances; yea, the history of the Church proves that it is in the wilderness, in times of suffering and persecution, that she has sung the sweetest. And it is so also in our individual experience.   It is not always when we are settled on our lees, and everything goes well with us outwardly, that the melody of praise and true worship ascends on high.   God has often to allure His people into the wilderness in order that there, under the sense of outward need and isolation, shut up to none but Him, our hearts may respond to His wondrous Word and works with true psalms of prayer and adoration.

The song itself is in keeping with the surroundings under which it originated. It begins with an invocation of the name Elohim. This is the name of the Almighty God of Majesty, and sets forth just the aspect of God's character which the lonely, helpless fugitive would lay hold of. "O God, I am in a wilderness, the place of need and danger, and myself helpless, but Thou art Elohim the Almighty, who has created the heavens, and with whom nothing is impossible." It is the name of God which first appears in the page of revelation, and which is most frequently in the plural—not the plural of majesty, as some have suggested, but containing the first Old Testament hint of the doctrine of the blessed Trinity, which is more fully unfolded in the New Testament. And Thou Elohim, in all the fulness of Thine infinite resources, in all Thy might and majesty, *art my God.* Oh, what wonderful words these are for a poor frail man on earth to use! Presumption, the world calls it, but, blessed be His holy Name, it is the kind of presumption which He Himself encourages. Does He not say hundreds of times, "I am the Lord *thy* God"? And what is the prayer of this Psalm but the response of faith, which, taking Him at His word, looks up to heaven and says, *"my* God," in answer to His own word, "THY God"? But whatever hesitancy God's people may have had before to such individual appropriation of the great God, and in addressing the Lord of heaven and earth as their very own, that hesitancy has been for ever removed by the message sent to us by the risen Christ. "I ascend unto My Father and your Father, and to My God and your God." Henceforth the weakest and least of "His brethren," to whom the message was sent, can look up to heaven in the full assurance of faith, and say to the Lord of all, *"my* God."

And what fulness there is in the little word "my"! It is the expression of faith, and the mark of personal religion, which recognises my own separate and individual relation to the living God. It is the feeble hand of man stretched out in the power of God, laying hold on His strength to be at peace with Him. It is the link forged by God's own Spirit, which unites God's Almightiness with human weakness and frailty, and which, in New Testament language, enables a worm of dust to say, "I can do all things through Christ who strengtheneth me."

"Early," or "diligently, earnestly [literally, 'with the breaking in of the morning'] will I seek Thee." David knew that Elohim was *his* God, and although he was in the wilderness, and although, outwardly, God's face seemed for the time to be turned away from him, he was not going to give himself up to doubt and despair; rather would he turn more earnestly to seek God, until His face should again be lifted upon him, and the vision of His glory, which he had so often seen in the sanctuary, be granted him in the very wilderness. The earnestness of his seeking after God is expressed in the words that follow— *"My soul thirsteth for Thee."* The emphasis is on the word "Thee," which is repeated three times in the first verse. It reminds us of the words in another psalm:

"My soul thirstest for God, for the living God;
When shall I come and behold the face of God?"
(Psa. xlii. 2.)

Thirst is a figure of speech often used in the Scriptures to express intense desire for something indispensable, and the indispensable to the Psalmist is God; without Him he cannot live. And the intense desire and emotion of his soul strongly affects his body. *"My flesh,"* too, he says, all that is within me, my whole being, *"longeth for Thee, in a dry and weary land without water."*

Here is the terrible moral desert of which the wilderness of Judah was the outward and visible type. It still graphically describes this present evil world in its moral and spiritual relations to the child of God.

1. It is a "Dry Land." Not only is there no moisture or sustenance to be drawn from it, but it is "a land of drought," as the same expression is elsewhere rendered [3]— "a drying-up land," which absorbs every drop of moisture which may perchance come in contact with it, and yet itself remains the same arid waste. There is no child of God but knows from painful experience the truth of this part of the picture. Not only is there no nourishment for the life of God in our souls to be drawn from this world, but we feel on the other hand its terrible drying-up influences upon us, so that, but for the constantly fresh supplies of His grace, and the continual descent of His Holy Spirit, we would become parched by reason of our very contact with it.

2. It is "a weary land" [4] of toil and pressure, a veritable land of the shadow of death, in which life itself is an almost unendurable burden to millions who are not cheered with a hope beyond the grave, and who have not learned the secret of the Apostle's words, that "the sufferings of this present time are not worthy to be compared with the glory which shall be revealed in us."

3. And there is "no water" in it, nothing that can alleviate the distress it occasions, or satisfy even the thirst which it itself creates All seek for it Some rush hither and thither in mad pursuit of imaginary fountains at which

---

[3] Jer. ii. 6.

[4] This word is applied to David and the people with him, in 2 Sam. xvi. 14, when he fled for refuge in the wilderness on the rebellion of Absalom—the occasion, most probably, when the Psalm was composed.

to drink and be satisfied, but only to have all their hopes disappointed, and to find in the end that what they were following was a *mirage* of their fancy, and what they were digging were "broken cisterns that can hold no water" Oh, ye sons of men, believe it, there is a place in the human heart which all the world's pleasures, and riches, and fame cannot satisfy, for over all that is of the world the words of Christ are written, *"Whosoever drinketh of this water shall thirst again, but whosoever drinketh of the water that I shall give him, shall never thirst; but the water that I shall give him shall be in him a well of water, springing up into everlasting life."*

These, then, are the conditions in which the Psalmist, looking upon the world with eyes enlightened by God's Spirit, found himself, and from the wilderness of his outward and inward need he looks up to Him from whom alone his help can come, even to Elohim, the Almighty One, the Maker of heaven and earth. And God was found of him, as He will ever be found of those who seek Him with their whole heart, for we remember His many answers to those who, like the Psalmist, thirst for Him in a dry and weary land where no water is. Here is one: "The poor and needy seek water and there is none, and their tongue faileth for thirst. I, Jehovah, will hear them. I, the God of Israel, will not forsake them. I will open rivers in high places, and fountains in the midst of the valleys. I will make *the wilderness a pool of water, and the dry land springs of water."* This, though primarily spoken of Israel and Palestine, and yet to be literally and spiritually fulfilled in the future history of that land and people, is yet true also to all who thirst for God in all ages. We think also of the promise in Isa. xliv., "I will pour water upon him that is thirsty, and floods upon the dry ground," and of the words of our Lord Jesus, who on that great day of the feast, stood and cried, "If any man thirst let him come unto Me and drink. He that believeth on Me, as the Scripture hath said, out of his belly shall flow rivers of living water."

That God did thus draw nigh to David, and satisfy the longings of his heart, is seen from all the rest of the Psalm. The second verse reads in the Authorised Version as if it were the continuation of the intense desire and prayer expressed in the first verse, but to get at the sense of the original the sentences must be transposed. The rendering is improved in the Revised Version. The order of the words in the Hebrew is this:

"So in the sanctuary have I beheld Thee,
In order to see Thy power and Thy glory."

It seems to me clear that it is no longer a prayer, but a rapturous exclamation at the vision of God's glory granted to him, there and then, in the wilderness. The "so" is both beautiful and forcible. "Even in the same beauty and loveliness, was I wont to gaze upon Thee in the sanctuary, beholding Thy power and Thy glory dwelling between the cherubim; but now I know that Thou art a God who revealest Thyself in all places to those who thirst for Thee, for I have seen Thy glory, even in the wilderness." Does it seem to us too abrupt a transition from the first to the second verse? Then let us remember that this like the other Psalms, is no mere poetic production composed for effect, perhaps at one sitting. The words we are considering have not only been *written* by David, but they have been, so to say, enacted in him, and as the expressions were wrung of his inmost experience they were caught up, and crystallised, and preserved by God's Spirit for the instruction, or warning, or encouragement of God's people in all times. Not long ago a learned gentleman remarked to me that the Psalms were a literary puzzle to him. "I can understand," he said, "the classics of the Greeks or Romans, or the lyrical writings of our modern poets: there is always a certain method and continuity of thought in them, but in most of the Hebrew Psalms there seems no harmony or sequence. They seem like so many disjointed fragments, some of them mere ejaculations, put together without any apparent connection. There is, for instance, a sigh, a prayer, a song of praise, a moan of despondency, and a shout of victory, all mingled together!" I ventured to say to him that the reason for it was that the Psalms were not mere literary productions, but expressions and records of real life, and their harmony is not discoverable by the rules and principles of literary art, but by the test of actual life and experience. They correspond in this respect to the life of the Christian, which is also made up, not only of prayer, し . f one continuous song of praise, but of many groans, and prayers, of songs of deliverance, moans of distress, and shouts of victory, all mingled together, and often without apparent harmony or order of sequence, but all the time working out together one beautiful pattern, the real harmony and interdependence of which we shall behold with wonder by and by. Sometimes in one verse we have the history of a mighty conflict, and we can follow the Psalmist descending into the valley of humiliation, and emerging again on the mountain top of communion and joy in the Lord.

Once his soul was enraptured with the beauty of the Lord, and his eyes were opened to behold His glory, he seemed no longer conscious of the wilderness of his surroundings, but rather to overflow with praise and adoration to God, for His marvellous grace and condescension:

> *"Because Thy lovingkindness is better than life,*
> My lips shall praise Thee."

The Hebrew word *"Chesed,"* translated "lovingkindness," is not uniformly rendered in the English Bible. It is of deep significance, though its meaning is akin to the old-fashioned English word "grace." It is always used of God's dealing in favour towards the unworthy and rebellious, and may be said to describe His undeserved mercy and compassion to man. There is an element in this word, especially when, as an adjective, it is used to describe the character of God, which has in it the hint of the *self-humbling* of God for man's salvation, the climax of which is reached in Him who is the *"Chasid,"* "Holy One" (Psa. xvi. 10; lxxxix. 19), because He was the meek and lowly of heart. It is, I suppose, on account of its depth of meaning, that the translators were at a loss how to express it in English. Frequently they have rendered it by the word "mercy," sometimes by the word "grace," often by the phrase "lovingkindness," and once at least (Psa. cxvii. 2) it is translated by the words "merciful kindness."

And this undeserved favour of God is *"better than life,"* because without it life itself is wretchedness, and because it has to do not only with the life that now is, but also with that which is to come. Oh, reader, have you laid hold of this marvellous grace of God, and has it brought salvation to you? And if it has, does your soul sufficiently dwell upon it, so that by contemplating its height and depth, and the smitten Rock through which it flows, you too, like the Psalmsit, look up to Him continually, saying, *"My lips shall praise Thee"?*

The fourth verse begins with the same word as the second. " *'Thus'* [or *'so'*] *will I bless Thee while I live."* " 'So,' or after this manner, did I behold Thee in the sanctuary," and "so," with my eyes fixed on Thy Glory, and at every remembrance of Thee, "will I bless Thee.".

The word translated "while I live" is, literally, "in my life," but it means both, "as long as I live, and with all the power of my life." It is a solemn resolution on the part of the Psalmist to bless God all his days, and that, not with his lips only, but *with his life* also, by giving himself up to God. This is also expressed in the words, *"I will lift up my hands in Thy Name,"* which is an idiom denoting both service and worship, which two must ever go together.

In the fifth verse we see the vital connection between a right condition of soul, and readiness of mouth and lip to show forth God's praise:

"My soul shall be satisfied as with marrow and fatness,
And my mouth shall praise Thee with joyful lips."

One of the dangers against which we must all guard is the use of expressions of praise and prayer which do not answer to our true condition, and do not really utter the experience of our hearts, for in that case it is neither praise nor prayer, but dead formality, which is an insult to the majesty of God. Why is it that sometimes the holiest and most solemn words and expressions fall from our lips flat and lifeless, and without the power to touch the hearts of those who listen to us? Is it not for the very reason that our own hearts are not at rest in God at the time, and that we ourselves are not satisfied? Oh, my brethren, let us never utter a "Hallelujah," or "Praise the Lord," if we are not ready, like the Psalmist, to add at the same time, "Bless the Lord, *O my soul."* On the other hand, out of the abundance of the heart the mouth must speak, and when my soul is in the banqueting chamber of the King, partaking of the feast of fat things, which in His grace and love He has Himself prepared; when my soul is satisfied as with marrow and fatness, I cannot help myself, "my mouth must praise Thee with joyful lips." By taking the fifth and sixth verses together, we also find the true secret of satisfaction:

"My soul shall be satisfied as with marrow and fatness,
And my mouth shall praise Thee with joyful lips—
When[5] I remember Thee."

"When I remember Thee!"—the secret and source of satisfaction is not in myself, but in Him. Only in the living God, "my exceeding joy"; and more especially in the remembrance of Him who loved me unto death can I find rest to my heart and peace to my soul. When I remember myself, or look into my own heart, I find no cause for satisfaction. When I look down on my present wilderness surroundings; or around me on my fellow-believers; or on a marred and distracted Church; or on a world lying in the hands of the wicked one, there is everything to make me unhappy, and to take satisfaction from me; but when I look up, "when I remember Thee, Lord Jesus, Thy power and glory, Thine everlasting unchangeable love, Thy life and death, Thy resurrection and ascension, Thy life of intercession for me, Thy coming again when mine eye shall behold Thee as Thou art—oh, then, my heart is overwhelmed with joy, and my soul is satisfied as with marrow and fatness." That was indeed good advice, given by Robert Murray McCheyne, that for one look at self we should give ten at our Lord Jesus.

"When I remember Thee on my bed,
And meditate on Thee in the night watches."

What a beautiful glimpse we get in the Davidic Psalms of the inner life of the sweet Psalmist of Israel. It is for this, as for so many other reasons, that David is such a beautiful type of His great Son and Lord, and that so many of his experiences merge into the experiences of Messiah the King, who is the true Man after God's own

---

[5] The conjunction *im* has various significations. It also means "if," "as often," "nevertheless," &c.

heart. Early in the morning [6] (ver. 6) his soul is athirst
for God. The day passes, what does this king and warrior,
with the crowd of business pressing on him, do? Listen.
"On Thee do I wait all the day" (Psa. xxv. 5). Here
in our Psalm night is upon him. He is a fugitive in the
wilderness, possibly fleeing from his own rebellious son.
He is surrounded by many enemies and dangers. How
many things we should naturally suppose would crowd
into his thoughts, but what does he do? *"When I remem-*
ber Thee," he says, *"upon my bed,"* and the blessed remembrance of God crowded out all other thoughts from
his mind. The great thought and remembrance of God
takes such possession of him that he cannot sleep. What
does he do? *"I meditate on Thee in the night watches."*
In silent meditation on God he finally falls asleep: *"And*
when I awake," he says, *"I am still with Thee!"* (Psa.
cxxxix. 18).

It is in such a life, lived in the presence of God, that
we find the secret of satisfaction, and the power to lift
up our hands in God's Holy Name, both in worship and
in service.

Part of the Psalmist's meditation was evidently on
God's great goodness, and on the deliverances which he
had experienced in the past, which awoke in him trust
for the present and hope for the future. This he expresses
in the next verse:

"Because [*or 'for'*] *Thou hast been a help to me;*
   Therefore [*or 'and'*] *in the shadow of Thy wings will I rejoice."*

---

[6] This is the literal meaning of the Hebrew, as already observed
above, but the word has also the secondary sense of "diligently,"
"earnestly," because the diligent man is one who rises early in
the morning.

As much as to say, "Thou, O Lord, hast been my help
and deliverer in the past, and in Thy tender sheltering
protection will I still trust and rejoice."   It was not the
first time that David was a fugitive and in danger.   Long
before he had to flee from his wicked son over the brook
Kidron, "towards the way of the wilderness" (2 Sam.
xv. 23-28), he had to wander many a day in the wilderness of Ziph and Engedi, and to hide in dens and caves of
the mountains; and long before the formidable rebellion,
and the wicked counsel of Ahitophel, by which he was
brought into this present danger, there had been those
"who sought his soul [or 'life'] to destroy it," but out of
all his afflictions the Lord had delivered him, and fulfilled
His word to him by bringing him to the throne, and subduing his enemies under Him.   And now, although the
danger and toil in which he found himself was the direct
outcome of his great sin (2 Sam. xii. 1-14), and although,
in bitter shame and humiliation, he again and again confessed his grievous failures, he had nevertheless learned
the secret of the Lord towards them that fear Him, which
is His faithfulness, and the immutability of His covenants and promises; and as he remembers God, and
meditates on Him, his faith grows stronger, and his hope
brighter, he remembers *the sure mercies of David,*
and the everlasting covenant, ordered in all things and
sure in spite of the fact that "he and his house were not
so with God," until, in full assurance, he utters his confidence that as God had been his help hitherto, so under
the shadow of His wings he would continue to rejoice.
It was on the same principle that the Apostle reasoned
after being once "delivered out of the mouth of the lion,"
when he said: "And the Lord shall deliver me from every
evil work, and will preserve me unto His heavenly kingdom, to whom be glory for ever and ever.   Amen."

But not only on past experiences is his hope based, but
also in a present abiding fellowship with God.

> *"My soul," he says, "followeth hard after Thee;*
> *Thy right hand upholdest me."*

Rich and beautiful is the thought which is brought before
us in the Hebrew word translated "followeth hard." Its
precise meaning is "to adhere," "to cleave," "to be inseparably joined," and thus it expresses the most intimate
possible relationship between the soul and God. The
figure is probably taken from Gen. ii. 24, where the word
is used for the first time. There is no nearer relationship
than that of marriage, which is ideally and scripturally an
indissoluble bond, deliberately entered into by two parties
for life. "Therefore shall a man leave his father and
mother, and shall cleave [or 'be inseparably joined'] to
his wife, and *they two shall be one flesh."* It is for this
reason that marriage forms such a perfect type of the
great mystery of "Christ and the Church" (Eph. v. 25-
33), and sets forth the blessed spiritual reality that "he
that is joined to the Lord is one spirit" (1 Cor. vi. 17).

Let us for a moment consider what is implied in this
blessed spiritual relationship of marriage to the Lord.
To touch on the lesser, or human side, first, it means that
my soul has made Him her deliberate choice, has set all
her affections upon Him, and is determined henceforth
to be inseparably joined to Him. Like Ruth who *"clave"*
(same word in Hebrew) to Naomi, I say to my heavenly
Bridegroom when my love is tested: *"Entreat me not to
leave Thee,* or to return from following after Thee, *for
whither Thou goest"*—even though it may lead to shame,
poverty, and suffering; even though Thy way be through
Gethsemane, and even Golgotha—there, by Thy grace,
"I will go, and where Thou lodgest"—even though it be
without the camp, *"I will lodge"*—gladly bearing with Thee

Thy reproach (Heb. xiii. 11, 13). *"Thy people"*—though they be the poor, the weak, and despised of the world; though they be men of other nations and different colour, and however unlovely in themselves, *"shall be my people, and Thy God"*—in the new light and glory in which Thou has revealed Him to me, *"shall be my God. Where Thou diest"*—even though on a cross of shame on Calvary, *"will I die, and there,"* in Thy sepulchre, *"will I be buried. The Lord do so to me, and more also, if ought but death part Thee and me."*

But this is like putting the moon before the sun, for what is my love and devotion to Christ but a faint echo and response of His infinite and everlasting love to me? Let me, then, rather think of what this blessed relationship implies on His part. It means, "that Christ loved the Church, and gave Himself for it" (Eph. v. 25); and not only the Church colectively, which is His Bride, but *"He loved me,* and gave Himself for me" (Gal. ii. 20). And having shed His life blood to win me to Himself, that I should share His kingdom and glory, He will never part with me. This brings me to another obligation which He assumed when, in His condescending grace, He entered with me into this union, and that is *protection.* In this respect the figure in the verse is perfect: "My soul cleaves, or is joined to Thee, as if in marriage; *Thy right hand upholdeth me."* I am the weak one, and all I can do is to cleave to or follow hard after Him; but He is the El-Gibbor, the Mighty One, and His right hand shields and protects me.

In the Song of Songs we get a glimpse of the Church as a whole, coming up from the wilderness, leaning on the strong arm of the Beloved (Cant. viii. 5), but here in this wilderness Psalm we have the same truth under the same figure in reference to the individual—the weak soul upheld and led by her heavenly Bridegroom. In this very relationship may Christ's people read their eternal safety, for what God hath joined together no one shall succeed in putting asunder. Has the God of Israel ever yet given a bill of divorcement to a soul that trusted Him, however feebly? "I hate putting away, saith the Lord" (Mal. ii. 16). Remember that Rom. viii., too, is a wilderness chapter, for the land of groaning and strife; and yet even there, with deadly enemies both within and without, we are taught to sing: "Who shall separate us from the love of Christ? Shall tribulation, or distress, or persecution, or famine, or nakedness, or peril, or sword? Nay, in all these things we are more than conquerors through Him that loved us."

The next two verses describe the lot of the enemies of God's people. Secure in the protection, and happy in the fellowship of the Lord, to whom he feels himself inseparably joined, the Psalmist turns round and beholds the formidable array of his many and implacable foes, who are ready to come upon him, not only "to eat up his flesh," but to *"seek his soul"*; and, with a defiant and contemptuous gesture, which we can almost see in the peculiar force of the expressions he uses, he says (I translate literally): *"And as for these—suddenly destroyed shall they be that seek my soul."* Like Korah and his company, on whom the earth opened suddenly, so

"Shall they come into the lower parts of the earth;
They shall fall [or, literally, 'be poured out'—that is their blood
'like water, upon the hands of the sword' ;
They shall be a portion for foxes" [or jackals"].

—those unclean animals who feed on unburied carcasses. This will be the final lot of our great adversary and his confederederates of wicked spirits and wicked men. Even now are we more than conquerors in spite of them, but soon God shall finally bruise Satan under our feet, and we shall be wholly rid of even the presence of our adversaries. In the last verse we have Hope viewing the future from the observatory of Faith. Just now David is a fugitive in the wilderness, disowned by the greater part of the people who have chosen to follow the usurper, but his title to the throne is too deeply rooted in the covenant faithfulness of God to be set aside by any combination of men or devils; and looking at it from the standpoint of God's promise he is still *"the King,"* and is confident that he shall yet again be openly declared as such, and *"rejoice in God,"* and that those who have *"sworn"* allegiance to Elohim and His Anointed by following Him even in the wilderness *"shall glory,"* or make their boast over their enemies, whose lying mouths shall be forcibly *"stopped."*

But behind the historical foreground of David there is "David's greater Son," many of whose experiences, as already stated, were foreshadowed by the sweet Psalmist of Israel; and this verse especially reminds us of Psa. xxi., where we read that:

"The King [Messiah] shall joy in Thy strength, O Lord; and in Thy salvation how greatly shall He rejoice!

Thou hast given Him His heart's desire, and hast not withholden the request of His lips.

For Thou preventest Him with the blessings of goodness; Thou settest a crown of pure gold on His head.

He asked life of Thee, and Thou gavest it Him, even length of days for ever and ever.

His glory is great in Thy salvation; honour and majesty hast Thou laid upon Him.

For Thou hast made Him most blessed for ever; Thou hast made Him exceeding glad with Thy countenance.

For the King trusteth in the Lord, and through the mercy of the most High He shall not be moved.

Thine hand shall find out all Thine enemies; Thy right hand shall find out those that hate Thee."

He, too, is now disowned, and especially by Israel, and those who sware allegiance to Him have to follow Him outside the camp, or into the wilderness; but soon He shall be manifest to vindicate His right in the power of God, and we too, however despised now, shall be manifested with Him in glory, and then the mouth of him who was a liar from the beginning, and of all his confederates in the great rebellion against the true King, shall be forcibly stopped.

VII

ZION'S GOD THE CONFIDENCE OF ALL THE ENDS OF THE EARTH

PSALM LXV

"Praise waiteth for Thee, O God, in Zion:
And unto Thee shall the vow be performed.
O Thou that hearest prayer,
Unto Thee shall all flesh come.
Iniquities prevail against me:
As for our transgressions, Thou shall purge them away.
Blessed is the man whom Thou choosest and causeth to approach
        unto Thee,
That He may dwell in Thy courts:
We shall be satisfied with the goodness of Thy house,
The holy place of Thy temple.
By terrible things Thou wilt answer us in righteousness,
O God of our salvation:
Thou that are the confidence of all the ends of the earth,
And of them that are afar off upon the sea:
Which by His strength setteth fast the mountains;
Being girded about with might:
Which stilleth the roaring of the seas, the roaring of their waves,
And the tumult of the peoples.
They also that dwell in the uttermost parts are afraid at Thy
        tokens:
Thou makest the outgoings of the morning and evening to rejoice.
Thou visitest the earth, and waterest it,
Thou greatly enrichest it:
The river of God is full of water:
Thou providest them corn, when Thou hast so prepared the earth.
Thou waterest her furrows abundantly;
Thou settlest the ridges thereof:
Thou makest it soft with showers;
Thou blessest the springing thereof.
Thou crownest the year with Thy goodness;
And Thy paths drop fatness.
They drop upon the pastures of the wilderness.
And the hills are girded with joy.
The pastures are clothed with flocks;
The valleys also are covered over with corn;
They shout for joy, they also sing."

ZION'S GOD THE CONFIDENCE OF ALL THE ENDS OF THE EARTH [1]

PRIMARILY this Psalm sets forth the blessedness of restored and converted Israel when the Lord shall establish and make Jerusalem a praise in the earth, and when "Zion" shall be, as never before, the earthly centre for the praise and worship of the one true God. Then "the vow" of national fidelity and obedience to God which Israel took upon himself "shall be performed," not in the legal spirit of bondage, in which they found it impossible to fulfil God's holy requirements, but in the spirit of liberty, when the laws shall be put in their inward parts, and written on their hearts. And then—when the relations between God and His Israel are restored—"all flesh," or, as it is expressed in ver. 5, "all the ends of the earth," shall come and put their confidence in Jehovah.

"I am a Prayer"

But it is not merely from its future prophetic point of view that I want to deal with this Psalm, but to show also its present spiritual application to all the true people of God now.

There are two Psalms which begin very much alike, namely the lxii. and the lxv. In both we have in the very first sentence the Hebrew word "Dumiyah" (translated in

---

[1] The exposition of the first three verses of this Psalm—now somewhat altered—appeared as "Notes of an Address" in "The Scattered Nation" in July, 1897. The whole of the Psalm is now written out for the first time.

the Authorised Version by the words "is silent"), as denoting an attitude in relation to God—in Psa. lxii. in relation to prayer, in lxv. in relation to praise.

First, in relation to prayer, "Truly my soul is silent before God," or, "Only upon God my soul doth silently wait" (Psa. lxii. 1). It is a very great comfort for God's people to remember, that, apart from their prayers, there is such a thing as *they themselves* being a prayer. I do not know if you have ever come across an expression in the Bible which is one of the most precious to me. It is in Psa. cix. 4. The speaker in Psa. cix. is the Messiah, the Lord Jesus Christ. It is He only who has a right to utter His curse and imprecation against sin and cruel hatred of the Righteous One as described in that Psalm; and the primary subject of that Scripture is most probably Judas (Acts i. 20). But we read in ver. 4, "For my love they are my adversaries: but I"—then, you note, there are three words in italics which are not found in the original—"I . . . prayer." The *"am"* must be supplied. I remember this verse being first pointed out to me by a rather sceptical Jew who thought David had made a slip here in his composition; that he could not have meant exactly that he was a prayer, but that he was praying, as it is rendered with the italics in the Authorized Version. I am sure it is not a slip, but that it is actually what it says.

In reference to our Lord Jesus Christ, how beautiful and true this is. He *was* prayer. Not only did He pray, not only was He pre-eminently the Man of prayer, spending all nights in prayer and intercession, but He was a prayer, even as He speaks of Himself by the Spirit, in Psa. xxii. "But Thou art He that took me out of the womb. Thou didst make me hope when I was upon my mother's breasts. I was cast upon Thee from the womb: Thou art my God from my mother's belly." Look at the infant, to use the figure suggested in these verses of Psa. xxii. If it received the attention of its mother only when it cried I suppose it would be very badly off indeed. But the infant, by reason of its helplessness and need, is continually a prayer. Before it asks it receives.

More helpless than infants are we in relation to God, and in relation to the great issues of life, but more constant and more tender than the love of a mother to her child is the love of God our Father toward His children. We are always poor and needy, but our Father thinketh upon us. "How precious also are Thy thoughts unto me, O God! how great is the sum of them! If I should count them they are more in number than the sand: when I awake I am still with Thee."

"I am a prayer." "My soul silently waiteth before God: from Him cometh my salvation."

Or, to pass from the figure of the helpless infant to the wretched beggar outside the rich man's gate. The rich man comes forth, and, if there be any of the compassion of God in his heart, does that beggar need to speak, or is it only the beggar's words that he heeds? No, he himself is a prayer. His wretched appearance pleads for him; his tattered garment pleads for him; his pinched face, his withered hand, his feeble step, plead for him. The following incident is related in connection with the Irish famine: "Leitch Ritchie, a well-known Scottish literary man, talking of his experiences in Ireland, stated that one man whom he saw sitting on the ground with his back to the wall attracted his attention by a degree of squalor in his appearance which he had not before observed in the country. But, unlike other Irish beggars, the man was strangely silent, and, struck by this, Mr. Ritchie asked him whether he was begging. 'Of course 'tis begging I am,' said the man. 'But you do not utter a word,' said Mr. Ritchie. 'Arrah, is it jokin' yer honner is with me?'

said the beggar. 'Look there,' and he held up the tattered remnant of what had been a coat. 'Does yer see how the skin is spakin' through the holes of me coat; and the bones crying out through me skin? Look at me sunken cheeks, and the famine that's starin in me eyes. Man alive, isn't it beggin' I am, with a hundred tongues!'"

And all this is true of us in relation to God, only if our hearts go out to Him in desire and love, we are not only beggars at His gate, but those whom He is not ashamed to call children; and we remember His word, that as a father pitieth his children, so Jehovah pitieth them that fear Him.

But if what I have just said is true in relation to prayer, it is also true in relation to praise; and in this connection the same word is used in the sixty-fifth Psalm: "Praise silently waiteth before Thee, O God, in Zion": or, as another has rendered it, "Before Thee silence [or 'resignation'] is as praise, O God, in Zion." [2]

Here, again, I would say that not only is it our privilege to *speak* His praise, but there is such a thing as His people *being* to the praise of His glory, because they have trusted in Christ, and are walking with Him in light.

You may very probably have noticed a rather remarkable expression in Neh. xii. in connection with the solemn thanksgiving after the completion of the building of the wall of Jerusalem. On that day the priests and the Levites were divided into two parties to form a procession around the wall. But, in addition, we read in ver. 31,

---

[2] Most probably the blessed condition of the restored people is what is meant—their faith and restful confidence in God; their prayerfulness (ver. 2); their fidelity and obedience to God—their whole life, when upon everything they do and have shall be written "Holiness to Jehovah" (Zech. xiv. 20)—shall be as an acceptable offering of praise—a silent cloud of incense sending up a sweet savour into His nostrils.

Nehemiah says: "Then I brought up the princes of Judah upon the wall, and appointed two great"—then there are five or six words in italics, which are also not found in the original—literally, "two great thanks." These princes did not utter a word. They walked in silence after the priests and Levites as representatives of the whole people, and God knew the thankfulness of heart which this silent procession was meant to express.

And truly it has been well said if there are prayers which cannot be uttered, there are also praises which cannot be expressed in words, but which He who searches the heart knows. It is what we *are,* and the attitude of our hearts, of which God takes more note than of our words. And this will be the case with Israel by and by, when restored and blessed.

The Vow

"And unto Thee shall the vow be performed."

This, as already explained, refers to the national vow of Israel. Israel entered into covenant relationship with God, and undertook certain obligations. We read, for instance, in Deut. xxvi. of the solemn transaction when the covenant was made with them nationally, "Thou hast avouched Jehovah this day to be thy God, and to walk in His ways, and to keep His statutes, and His commandments, and His judgments, and to hearken unto His voice. And Jehovah hath avouched thee this day to be His peculiar people as He hath promised thee, and that thou shouldest keep His commandments; and to make thee high above all nations which He hath made, in praise, and in name, and in honour; and that thou mayest be an holy people unto Jehovah thy God, as He hath spoken." We remember also their too quick response when the words of the covenant were read to them, "All that Jehovah our God hath said we will hearken and do."

This was the solemn vow made, but they have never yet fulfilled it; they have never yet hearkened or been obedient to God as a nation. But the vow shall yet *be performed*. The stony heart shall be taken from them, and a new heart be given them. God's laws shall be written *within* them, they shall do His will; and Israel will yet answer to the ideal which God has set before them in His Word. And then it is that praise shall silently go up to God from Mount Zion.

"All Flesh"

The blessed issue of Israel's restored relations to God is that all the ends of the earth shall learn to know Him.

> "O Thou that hearest prayer,
> Unto Thee shall all flesh come."

Here we have an invocation of God by one of the most precious of His names by which he has been pleased to reveal Himself to man. "Hearer of prayer," this is the literal meaning of the first of the two lines of which the second verse consists. "Hearer of prayer"—this is how our fathers knew Him; this is how we too have learned to know Him, and this is how by and by "all flesh" shall know Him.

Experimentally, however, we only know God as the Hearer of prayer *if we are men and women of prayer*. Alas! how many even Christians there be who have not because they **ask not; or ask** and receive not because they do not really pray, but ask *selfishly*, "that they may spend it on their own pleasures." And how short we all come of **the apostolic exhortation** to pray *always*, "with all prayer and supplication- *in the spirit,* and watching thereunto with all perseverance and supplication for all saints." Lord, teach us to pray; yes, always to pray and never to faint; and help us to know Thee, not only from Thy words, and from the testimony of Thy saints in all ages, but *from our own experience,* that Thou art the Hearer of prayer! The juxtaposition of the two names in this short verse—the name for God and the name for man —is very beautiful. "Hearer of prayer" is the name for God, and the name for man is "flesh." Now, the term "flesh" stands sometimes for the sinfulness or corruption of our nature—the "old man" in the believer which must be put off, and to the promptings of which we may not yield; but more often it is the term used to describe the *weakness,* the helplessness, and the transitoriness of human nature. "All flesh is grass, and all the goodliness thereof is as the flower of the field." Our Lord Himself gave us a definition of flesh in this sense when He said "the flesh is weak." And in this our helplessness and need to whom shall we go?

Blessed be His Holy Name. He knoweth our frame, He remembereth our weakness and frailty, and just because we are "flesh" we may cast ourselves upon Him. Blessed weakness if it only lays hold of His Almightiness! Blessed helplessness if it only leads to a complete dependence upon Him—if it can only appropriate His Word, "My grace is sufficient for thee, for My strength is made perfect in weakness."

But, as already indicated, the words form a prophecy, "Unto Thee all flesh"—that is, all men, all nations—"shall come," in contrast to the present, when only *some* have by His grace been brought to know and trust in Him. Yes, there is a time coming, and it is closely connected with the blessing and salvation of Israel, when the glory of Jehovah shall be revealed and *all flesh* shall see it together, and when the knowledge of the One true and living God shall cover the earth as the waters cover the sea.

God's Remedy for Sin.

The next verse speaks of the great obstacle in the way of "all flesh" coming to God, and how alone this obstacle can be removed. This short verse forms, perhaps, one of the most comprehensive statements to be found in Scripture on this subject.

"Iniquities prevail against me."

You have, perhaps, noticed the alternative readings which are given in the margin. It shows the difficulty which the translators felt in giving exactly the idiom to be found in the original, and I think that idiom is not fully grasped even in the suggestions given in the alternative readings, either in the Authorised or Revised versions. If we take one of the suggestions in the margin—namely, "matters of iniquity"—I should be inclined to take it in the sense of "that which concerns iniquity"; and the words rendered "prevail against me" literally mean "are too strong for me," "have overpowered me," like some mighty giant against whom I am altogether helpless. In this sentence, my dear friends, we have a confession of human helplessness in the great matter of sin. Men may cavil at what they are pleased to call the *theory* or the doctrine of sin, but the fact and power of sin none can deny.

The word *avon*, translated "iniquity," describes sin in its radical sense. Here it is, a terrible reality—"sin," "iniquity"; but what I am to do with it, how I am to rid myself of it, I know not; "it is beyond me." I am powerless to devise means to free myself from it, or to discover a way by which sin can be atoned for and put away. O wretched man that I am, who shall, or can, deliver me? Blessed be God, the next line tells me: "As for *our transgressions*" (which is the synonym for "iniquities" in the first line), *"Thou atonest for them."* If the first line is the confession of man's helplessness in the matter of sin, the second line is the utterance of a man enlightened by the Spirit of God to see how sin *is* put away. We are reminded of Abraham's reply to Isaac, "The Lord shall provide Himself a lamb for a burnt-offering."

Yes, that which man could neither discover nor devise, and which could never have entered into his heart, *God has provided,* and that from eternity. The parallelism in this verse is perfect.

> *"Iniquities have overpowered me;*
> *Our transgressions Thou shalt atone for."*

Thus the word "transgression" is the synonym for "iniquity" and "Thou" is in contrast to "me." The *"Thou"* is very emphatic, and therefore rightly rendered by some critical expositors as *"Thou, even Thou."* And if we want to know how God atones for sin, the answer is to be found in the very word used in the original, and translated "purge away" in the Authorised Version. It is the word *"kaphar."*

In the Psalms it is found only three times. In this Psalm, in Psa. lxxviii. 38, where it is rendered "forgave," and in Psa. lxxix. 9, but it is a Leviticus word—that is, wherever you have the word for *atonement by blood* in the Book of Leviticus it is this word which is used. The primary idea is that of "covering," the hiding of sin from the eyes of God; the hiding of the guilt of sin from the avenging justice of God. "As for our transgressions, *Thou* shalt atone for them." Blessed be God! in the light of the fuller revelation of the New Testament; in the light of Calvary and the precious blood which came forth from the side of our Saviour, we know how God purges our sin, and cleanses away our iniquity.

The Spiritual Priesthood.

The great obstacle being removed, the way is open for communion and fellowship, the blessedness of which is set forth in the fourth verse.

In contemplating this verse we cannot but pause in amazement, and marvel at the fulness and riches of revelation which the Spirit of God has been pleased to store up in one brief passage of Scripture, consisting in the original of only ten words. Luther said of the Book of Psalms that it was the whole Bible in small compass, "for in it all things that are contained in the whole Bible are given to us in the most wonderfully brief and sweet manner condensed into a most beautiful manual." Sometimes this is almost true of a single Psalm in this precious collection, and occasionally we seem to see the whole plan of God in the salvation of man compressed in one verse, as is the case with the one before us. In this verse we see, as it were, two eternities centre—the eternity that is past, and the eternity that is to come. It begins with a beatitude—"*Ashrey*"—which is a plural vocative. "Oh, how blessed!" as if the Spirit of inspiration Himself were at a loss to describe fully the heights and depths of the blessedness of a man in such a case. "Oh, how blessed!" or "Oh, the blessedness!" God never blesses His people but what He blesses them much. Yes, to an extent that human language utterly fails adequately to describe. As yet we may not have fully comprehended, much less experimentally entered into, all that is ours in Christ Jesus our Lord, as the result of His redeeming work, but of this be assured, my fellow-Christian, that if you are an object of His grace, and know that Christ has undertaken for you in "matters of iniquity," you are one of those of whom the Lord says, "Oh, how blessed!" and through all eternity you will not cease to marvel at "the greatness of His goodness, which He has safely hid for them that fear Him, and which He has wrought for them that trust Him before the sons of men."

But let me show you the primary significance of this verse, and its concrete connection with the past and

future history of the Jewish people. In examining the
words carefully, we find that they describe the calling
and privileges of the priesthood. The sons of Levi were
chosen to be a special tribe above the others, and from
that tribe the Aaronic family was chosen to stand in a
position of special nearness to God. They were "chosen,"
and by means of ceremonial consecration and cleansings,
were "made nigh." They "dwelt" about the courts of
God's House, and were "satisfied" with its good and
bountiful provision of "holy things."

But the language, though borrowed from the privileges
of the Aaronic priesthood, is used only in a figurative
sense to set forth the greater spiritual priesthood of Israel
in the future. God's original purpose in the election and
call of Israel is thus stated in Exod. xix. 5, 6: "Now
therefore if ye will obey My voice indeed, and keep My
Covenant: then ye shall be a peculiar treasure unto Me
above all peoples; for all the earth is Mine. And ye shall
be unto Me a kingdom of priests and an holy nation."
Here we have a summary of Israel's high calling. It is
chosen and separated from all other nations that it may, in
a peculiar sense, be a people of God's own possession.

Secondly, because as a nation it is God's "peculiar
treasure" it must be holy even as He is holy, so that in
their whole work and conversation, and in their very national and social institutions and ordinances they might
show forth His praises, and be the medium of blessing
to all nations.

Thirdly, as a holy and priestly people Israel is called
to the great privilege of direct and personal dealings with
God—to draw near to Him in worship with their gifts and
sacrifices, and to receive the gifts of His grace and blessing from His all-bountiful hand. But Israel so far has
not apprehended that for which they were apprehended
of God. At the foot of Mount Sinai Israel was, so to

say, put on its trial with a view to make it manifest to themselves and to the world that they were not yet able to respond to their high calling. Instead of being able to bear the revelation of God's holiness and to draw nigh as "the priests of the Lord" to hear His voice and to receive His law, we read that when "all the people saw the thunderings and the lightnings, and the voice of the trumpet, and the mountain smoking, . . they trembled and stood afar off. And they said unto Moses, Speak thou with us, and we will hear: but let not God speak with us, lest we die" (Exod. xx. 18, 19).

Thus Israel themselves acknowledged their inability for direct and immediate fellowship with God, and instead of taking their place as priestly mediators between God and the nations, they themselves confessed their need of a mediator.

But one of the chief objects which God had in this self-revelation to them on Sinai was to bring them to just such a knowledge of themselves, and it was after this solemn confession on the part of the people at the foot of Mount Sinai that the Aaronic priesthood was appointed, which was parenthetical and temporary, and had to do only with Israel, and with special appointments and institutions in Palestine. And this Aaronic priesthood, summed up as it was in the person of a High Priest, while appointed of God to meet Israel's felt need of a mediator between God and them, was designed also to foreshadow, not only some of the aspects of the everlasting Priesthood of Him who ever liveth to make intercession for us, but to be a continual reminder of God's purpose with the nation as a whole, and to teach them the meaning of priesthood, which is to be chosen, to be "His," to be "holy," and to "draw near," unto Him (Num. xvi. 5). To the ultimate realisation of this purpose of God in the whole nation the prophetic Scriptures bear unanimous witness.

Thus Isa. lxi., speaking of that future day, says: "Ye shall be named the Priests of Jehovah; men shall call you the Ministers of our God": and in the Book of Zechariah we have this truth beautifully unfolded to us in chap. iii. There we get in the person of Joshua the high priest, who is a type and representative of the whole nation, a picture of Israel in their present condition, clothed in filthy garments. Then we see a wonderful transformation taking place. The filthy garments are taken from him, and instead he is clothed with beautiful garments, or "rich apparel," as it is in the Revised Verson, most probably the garments of glory and beauty which the high priest wore.

There was yet lacking one thing to finish the high-priestly outfit, namely, "the mitre," to which was fastened the golden plate on which was graven "Kodesh la-Yehovah"—"Holiness to the Lord." And the prophet seeing this, breaks in with the petition, "Let them set a fair mitre upon his head." That the subject is not Joshua, but the people whom he represents, must be apparent to all students of the Scripture, for when we come to the end of the chapter we have the Divine explanation of the whole vision in the words: "I will remove the iniquity of that land in one day." Then, once Israel is thus stripped of himself, and clothed in the righteousness of the Messiah, he enters on his priestly mission. This is brought out clearly in the next chapter (Zech. iv.) where Israel, under the symbol of the restored candlestick, is fulfilling his mission on earth of being the light of the world. Yes, Israel will yet be a nation of priests, and it is primarily in relation to this nation that the beautiful prophetic words in this Psalm are spoken.

But remember, dear Christian reader, that we, as believers in the Lord Jesus, are now, in relation to spiritual blessings, put in the very position that Israel as a nation will occupy by and by. Hence these words equally describe the high calling and privileges of every one who belongs to Christ now.

Thus the Apostle Peter, addressing all believers, says, "Ye are a chosen generation, an holy nation, a peculiar people; that ye should show forth the praises of Him who hath called you out of darkness into His marvellous light." Here believers in Christ are put by God into the very position which Israel should occupy, and will occupy by and by. "This people have I formed for Myself: they shall show forth My praise," said God of Israel. "That ye might show forth the 'praises' or 'excellences,' of Him who hath called you out of darkness into His marvellous light."

The time of Israel's unbelief is thus being filled up, during this interval of Israel's backslidings and dispersions, by the faith, the worship, the spiritual sacrifices, and service of all who believe in Christ, of whatever nation they may be. Let us enter, then, into this blessedness, and see what it means.

> *"Oh! how blessed is the man whom Thou hast chosen"* [*or* *"choosest"*].

This is the first step in this blessedness; it is the initial blessing which carries with it a whole train of blessings, and remains in itself the most precious of all. Let me attempt to illustrate it by an imperfect, homely simile. An illustrious prince sets his affections on some lowly maiden. She will, no doubt, receive many gifts and presents, but why does she get them? and are not all these gifts, however precious in themselves, as nothing in her eyes compared with himself, and the assurance that she is indeed the chosen bride? It is even so with us and our heavenly Bridegroom. We were not only in a lowly, but a fallen state, and yet, blessed be His Holy Name! from eternity He loved us and chose us to be His for ever. Since bringing us to Himself He has simply loaded us with blessings and benefits, and yet would we not gladly exchange the "all things" that are ours in Him, for Himself, and for the assurance expressed in the words, "My Beloved is mine and I am His"? "Oh! how blessed is the man whom Thou choosest!"

I am afraid many lose the blessedness of this grand and comforting truth, because it is merely grasped with the mind, or turned into a subject for discussion, instead of resting their hearts upon it, and turning it into a subject for adoring praise and gratitude, as did Paul, when he bursts out in that adoring song in the first chapter of his Epistle to the Ephesians: "Blessed be the God and Father of our Lord Jesus Christ, who hath blessed us with all spiritual blessings in heavenly places in Christ: *according as He hath chosen us in Him before the foundation of the world,* that we should be holy and without blame before Him in love."

Of Israel it is said that they are the chosen people, and in the very terms we imply privilege and blessing. We also are a chosen generation, an "elect race," and if Israel, who in the first instance were chosen merely nationally in relation to the earth, and to Palestine—if their choice can be spoken of as something great and blessed, how much more so the choice of those who from eternity, in Christ Jesus, were chosen in relation to spiritual and eternal privileges. Well may we exclaim, "Oh! how blessed is the man whom Thou choosest!"

I cannot dwell on this point, else I might point out the responsibilities as well as the privileges attaching to the chosen people.

The next point of blessedness is contained in the words *"makest nigh."* This is the true rendering of the one word which is translated in the Authorised Version "causest to approach unto Thee."

Because God has chosen us, He has made us nigh. "I have loved thee," He says, "with an everlasting love, therefore with lovingkindness have I drawn thee," [3] "Whom Thou *makest* nigh." There is a great deal in this expression. It tells us that God has to *make* us nigh. It is evident then that man by nature is not nigh to God. It is a delusion on the part of men to believe, and to teach, that we are by nature nigh to God; that there is something in man which merely requires improving and developing, in order to make him meet for fellowship with the holy God. It is not so. Since the Fall there is an abyss, a gulf, as wide as the universe and as deep as hell, separating man by nature from God. But, blessed be His Name! even that gulf could not stand in the way between God and those whom He has chosen in Christ Jesus, so He devised means by which to make them nigh.

How does He make us nigh? The third verse explains it. "Matters of iniquity" stood between us and God. Man is powerless in regard to this matter. I know not what to do. I cannot bring myself nigh, but God makes us nigh. "Now, *in Christ Jesus,* ye who sometimes were far off *are made nigh by the blood of Christ.*" I have said that the historical foreground of the fourth verse is the Aaronic priesthood. How were they made nigh? They were chosen, but a number of ceremonial performances had to be undergone in order to bring them into the position of nearness to God. Was it not by blood shed, by the washing of the laver, by anointing oil? And what was the blood shed but the type of the more precious blood of our Saviour Jesus Christ? And what were the washing of the laver and the anointing with oil but types of the washing of regeneration and the renewing of the Holy Ghost,

---

[3] Or "Therefore have I extended, or *drawn out,* My lovingkindness unto thee."

which God hath shed on us abundantly through Jesus
Christ our Lord?

"Whom Thou makest nigh." The word, in the Hebrew,
means not only nigh, in the sense of distance; it is a
word, used by the Jews colloquially to this day, to express
blood relationship. We are made nigh not only in point
of distance, while before we were morally far from God,
but when we are made nigh to God, He sends His Holy
Spirit into our hearts and begins the work of regeneration
and sanctification. By the Holy Ghost who dwells in us,
we are brought into actual relationship with our Father in
heaven. "As many as are led by the Spirit of God, they
are the sons of God. For we have not received the spirit
of bondage again to fear, but we have received the Spirit of
sonship, by whom we cry, Abba, Father."

Then follows another stage of blessedness, *"That they
may dwell."* That is the purpose for which God has
chosen us in Christ Jesus, and for which He has made us
nigh—that we may dwell in His courts, the place of fellowship with God. Blessed be His Name! we are permitted not only to come into His presence and have an
audience with Him, the King of kings, at the close of
which we must withdraw. It is our privilege *"to dwell."*
Just as it was the privilege of the priesthood to dwell in
the courts of the temple, so it is our blessedness to dwell
even now in the courts of His house, in the very presence
of God.

I wonder how many of us have entered experimentally
into this blessedness of dwelling with God. I am afraid
some of us are sometimes driven by sorrow or trial to
come into God's presence. We know Him as a Refuge in
time of trouble; but do we know what it is to dwell in
His courts? "O God, Thou hast been our dwelling-place
in all generations" is the exclamation of Moses, the man of
God, and here the blessedness of dwelling in God is de-

scribed. May God teach even us to know this. We need God as our dwelling-place, for His children must have a place of refuge and of safety. We need Him, because it is only when we dwell in God that we are freed from the spirit that prevails around us.

This Psalm goes on to speak of strife of tongues and tumults of the peoples which God will ultimately still; but even now, in proportion as our hearts àre fixed on God and we live in His presence, are we freed from that spirit of strife and of hurry and worry which prevails in this world.

But this beautiful verse, which tells us of the origin of the blessedness of God's people in the eternity that is past, when He hath chosen us in and for Himself before the foundation of the world, does not stop without giving us a glimpse into the eternity that is to come. The last part takes us to the future. *"We shall be satisfied with the goodness of Thy house, the holy place of Thy temple,"* or perhaps more correctly "with the holiness of Thy temple."

"We shall be satisfied"—that is a beautiful promise, and something to look forward to. It is in contrast to the present. Now, we may be satisfied by anticipation; by having our heart fixed upon the future, "We rejoice in the hope of the glory of God." And it is in proportion as our hearts are thus fixed upon the future that we are satisfied now; but, in actual realisation and consummation, satisfaction comes by and by. "We shall be satisfied." "As for me," says the Psalmist, "I shall behold Thy face in righteousness: I shall be satisfied when I awake with Thy likeness."

And not only shall we be satisfied then with "the goodness of His house," but also "with the holiness of His temple." God's house always remains His temple. However much liberty and access there may be for the children of God, His dwelling is now and ever will be through eternity the place of reverence and of worship, the place where cherubim and seraphim, as well as the redeemed, must cover their faces and cry, "Holy, Holy, Holy is Jehovah of Hosts, all the earth is full of His glory!" But there is this difference between the present and the future, that while now the remembrance of the absolute holiness of God sometimes takes satisfaction from our hearts, because even the holiest of God's people must say that "there is none holy as the Lord"; and the more the light of God shines into our hearts, the more do we have revealed to us the great contrast between God who is perfectly, absolutely holy, and us, who, though redeemed and possessed of a new nature, still carry about with us this body of death with its disposition to sin. But by and by when we see Him as He is, and are conformed perfectly to His image, not only will the *goodness* of God minister to our satisfaction, but the very holiness of God will form the chief element in the fulness of the blessedness of His saints. It is our privilege now to dwell *in the courts* of God's house; the utmost limit to which we can go while on earth; but between the courts and His immediate presence there is still a veil. In the spirit we know that we can enter even now into the Holiest; but I am speaking of the veil of our flesh, the veil of this body of death which we still carry with us. When this veil is removed, when, instead of this mortal, we put on immortality, and instead of this body of humiliation and corruption, we are clothed upon with incorruption; then in actual presence we shall be brought into His house, we shall sit at His table, and behold His face in righteousness. Not till then shall we know in its fulness the depth and height of the blessedness of those whom God has chosen, and made nigh to dwell in His presence.

Jehovah the Confidence of all the Ends of the Earth.

The next short strophe, consisting of vers. 5-8, speaks of the wonderful interpositions of God on Israel's behalf at the second coming of Christ, through which Israel itself shall at last learn to know Him as the God of their salvation, and all "the ends of the earth" to put their trust "in Him."

"By terrible things [or 'deeds'] of righteousness
Wilt Thou answer us,[4]
O God of our salvation.
The confidence of all the ends of the earth,
And of the furthest sea.
Who settest fast the mountains by His strength,
Being girded with might.
Who stillest the roaring of the seas, the roaring of their waves,
And the tumult of the peoples.
They also that dwell in the uttermost parts of the earth are afraid
of Thy tokens.
The outgoings of the morning and evening
Thou makest to rejoice" [or "shout for joy"].

The "terrible things" or "deeds" which will mark once more the baring of God's arm on Israel's behalf will be in "answer" to the prayers of the godly remnant at the time of the end, who will bring to His remembrance "the great and terrible things" which He wrought in the sight of Egypt, and the nations, when He delivered their fathers from their oppression by Pharaoh, of which Divine acts the same word is used (Deut. x. 21). And one

---

[4] Hengstenberg paraphrases "Thou impartest to us when we pray to Thee in our own trouble astonishing deliverances." In "terrible" reference is made to such events as happened before and after the departure from Egypt, as Calvin puts it: "O Lord, Thou hearest us always, so that Thy power now appears in wonderful deliverances as it did formerly when our fathers went out of Egypt."

sample of such a prophetic prayer to which such mighty answer will come we find in Isa. lxiv. 1-3:

> *"Oh that Thou wouldest rend the heavens,*
> *That Thou wouldest come down,*
> *That the mountains might quake at Thy presence. . . .*
> *To make Thy name known to Thine adversaries*
> *That the nations may tremble at Thy presence.*
> *When Thou didst terrible things which we looked not for,*
> *Thou camest down;*
> *The mountains shook at Thy presence."*

And, as the "terrible things," or "awe-inspiring deeds," which He wrought in olden times in Egypt at the Red Sea, were all "in righteousness" as judgments on the oppressors of His people, and in vindication of His character in the sight of Israel, and the nations who witnessed them, so that Moses, contemplating those great Divine acts, was constrained to exclaim, "A God of truth and without iniquity; righteous and upright is He"; so in the future also, when God shall once more arise to shake terribly this earth, and when the vials of His wrath shall be poured on the nations containing "the seven last plagues," which are so remarkably analogous to the plagues of Egypt, they who shall have gotten the victory over Pharaoh's antitype shall "sing the song of Moses, the servant of God, and the song of the Lamb" in celebration of this same character of these judgments, saying, "Great and marvellous are Thy works, O Lord God Almighty: righteous and true are Thy ways, Thou King of the ages. Who shall not fear Thee, O Lord, and glorify Thy name, and worship before Thee; for Thy righteous acts have been manifest" (Rev. xv. 3, 4).[5]

But there is a gracious end in His very judgments, for the blessed issue of it all shall be that He who, by reason

---

[5] De Burgh.

of His judicial and redemptive self-attestation, manifests Himself as the God of "our" (*i. e.,* Israel's) "salvation," will also become known as the confidence of *all the ends of the earth,* and of them even who dwell by the furthest sea.[6] Yes, at last when these great judgments come on the earth shall the inhabitants of the world learn righteousness (Isa. xxvi. 9). In Himself *potentially* Jehovah is ever the confidence of the ends of the earth, for, as Hengstenberg observes, "even the rudest heathen has in God the foundation of his existence, receives from Him all that is requisite for his life, and without Him must perish." But what He ever was, and is, that He shall hereafter be universally *recognised* and joyfully *acknowledged* to be, and all men shall experimentally learn that, both in reference to their physical and to their higher spiritual life, it is in Him that they live and move and have their being.

"All the ends of the earth shall remember and turn to Jehovah,
And all the kindreds of the nations shall worship before Thee.
For the kingdom is Jehovah's,
And He is ruler over the nations" (Psa. xxii. 27, 28).

And what a refutation a Scripture like this is to the shallow infidel assertion one sometimes hears, that in the Old Testament God is spoken of as the tribal and national God of the Jewish people. It is true that for centuries God limited the knowledge of Himself to one land and one people on this earth; but, as I have elsewhere shown,[7]

---

[6] *"Yam rehokim"* doubtless means "the sea of those afar off," and denotes those who dwell on the most distant sea, just as "the ends of the earth" denote those who dwell on its utmost extremity. The mercies of God are co-extensive with human needs, or, as Luther observes, "One may run over the wide world even to its utmost extremity, yet Thou art the only foundation on which the trust of man's heart can stand or remain."—*Hengstenberg.*

[7] See exposition of the second part of Psa. xlv. and the Commencement of the Hallel.

the very limitation was designed with a view to the better accomplishment of His ultimate purpose of its universal diffusion. "The light is focused and set in a tower that it may shine out over sea and storm; the fire is gathered into a brazier that it may warm all the house"; [8] and so one people is chosen and disciplined that through His self-revelations in its midst "all the ends of the earth should eventually learn to put their trust in Him."

And that Jehovah alone is worthy to be the confidence of all the ends of the earth, and can never fail those who put their trust in Him, is proved by His omnipotence, which is demonstrated by the fact that He "setteth fast the mountains," supposed to be the most secure objects in nature; and controls and stills the roaring of the restless, tumultuous "sea."

"Two mighty things are selected to witness to the Mightier, who made and manages them. The firm bulk of the mountains is firm because He is strong. The tossing waves are still because He bids them be silent. How transcendently great, then, is He, and how blind those who, seeing hill and ocean, do not see God! The mention of the sea, the standing emblem of unrest and rebellious power, suggests the 'tumult of the peoples,' on which similar repressive power is exercised. The great deeds of God, putting down tyranny and opposition to Israel, which is rebellion against Himself, strike terror, which is wholesome and is purified into reverence, into the distant lands; and so from the place where the sun rises to the 'sad-coloured end of evening' where it sinks in the west—i. e., through all the earth—there rings out a shout of joy. Such glowing anticipations of universal results from the deeds of God, especially for Israel, are the products of diseased national vanity, unless they are God-taught appre-

---

[8] Alexander Maclaren.

hension of the Divine purpose of Israel's history, which shall one day be fulfilled, when the knowledge of the yet more wondrous deeds, which culminated in the Cross, is spread to the ends of the earth and the remotest seas." [9]

But the mountains may signify here, as in some other Scriptures, the great worldly kingdoms (Isa. xli. 15), even as the sea symbolises in prophecy Gentile world-power (Dan. xii., &c.), but be this as it may, the "tumult of the peoples," which God shall finally quell, is that of the confederate nations who shall be gathered in their final attempt to "cut off Israel from being a nation, that their name be no more in remembrance" (Psa. lxxxiii). "And as in their former deliverance Israel's cause was *the cause of God* in the earth, so will it be again; only that then the controversy was limited to Egypt and Canaan, while hereafter its decision will affect all the nations of the world. Then at these His "tokens" shall they that dwell in the uttermost parts be afraid, "and from the rising to the setting of the sun He shall be praised."

And now we come to the last strophe which gives us a beautiful glimpse of the productiveness of the soil, and of the plenty and prosperity which shall then characterise the earth when the covenant relations between God and His people are restored, and when the double curse which has rested upon "the land" shall be removed.

> *"Thou visitest the earth and waterest it.*[10]
> *Thou greatly enrichest it:*
> *The river of God is full of water;*
> *Thou providest them corn when* [*or* 'for'] *Thou hast so
>   prepared it.*
> *Thou waterest her furrows abundantly;*
> *Thou settlest the ridges thereof;*
> *Thou makest it soft with showers;*

---

[9] Alexander Maclaren.

[10] The margin of the Authorised Version reads, "after Thou hast made it to desire [rain]." Delitzsch renders, "that it should overflow"; and Hengstenberg, "and sendest it a flood." The

Thou blessest the springing thereof,
Thou crownest the year of Thy goodness [*or 'with Thy*
goodness'],
And Thy paths drop fatness:
They drop upon the pastures of the wilderness;
And the hills are girded with joy.
The pastures are clothed with flocks;
The valleys also are covered over with corn;
They shout for joy, they also sing."

He who shall visit the people, and manifest even to the most distant nations His glory, shall also "visit" the earth,[11] or "the land," and His gracious presence shall be as life, and His favour as showers of refreshing rain, both spiritually to the people and literally to the land.

Yes, creation itself shall then be delivered from the bondage of corruption into the glorious liberty of the children of God, and one of the blessed consequences will be fruitful seasons and abundant harvests: Palestine, which in consequence of the sin of the people has so long been desolate, will then answer to its original description as "a land of hills and valleys, and which drinketh water of the rain of heaven. *A land which Jehovah thy God careth for: the eyes of Jehovah Thy God are always upon it* from the beginning of the year even unto the end of the year" (Deut. xi. 11, 12)—so that the whole of it "shall be one circle of bounty, and the revolutions of the seasons mark the course of Him 'whose paths drop fatness'—the gracious Giver of all

---

word is וַתְּשֹׁקְקֶהָ (*Vat' shok' Keah*), which Gesenius takes to be the Pil. future of שׁוּק —(*shuk*), i.q. שָׁקַק (*shakak*), "to run," and thence "run over," "overflow," or to run after and have desire. But the more satisfactory derivation is to regard שׁוּק (*shuk*) here as another form of שָׁקֹה (*shakoh*), "to drink" and "give to drink," or "to water."

[11] "*Eretz*," though meaning both "earth" and "land," usually stands for the land of Palestine, which will then be conspicuous for its fertility and productiveness, even as "the people" shall be pre-eminent for spiritual blessing and fruitfulness unto God.

good things, who leaves the impress of His steps as He passes in blessing and plenty. Joy shall then fill every heart—the joy of men rendered happy by abundance and prosperity."

And the power and goodness of the bountiful Giver will then be universally recognised and celebrated in the bounties of His providence, even as the spiritual blessings, of which they will then be the outward pledge and accompaniment, will be thankfully acknowledged as the gifts of His grace. It is beautiful to note the frequent repetition of the blessed "Thou" as we read these last lines. "*Thou* visitest the earth. . . . *Thou* greatly enrichest it. . . . *Thou* providest them corn when *Thou* has so prepared it. . . . *Thou* waterest. . . . *Thou* settlest the ridges thereof. *Thou* makest it soft with showers. *Thou* blessest the springing thereof. *Thou* crownest the year of Thy goodness," that is with a plentiful harvest, so that "the pastures are clothed with flocks," and "the valleys are covered over with corn." On which it has been truly remarked that "the Psalmist represents the Divine Husbandman as lovingly and patiently attending to all the steps of the process needed for the great ingathering. *He* guides the showers, *He* fills the little valleys of the furrows, and smooths down the tiny hills of the intervening ridges. *He* takes care of the germinating seed, and *His* sunshine smiles a benediction on the tender green blade as it pricks through the earth which has been made soft enough for it to pierce from beneath. This unhesitating recognition of the direct action of God in all 'natural' processes is the true point of view from which to regard them. God is the only force; and His immediate action is present in all material changes. The Bible knows nothing of self-moving powers in nature, and the deepest conception of God's relation to things sensible knows as little. There is no power but of God, is the last word of religion and of true philosophy."

VIII

THE COMMENCEMENT OF THE HALLEL

PSALM CXIII

"Praise ye the Lord.
Praise, O ye servants of the Lord,
Praise the name of the Lord,
Blessed be the name of the Lord,
From this time forth and for evermore.
From the rising of the sun unto the going down of the same `
The Lord's name is to be praised.
The Lord is high above all nations,
And His glory above the heavens.
Who is like unto the Lord our God,
That hath His seat on high,
That humbleth Himself to behold
The things that are in heaven and in the earth?
He raiseth up the poor out of the dust,
And lifteth up the needy from the dunghill;
That He may set Him with princes,
Even with the princes of His people.
He maketh the barren woman to keep house,
And to be a joyful mother of children.
Praise ye the Lord."

VIII

THE COMMENCEMENT OF THE HALLEL

THE Hallel consists of a series of six Psalms, beginning with the one hundred and thirteenth, and ending with the one hundred and eighteenth. *Hallel* means "praise," and although the whole Book of Psalms is pervaded by a spirit of fervent praise and adoration of Jehovah's Name, this short series are especially called so because they were the public praise, sung in circumstances of joyous solemnity in the Temple courts, at the three great —Passover, Pentecost, and Tabernacles—when all the men of Israel had to appear before the Lord.

But it is especially in connection with the Passover that the Hallel has always been associated in the minds of Jews, and to this day it figures very prominently in the "Haggada," or ritual for the Passover evening, when, in all the ends of the earth, scattered Israel meet around their family board, to "show," or "tell forth," [1] by means of a commemorative meal, the wonders which God wrought for them in the past, and the story of the typical redemption.

According to the old Rabbis the Hallel celebrates the praises of God in connection with five things—the deliverance from Egypt; the dividing of the Red Sea; the giv-

---

[1] This is the meaning of the word *Haggada,* and it is remarkable that we should find such a clear echo of it in the words of our Lord when, during His last Paschal Supper with His disciples, He took bread and broke it and said, "This is My body given for you," and again the cup after supper, saying, "This cup is the new covenant in My blood . . . for as often as ye eat this bread and drink the cup ye proclaim [or 'tell forth,' or 'announce'— καταγγελλετε]—the Lord's death till He come" (1 Cor. xi. 23-26).

ing of the law; the resurrection of the dead; and the lot
of the Messiah. In connection with the Paschal supper,
the Hallel used to be divided into two parts:—the first
half, consisting of the first two of the series, being sung
or recited at an early part of the service, before the second
wine-cup, and the second half, consisting of the last four
of these six Psalms, after the fourth or last cup which
had to be drunk, or tasted, in the course of the service.
On the night on which our Lord Jesus kept the Passover
for the last time with His disciples, when He turned the
service in commemoration of deliverance from Egyptian
bondage into the blessed ordinance which should henceforth "show," or "tell forth," the greater spiritual redemption accomplished by the breaking of His own body, and
the shedding of His precious blood, we read in Matt. xxvi.
30, and in Mark xiv. 26, that having sung a hymn (or
"psalm"), they went out into the "Mount of Olives," that
He might finish His redeeming work by the awful transactions of Gethsemane and Calvary. That "hymn," or
"psalm," as Lightfoot has long ago pointed out, was nothing else than the conclusion of the Hallel,[2] and as we study
its climax (Psa. cxviii.)—which is nothing less than a prophetic drama, setting forth, among other things, how the
"stone" which "the builders" were now rejecting would
yet be made the "Head Stone" of the corner, and be ac-
claimed by the same nation with shouts of "Hosanna!
Blessed be He that cometh in the Name of Jehovah"—
we can imagine something of the thrill that would go
through the heart of our Saviour, who, for the joy that
was set before Him, was just about to go forth to endure
the cross, despising the shame. But it is only of the

---

[2] See the chapter on "The Conclusion of the Hallel—a Prophetic
Drama," in my book, "The Ancient Scriptures and the Modern
Jew."

beginning, or what may be viewed as the *prologue* to the Hallel, that I want to speak now.

Although in itself full of praise, the Hallel was turned by the worshipful through of Levites and Israelites in the Temple courts into one continuous Hallelujah. The manner in which it was used on those joyous occasions was responsive. The custom was for the people to repeat the whole of the first line of these Psalms after the Levites, and then to respond with an "Hallelujah" after each of the subsequent lines; thus the Levites would begin with the word '"Hallelujah," which forms the first line in the Hebrew, and the people would respond "Hallelujah"; then the Levites would chant "Praise ye, servants of Jehovah," and the people would respond "Hallelujah"; the Levites would continue, "Praise the Name of Jehovah," and the people would respond, "Hallelujah"; and so on throughout the series. But now to open the contents of the 113th Psalm.

As it stands in the English the nine verses divide themselves into three equal parts, the *first* part being *the call to praise;* the *second* setting forth the *praiseworthiness of Jehovah because of what He is;* and the *third* setting forth His praiseworthiness more especially *because of what He does.*

THE CALL TO PRAISE

"Hallelujah!" This is the watchword of God's redeemed people, and is put into our mouth by His Spirit, so that we may stir up *one another* to praise His most blessed name. "Hallelujah! praise *ye* Jehovah." Of the Seraphim we read that "one called unto another," as if to provoke one another unto the holy service of crying, "Holy, holy, holy, is Jehovah of Hosts, the whole earth is full of His Glory." And saints, too, are exhorted when they assemble themselves together (Heb. x. 24, 25) "to con-

sider and to *provoke* one another," not in the way in which
Christians do, alas! often "provoke" one another, but
"unto love and to good works" among themselves, and
unto fervent praise, and the worship of God our Saviour.
Yet, let us remember that we can never effectually utter
the words, "Hallelujah, praise ye Jehovah," to others, if
we are not in a condition at the same time to say, "Praise
Jehovah, *O my soul.*"

"Praise ye, servants of Jehovah."

Primarily, it is Israel who is thus addressed, even as we
read in Psa. cxxxvi., that He brought them out of Egypt,
and led them through the wilderness, and smote great and
famous kings, that He may give their land as an heritage
unto *"Israel His servant";* and the Rabbis, in speaking
of the appropriateness of this Psalm for the Passover,
point out the emphasis on the words, "Ye servants of
Jehovah," as if intended to remind them that now being
freed from Egypt they are no longer servants of Pharaoh.

And if we ask, *How* did Israel, who were in bondage in
Egypt, become servants of Jehovah? the answer is, that
they were constituted so by very reason of their redemption; and the same is true of us: "Ye were the servants
[bondsmen] of sin," says the Apostle (Rom. vi. 20, 22)—
a bondage more terrible and degrading than the servitude
of Egypt—"but now, being made free from sin, and having
become bondmen to God, ye have your fruit unto sanctification, and the end life eternal."

The process is that of an exchange of service, being set
free from the tyrannical "power [or 'authority'] of darkness" we are immediately called into allegiance to "the
Son of His love," in whose service we find perfect freedom.

And it was in the spirit of sonship that Israel was called
to serve God, as may be gathered from the message addressed to Pharaoh, "Thus saith Jehovah, *Israel is My*

son, My firstborn, and I say unto thee, *Let My son go that he may serve Me"* (Exod. iv. 22, 23); and to us too our Father comes, saying, *"Son,* go work to-day in My vineyard"; and it is only when we serve in this free, filial spirit, like our Lord Jesus, the eternal Son of God, who, when He girded Himself with a towel, to perform one of the meanest offices of a servant, did so in the full consciousness of His Divine Sonship, "knowing that the Father hath given all things into His hands, and that He came from God and went to God"—it is only then, I say, that our service is effectual and pleasing in His sight.

And the service of Jehovah consisted not merely in work, but also in worship.

Here in our Psalm it is to the holy service of praise that God's servants are called. The seraphim have each of them six wings, but four of them they employ in covering their faces and feet, in lowly worship and adoration of the God whose glory fills the universe, and "with twain" they do fly, to accomplish God's errands. May we learn from them how to combine the spirit of worship with our service, so that in worshipping we may serve, and in serving we may worship!

"Praise the Name of Jehovah."

The *Name* stands for Himself—His glorious character and Divine nature; and if we want to know what is included in it, we must gather up the various attributes scattered for us over the pages of Scripture, which are like the golden letters by which "the Holy Name" is spelled.

Think, then, of the eternity and unchangeableness of His nature, of His wisdom, power, righteousness, justice, goodness, love, and truth, all blended in beautiful harmony, and "praise the Name of the Lord."

But it is perhaps the Name *"Jehovah"* that we are called upon in this Psalm to praise—that Name which was first brought into display in connection with the typical redemption from Egypt which the Hallel specially celebrates. Thus, when God's time came to lead His people out of Egypt, He said to Moses, "I am Jehovah; and I appeared unto Abraham, unto Isaac, and unto Jacob as El Shaddai (the God Almighty), but by My Name Jehovah was I not made known to them." This does not mean that God had not previously spoken of Himself by that Name to the Jewish Fathers, for as a matter of fact the Name Jehovah occurs from the second chapter of Genesis onwards, but until He appeared as Israel's *Redeemer* in faithfulness to His covenants and promises, they did not know Him *in that character,* for Jehovah may be said to be the *personal Name of the God of the history of redemption* which, in as far as it is unfolded in His dealings with Israel, only begins with the exodus and the passover, which is regarded in Scripture as the birth of the nation (Psa. cxiv. 1; Hosea xi. 1), and "the beginning of months and commencing of days" of Israel's history. From that time on the Name Jehovah has become the "strong tower into which the righteous runneth, and is set aloft"— safe from the great adversary who seeks his destruction; therefore, oh "ye servants of Jehovah," who know the secret of His covenant faithfulness to them that fear Him, "praise the Name of Jehovah!"

THE DURATION OF GOD'S PRAISE

The second verse speaks of the *duration* of the praise due to Jehovah's Name—

"Blessed be the Name of Jehovah from this time forth and for evermore."

"From this time forth"—that is when it is to begin. In relation to Israel there is both an historical and prophetical point of time in the words *from this time*. The historical goes back to the typical redemption from Egypt, which, as already stated, was the starting point of their national history. "From that time forth," from the very beginning of their national career, and by very reason of their redemption, they were called to the service of Jehovah, part of which blessed service was to praise His Holy Name. But alas! Israel, in the past, excepting the little godly remnant, did not apprehend their high calling of God, nor respond to the blessings and privileges which were theirs by covenant right, and their history so far is for the most part a history of failure. Has, then, the purpose of God in the call and miraculous preservation of the nation been frustrated? or has it exhausted itself with the birth of Messiah? Oh no; "this people have I formed for Myself, *they shall show forth My praise.*" There is also a prophetical point of time in this Hallel, as may be seen more especially in the last two Psalms of the series, and "from this time forth," marks the day of the future spiritual birth of the nation, when through the grace of Christ they will enter into experimental knowledge of the blessings of redemption which were only prefigured when God took them by the hand to bring them out of Egypt. It is then—when the prophetic climax of the Hallel is reached in their actual experience; when the stone which the builders refused has at last become the head stone of the corner, and Israel cries to the One who was pierced, "Hosanna! Blessed be He that cometh in the Name of Jehovah!" (Psa. cxviii. 21, 26)—that they will begin to show forth God's praise, and call not only upon one another, but upon all the nations of the earth to magnify Jehovah with them, and to exalt His Name together; then, in regenerated Jerusalem, and in the courts of that temple, which shall be the central house of prayer for all nations, the Hallel shall again form the responsive song of praise, only not, as in the past, between the Levites and the people, but between Israel, who shall then be called the priests of Jehovah (Isa. lxi. 6), and the representatives of all the nations. [3]   Thus, to take the very heart of the Hallel (Psa. cxvii.), Israel will say—

"Oh, praise Jehovah, all ye nations,"

and the nations will respond—

"Hallelujah."

Israel will say—

"Laud Him, all ye peoples!"

and the nations will respond—

"Hallelujah."

Israel will say—

"For His grace [or 'mercy'] has finally prevailed over us,"

and the nations will respond—

"Hallelujah."

Israel will say—

"And the *truth [or 'faithfulness'] of Jehovah endureth for ever,"*

and the nations will respond—

"Hallelujah."

And how long is the Hallel to continue? *"For ever-more"*—eternally, through the ages of ages "the Name of Jehovah is to be praised," for when with the millennial

---

[3] "And it shall come to pass that every one that is left of all the nations which came against Jerusalem shall go up from year to year to worship the King, the Lord of Hosts, and to keep the feast of tabernacles" (Zech. xiv. 16).

period the song dies away on earth, it will be continued by the whole redeemed family in the new heavens and the new earth wherein shall dwell righteousness and praise "for evermore."

THE UNIVERSALITY OF GOD'S PRAISE

"From the rising of the sun to the going down of the same Jehovah's Name is to be praised" [or "praised be the name of Jehovah"].

This is a prayer, and at the same time a prophecy, linked as to the time of its fulfilment with two other prophetic utterances in reference to the future.   One is Isa. lix. 19-21 (R. V.), "So shall they fear the Name of Jehovah from the west, and His glory from the rising of the sun; for he (the desolator) shall come as a rushing stream, which the breath of Jehovah driveth.   And the Redeemer shall come to Zion, and unto them that turn from transgression in Jacob, said Jehovah."   The other in Mal. i. 11, "For from the rising of the sun, even to the going down of the same, My Name shall be great among the Gentiles."   Israel, as represented by its Psalmists and Prophets, knew nothing of a local or national God; in spite of what infidels and agnostics sometimes assert.   Israel *does* often speak of Jehovah as their very *own* God, but only in the sense in which the New Testament speaks of God as the Saviour or all men, *but especially of them that believe.*   For ages, He *was* their God only, and in the words of the Hallel, *"Judah was His sanctuary, Israel was His dominion,"* when the gods of the other nations were vile abominations —"the work of men's hands."   With right, therefore, could they cry to Him, "We are thine! As for our adversaries, Thou never bearest rule over them; they were not called by Thy Name," but at the same time they rejoiced in the expectation, and greeted from afar the promises of a time, when Israel and Jerusalem as the centre, the knowledge of Jehovah would radiate to all the other nations, and the glory of Jehovah would cover the earth, even as the waters covered the sea. And not only did they believe in a time when the Name of Jehovah—the one true and living God—would be universally known and praised by the nations, but they earnestly *prayed for it*. Now the Church of Christ is beginning slowly to respond to the call to prayer on behalf of poor Israel, but here is a sample of the earnestness with which Israel prayed for the Gentiles:

> *"Let the peoples [4] praise Thee, O God,*
> *Let all the peoples praise Thee;*
> *Oh let the nations be glad and sing for joy:*
> *For Thou shall judge the peoples with equity*
> *And govern the nations upon earth"* (Psa. lxvii. 3, 4).

And this, and similar prayers of Israel, were, as already stated, also prophecies of the time when, "From the rising of the sun, to the going down of the same, Jehovah's Name *shall be* praised"—even as our continual prayer, "Hallowed be Thy Name," is also a continual prophecy of the time when God's Kingdom *shall* come, and when His holy will *shall* be done on earth, even as it is done in heaven.

The Praiseworthiness of Jehovah, because of What He Is

This, as stated at the commencement, is the theme of the second of the three equal parts into which the pro-

---

[4] The plural "Amim" always designates the Gentile peoples in contrast to "Am," which always means Israel.

logue to the Hallel divides itself. The middle line of this
section (vers. 4-6) begins with a question—

"Who is like unto Jehovah our God?"

This may be described as Israel's challenge *to the nations,*
even *as it is the Christian's challenge* to all unbelievers.

"Who is like unto Jehovah?" Among all who were
called Gods, let them point us to one to be compared to
"our God"? To show the unanswerableness of this challenge, and the reason Israel has for glorying in Jehovah,
Scripture puts this question in different relations.

I. Who is like unto Jehovah our God, a *living God?*
The gods of the nations, as beautifully described in one of
the Psalms of the Hallel, are *"idols,"* the work of men's
hands (or brains) :

> "They have mouths, but they speak not;
> Eyes have they, but they see not;
> They have ears, but they hear not;
> Noses have they, but they smell not;
> They have hands, but they handle not;
> Feet have they, but they walk not;
> Neither speak they through their throat"— (Psa. cxv. 3-8).

"But Jehovah is the true God, *He is the living God and
King of Eternity;* at His wrath the earth shall tremble,
and the nations shall not be able to abide His indignation."
"He hath made the earth by His power, He hath estab-
lished the world by His wisdom, and by His understanding
He hath stretched out the heavens" (Jer. x. 10-12).

Not only can He speak, and has spoken to us words
of eternal life, "but who hath made man's mouth? or who
maketh the dumb, or the deaf, or the seeing, or the blind?
Have not I, Jehovah?" Yes, not only has He, "the seeing
and living one," an eye to see, but "He hath formed the

eye." Not only hath He an ear to hear, but He is the one "that planted the ear." *"To whom then will ye liken Me or shall I be equal? saith the Holy One.* Lift up your eyes on high, and behold who hath created these, that bringeth out their host by number; He called them all by name, by the greatness of His might"—"and for that He is strong in power, not one is lacking." "Have ye not known? have ye not heard? hath it not been told you from the beginning? have ye not understood from the foundation of the earth? it is He that sitteth upon the circle of the earth, and the inhabitants thereof are as grasshoppers; that stretcheth out the heavens as a curtain, and spreadeth them out as a tent to dwell in: that bringeth princes to nothing; He maketh the judges of the earth as vanity" (Isa. xl. 21-23, R.V.). "Therefore, Israel, trust thou in Jehovah; He is thy help and thy shield."

Hallelujah! for He is a living God.

II. Secondly, Who is like unto Jehovah our God, *a holy God?* This is the way Moses put it, in his song of triumph—"Who is like unto Thee, O Jehovah, among the gods? Who is like unto Thee, *Glorious in Holiness,* fearful in praises, doing wonders?" The gods of the nations were vile, and their worship was often accompanied by unspeakable impurities and abominations, which had a terribly debasing effect on their votaries. "They that made them became like unto them, so did every one that trusted in them." [5]

---

[5] "That a religion should concern itself with character is to us a matter of course; but this was far from being the case in the great world into which the young Christian Gospel made its way. In the civilisation of the Roman Empire—a civilisation, in some respects, more elaborate than ours—religion was something absolutely apart from morality. The priest and augurs of ancient Greece and Rome never for one moment regarded it as any part of their duty to exhort or help men to a purer life. Alike public

Holiness, as an attribute of the gods, never even entered into the heart of the heathen, and the idea never could have been evolved as a natural process among men who are innately strangers to it, and who, when they are brought face to face with it as a revelation, naturally *hate* it. But *"Thou art holy, O Thou that inhabitest the praises of Israel"*—"The Father of lights," in whom is "no darkness at all"—"dwelling in light which no man can approach unto." At the sight of Thy glory even an Isaiah falls down crying, "Woe is me, for I am undone"; and seraphim veil their faces, crying, "Holy, Holy, Holy is Jehovah of Hosts." And He is not only holy in *Himself,* but requires of those that worship Him to worship Him not only in the Spirit, and in truth, but *"in the beauty of Holiness."*

Hallelujah! for Jehovah our God is a Holy God.

III. Thirdly, Who is like unto Jehovah our God, a *gracious God?* This is how Micah puts it, "Who is a God like unto Thee, *that pardoneth iniquity,* and passeth by the transgression of the remnant of His heritage? He retaineth not anger for ever, because He *delighteth in Mercy."*

The Gods of the nations are represented as cruel and inimical to man's welfare. "Truly their rock is not as our Rock, even our enemies themselves being judges." Among the thousands of gods in ancient Greece there was not one that enshrined the attribute of Mercy, nor would those ancient great philosophers have bowed down before a god of compassion. *But Jehovah is a God of Love,* merciful and gracious, long-suffering, abundant in goodness and truth—who in order to save man gave His

---

life and private were steeped in a heartlessness of cruelty and an abandonment of vice such as we can hardly realise; but pagan religion made no protest, for, on the contrary, its mysteries often screened and its ministers sanctioned the grossest iniquities" ("The Fact of Christ," by P. Carnegie Simpson, M.A.).

only-begotten Son; whose compassion for them that fear Him is "as great" as the height of the heavens above the earth, and whose "pity" for man is like unto the pity of a father for his children.

Hallelujah! because Jehovah, our God, *is a Gracious God*.

But it is especially in connection with two wonderful facts about His character that our admiration of Jehovah is called forth in this middle section of the first Psalm of the Hallel. These two facts are: His infinite *exaltation;* and His marvellous *condescension*

> *"Who is like unto Jehovah our God;*
> *Who exalteth Himself to dwell,*
> *And who humbleth Himself to behold?"*

(*a*) His infinite exaltation: "He exalteth Himself to dwell." There is a certain greatness and majesty in the totality of nations viewed in themselves; but *"Jehovah is high above all nations"* (ver. 4). Yea, "before Him all nations are as nothing; they are counted to Him less than nothing and vanity," for "He doeth according to His will in the army of heaven and among the inhabitants of the earth; and none can stay His hand or say unto Him, What doest Thou?" Egypt's greatness and all its majesty availed as nothing when His time came to set the people free in the manner which the Hallel celebrates. Then look to the heavens above; "behold the height of the stars, how high they are," and how glorious, too, but

> *"His glory is above the heavens"* (ver. 4).

Oh, who can follow or even comprehend the height of His exaltation?

"Thus saith the high and lofty One that inhabiteth eternity, whose name is Holy, I dwell in the high and

Holy place"—"the heavens [6] are My throne and the earth is My footstool. What manner of house will ye build unto Me? and what place shall be My rest? For all these things hath Mine hand made, and so all these things come to be, saith Jehovah" (Isa. lvii. 15; lxvi. 1, 2, R. V.).

(b) But as is the height of His exaltation, so infinite is the depth of His condescension.

"Who humbleth Himself."

Blessed announcement at which to stop and respond with a "Hallelujah!" for here, O Lord, we behold the first steps in the process of Thy self-humbling for our salvation —of "Thy gentleness," which is designed with a view "to make us great." Shall we trace that downward look— those blessed downward steps on their way from the height of heaven to the "horrible pit and miry clay," where He finally found us?

Here in our Psalm it is described as an act of self-humbling on the part of God *"to behold these things which are in heaven,"* for, as has been well remarked, "in respect of God all created things are low, whether it is in earth or in heaven," and compared with His own absolute Holiness, especially since the great rebellion, and the introduction of sin, *"even the heavens are not pure in His sight."*

The second step is "that He humbleth Himself to behold the things that are in the earth." This is regarded not so much as an act of condescension as of *grace.* It *is* condescension, for in His vast infinite universe how insignificant is this earth, and what are all the inhabitants of this globe before Him but as grasshoppers. Well might the Psalmist exclaim: "When I consider the heavens the

---

[6] The word for heaven in the Hebrew is always in the plural.

work of Thy fingers; the moon and the stars which Thou hast made, what is man that Thou art mindful of him? and the son of man that Thou visitest him?" Rationalists sometimes argue from the fact of God's greatness against the *possibility* of His stooping to behold the very little, forgetting that the small is not always the insignificant, and that a minute object, by reason of its being "fearfully and wonderfully made," may have more of the interest and care of the Master worker centred on it, than vast objects whose structures are not so complex.

The Christian, on the contrary, finds an argument for the possibility of God's stooping to notice the little *in the very fact* that He is infinitely great. Only He who did spread out the heavens as a curtain, and create the stars, can come down to the simple "atom" and the extreme of littleness which man can *never* reach, any more than he can reach the other extreme of greatness. Does the tiniest insect testify less to the manifold wisdom and perfect skill of the Creator than the creation of a sun? And does not the microscope reveal as much of His power and beneficence as the telescope? But it is not of the physical, but of the moral and spiritual, that the Psalm speaks, and that is why I said that His humbling Himself to behold the things in the earth is regarded not so much as an act of condescension as of grace. Since the introduction and the development of the drama of sin on this earth, we would not have been surprised if a message had reached us to the effect that He has for ever turned away from this seat of apostasy those holy eyes, which are "too pure to behold evil, and cannot look upon iniquity," but no! He humbleth Himself still "to behold" this earth, and to behold it with the look of grace for man, as the last verses of the Psalm testify.

But only the first steps in the self-humbling of God our Saviour are noted in this first Psalm of the Hallel. The still downward course and climax of that blessed path we must trace in Scriptures like Psa. xxii. and Isa. liii. and in the Gospels, where we see the second person of the blessed Trinity—"Christ, who is over all, God blessed for ever," "emptying Himself" of His Divine prerogatives, and taking upon Himself the form of a bond-servant. And being found in fashion as a man, *"He humbled Himself and became obedient unto death, even the death of the cross."*

"Hast thou not heard that my Lord Jesus died?
   Then let me tell thee a stranger story:
The God of power, as He did ride
   In His majestic robes of glory,
Resolved to light; and so one day
He did descend, undressing all the way.

"The stars His tire of light and rings obtain'd,
   The cloud His bow, the fire His spear,
The sky His azure mantle gained;
   And when they asked what He would wear.
He smiled, and said as He did go
He had new clothes a-making here below."

But from the lowest depths of self-humiliation He ascended again to the highest height of glory, carrying with Him His glorified humanity in pledge of His eternal oneness with those whom He came to seek and to save. "Wherefore also God highly exalted Him, and gave unto Him the name which is above every name; that in the name of Jesus every knee should bow, of things in heaven and things on earth, and things under the earth, and that every tongue should confess that Jesus Christ is Lord, to the glory of God the Father" (Phil. ii. 9-11, R. V.).

Hallelujah to Him, who exalteth Himself to dwell, and in infinite grace humbleth Himself to behold!

THE PRAISEWORTHINESS OF JEHOVAH BECAUSE OF WHAT HE DOES

The praiseworthiness of Jehovah because of what He does: this is the theme of the last brief section of our Psalm. The descent of God forms the only way and means for the ascent of man. Having "humbled Himself to behold" us in our wretchedness and sin, He came to our rescue, and wrought for us a marvellous salvation. What a glorious transformation scene is that described in the last three verses, to which all the previous part of the Psalm leads up!

> *"He raiseth up the poor out of the dust,*
> *And lifteth up the needy from the dunghill:*
> *That He may set him with princes,*
> *Even with the princes of His people."*

The historical foreground is again Israel's deliverance from the bondage and degradation of Egypt, which is regarded as typical of the greater national redemption from the longer bondage of the future, when they shall no more say, "Jehovah liveth, which brought up the children of Israel out of the land of Egypt; but Jehovah liveth which brought up, and which led the seed of the house of Israel, out of the north country, and from all countries whither I had driven them." But, at the same time, let it be remembered that the national redemption of Israel has in it the promise, and sets forth the great *spiritual* redemption accomplished by Messiah for men of all nations. What is the bondage and degradation of Egypt but a type of the bondage and degradation of sin? And what is Pharaoh but a type of "the God of this world," who holds man captive at his will? Regarded in this deeper spiritual sense, there is no more beautiful Gospel text in the whole Bible than these last three verses of our Psalm, for they set forth the wonderful process of our salvation, from the moment when God finds us in the lowest depths, to the time when we shall be "presented faultless before the presence of His Glory with exceeding joy," and, together with Christ, "inherit the throne of glory" (1 Sam. ii. 8).

It tells us what and where we are by nature, and what we become, and the place we are brought to by grace.

What are we in ourselves?

(a) We are *poor*. "He raiseth up the poor out of the dust." When man was first created, he was made very rich and appointed lord of creation. "God blessed them, and God said unto them, Be fruitful, and multiply, and replenish the earth, and subdue it; and have dominion over the fish of the sea, and over the fowl of the air, and everything that moveth upon the earth" (Gen. i. 28). It is primarily in reference to this high appointment, which, however, is finally only realised in the "last Adam," "the Son of man," who is also the Son of God, that David sings: "Thou hast made him but a little lower than God: and crownedst him with glory and honour; Thou madest him to have dominion over the works of Thy hands; Thou hast put all things under his feet!" (Psa. viii., R. V.). But alas! very soon a most terrible catastrophe occurred. There came sin and the Fall, and man, by joining Satan in the great rebellion against God, brought himself judicially under the sentence of death; forfeiting also all his former estate. Since then all his real possession is "the dust"; for what are these words in the Psalm but an echo of Gen. iii. 19, *"Dust thou art, and unto dust thou shalt return"*? Yes, men may gather unto themselves all the treasures of the earth, but they can hold them no longer than they can hold themselves, and in the end, if their hearts be fixed on their earthly riches, they will carry out of this world nothing more than their own "dust" together with the terrible consciousness that before the God of judgment, whose really is the silver and the gold, they will have to give an account as to *what use* they have put that, which for a time was only entrusted to them.

(*b*) And we are not only poor, but we are also in a state of degradation. This is implied in the words: "He lifteth up the needy [or 'the beggar,' 1 Sam. ii. 8] from the dunghill." Sin is not only a crime, but it is a *loathsome moral filth* which has debased and defiled our whole being. "Out of the heart," says our Saviour, "proceed evil thoughts, murders, adulteries, fornications, thefts, false witness, blasphemies;—these are the things which defile a man." This is the moral leprosy which fits the sinner only to sit on the dunghill, outside the camp, crying, "Unclean, unclean" (Lev. xiii. 44-46). It is a most humiliating picture, but a true one, drawn by God's own hand, and describing the highly civilised and cultured man equally with the savage barbarian.

This is how and where God finds us, and what does He do for us?

I. *"He raiseth up* the poor from the dust." It is beautiful to observe how all the glory of our salvation is, in this passage, as everywhere else in Scripture, ascribed to Jehovah. Finding us deep down in the terrible pit, He does not come merely to lecture us on our bad behaviour, and to command us to get out of our deplorable condition as best we can. Oh no, this is the doctrine of Rabbinism, Romanism, and every other false system which denies man's utter helplessness, and is in opposition to the Gospel of God's *Grace*. The true Christ comes to us where we are, and by His power and love *"raiseth* up the poor from the dust, and *lifteth* up the needy from the dunghill."

I remember reading somewhere an address by a native preacher in China to his fellow-countrymen, in which he tried to show the difference between the false systems

with which they are familiar and the faith of our Lord
Jesus Christ, and this is how he described it: Once upon
a time, he said, poor man fell into a deep pit, and there
he lay at the bottom, bruised and bleeding. After a long
time, Confucius, passing by and hearing his moans, stopped
at the edge of the pit and looking down and seeing the
poor man's deplorable condition, he stopped to give him a
severe lecture. He told him he was stupid not to have
taken care of his steps, and now the best thing he could
do was to get out of that pit as soon as he possibly could.
Then Confucius walked off, leaving poor, helpless man,
bleeding, groaning, and dying, in the pit. Then after
a time, wise and kind Buddha passed that way, and
hearing the groans from that pit, and stooping down to
behold man's terrible condition, his heart was moved to
pity, and he not only lectured him, and gave him certain
good advice, but he stretched himself across the pit, and
put his arms down for man to lay hold of, so that he
might help him up. But his arms were not long enough,
and in the end he too had to pass on, leaving poor man
groaning, bleeding, dying, at the bottom of the pit. But,
he continued, after a time, Jesus Christ passed by, and
when He stooped down and saw the man in his helpless
and wretched condition, He did not, like Confucius, lecture him; He not only like Buddha, tried to reach His
arms down to him, but *He went down right to the bottom
of the pit, where man was,* and having found him, He laid
him on His shoulders rejoicing, and brought him up, and
healed him of his wounds. That Chinaman must have
studied the New Testament to profit. That is just what
our Lord Jesus did do. Who is it who, in the 40th
Psalm, says "He [God the Father] brought me up also
out of an horrible pit, out of the miry clay; and He set
my feet upon a rock, and establish my goings"? It is
Messiah, who, further down in the same Psalm, says, "Lo

I come, in the scroll of the book it is written of Me. I delight to do Thy will, O `My God ; yea, Thy law is within My heart." It was that love which passeth knowledge, and the acomplishment of the Father's will in our salvation, which brought the Holy One down to the very "dust of death" (Psa. xxii. 15) in order that He may raise up the poor out of the dust, and carry us safely into the Father's presence, saying, "Rejoice with Me; for I have found My sheep which was lost."

Hallelujah! What a Saviour!

II. And He not only raises us from "the dust of death," but He lifts us out of the dunghill of our old depravity and innate moral degradation, and this He does not only by justifying us before God, by His precious blood, and on the ground of His perfect righteousness, but by the work of sanctification, which is continually carried on in our hearts by His Holy Spirit, and by implanting in us the new law of the Spirit of life, which makes us free from the law of sin and death.

But there is a still higher climax in the transformation scene as described in this section of the Psalm. "Whom He justified them He also glorified." Not only has He loved us, and loosed us from our sins by His *blood,* but He makes of us a kingdom and priests—fit for fellowship with Him and His saints now, and to dwell with Him in glory hereafter. This is brought out in the 8th verse, "That He may set him with princes, even with the princes of His people," to which, in the original song of Hannah (of which this part of the Hallel is an inspired *echo*), there is an additional line, which reads: "And to make them inherit the throne of glory."

Next to our being "for ever with the Lord," and the unspeakable blessedness of gazing upon that face which was once marred for us "more than that of any other man," and of lying at the feet of Him who loved us unto death, will be the holy joy of belonging to the one glorious, glorified company of the redeemed, and of converse with the "mighty ones" and heroes in the faith. We "shall sit down with Abraham, Isaac, and Jacob in the kingdom of heaven"; with Moses, "the man of God," who, next to our Saviour, is perhaps the most prominent figure in the history of redemption; with Joshua, and with David, the sweet Psalmist of Israel, the shepherd king, who sang those wonderful songs which to all ages remain the deepest and highest expressions of penitence and faith, of true worship and rest in the Lord; with Isaiah, the comforter, and noble-hearted Jeremiah, who wept his heart out for his people in the Book of Lamentations; with the great apostle of the Gentiles, and the disciple whom Jesus loved; with warm-hearted Peter, who, once he was "converted" after his fall, was so fervent and fearless, and never grew tired in speaking of the "preciousness" of that Corner-stone to whom he points all men away from himself; with the other "apostles and prophets," and the blessed company of martyrs, who accepted not deliverance that they might obtain a better resurrection.

And what shall I say more? for time would fail me to speak of the many other "princes of God's people," in whose blessed company it will be our privilege to mingle. By faith we are already come "unto Mount Zion, and unto the city of the living God, the heavenly Jerusalem, and to innumerable hosts of angels, to the general assembly and Church of the firstborn who are enrolled in heaven, and to God the Judge of all, and to the spirits of just men made perfect, and to Jesus the mediator of a new covenant," but not until the resurrection morning, when "the Lord Himself shall descend from heaven with a shout, with the voice of the arch-angel, and with the trump of God," when we shall see His blessed face, and be like Him—shall we in actual presence and realisation

"sit down with princes, even with the princes of His people," at His own table in the kingdom of heaven.   Then
also, together with Him, we shall "inherit the throne of
glory," for "if we suffer with Him we shall also reign with
Him," and Christ shall yet say to those who have been
faithful unto Him, even unto death: "Ye are they which
have continued with Me in My temptations, and I ap-
point unto you a kingdom as My Father hath appointed
unto Me; that ye may eat and drink at My table in My
kingdom, and sit on thrones judging the twelve tribes of
Israel."   Oh, blessed compensations for the sufferings of
this present time! Oh, exceeding and eternal weight of
glory not to be compared with the "momentary lightness
of affliction" of our present wilderness state!

We now come to the last verse, which may be regarded
as the key to the special, or primary, sense of this part of
the Hallel, in relation to Israel as a nation:

"He maketh the barren woman to keep house [*or, 'to dwell in the
house'*],,
And to be a joyful mother of children. Hallelujah!"

The barren woman is frequently used in Scripture as
a figure of Zion in her present desolate and spiritually
unfruitful condition, but the miracle God wrought at the
beginning of Israel's history is to be repeated in the
spiritual sense on a national scale.

At the very commencement, when God called Abraham,
and said to him, "I will make of thee a great nation, and
in thee shall all families of the earth be blessed," we read:
"But Sarah was barren; she had no child"; and when
afterwards the promise of the seed was definitely given,
Sarah was "past age" to be delivered of a child (Heb. xi.
11). Humanly speaking, there seemed no probability in
the promises of God to Abraham, in which was involved

the blessing of the nations, ever fulfilling themselves, but
God stepped in, and by His grace and power began to
write over Jewish history, for the benefit of all nations,
the words first spoken to Sarah: "Is anything too hard
for Jehovah?" And because they judged Him faithful
who had promised "therefore sprang there, even of one,
and him as good as dead, as many as the stars in the sky
in multitude, and as the sand which is by the sea-shore
innumerable." Of this miracle in connection with their
origin, the godly remnant in captivity are reminded in
Isa. li., when God comforts them with promises of the
future, which also seem impossible of fulfilment as far
as human probabilities are concerned. I translate from
the Hebrew: "Hearken to Me, ye that follow after righteousness, ye that seek Jehovah, look unto the rock whence
ye are hewn, and to the hole of the pit whence ye are
digged; look unto Abraham your father, and unto Sarah
that bare you; for I called him when he was but one
(and that one 'as good as dead'; and as to Sarah, she
was barren and past age—but in spite of the apparent
impossibility)—'I blessed him and increased him.'" Now,
this miracle, says Jehovah, I am going to repeat spiritually
on an infinitely larger scale, "For Jehovah shall comfort
Zion; He will comfort all her waste places, and He will
make her wilderness like Eden, and her desert like the
garden of Jehovah; joy and gladness shall be found therein; thanksgiving and the voice of melody." Yes, Zion
now is like a "barren woman," and, like Hannah, who first
uttered these wonderful words of Hallel, she is "grieved
in spirit" (Isa. liv. 6), because her Gentile adversary
provokes her sore for to make her fret (1 Sam. i. 9) by
tauntingly saying of her, "This is Zion" (a dry, barren,
good-for-nothing place), "whom no man seeketh after"
(Jer. xxx. 17); but the barren woman who was for a
time put away, but never divorced, shall be made to dwell

as mistress in her own house again, and by God's power become "a joyful mother of children." "For thy Maker is thy Husband, Jehovah of Hosts is His Name, and thy Redeemer, the Holy One of Israel; the God of the whole earth shall He be called. For a small moment have I forsaken thee, but with great mercies will I gather thee. In a little wrath I hid my face from thee for a moment, but with everlasting kindness will I have mercy on thee, saith Jehovah thy Redeemer" (Isa. liv. 5-8).

This first Psalm of the Hallel ends as it began, with an "Hallelujah" to which our heart's response is "Hallelujah." "Blessed be Jehovah God, the God of Israel, who only doeth wondrous things, and blessed be His glorious Name for ever, and let the whole earth be filled with His glory.

AMEN AND AMEN."

IX

"SONGS OF ASCENTS"

PSALMS CXXIX AND CXXX

"Many a time have they afflicted me from my youth up, let Israel
   now say;
Many a time have they afflicted me from my youth up: yet they
   have not prevailed against me.
The plowers plowed upon my back; they made long their furrows.
The Lord is righteous: He hath cut asunder the cords of the
   wicked.
Let them be ashamed and turned backward, all they that hate
   Zion.
Let them be as the grass upon the housetops, which withereth
   afore it groweth up:
Wherewith the reaper filleth not his hand, nor he that bindeth
   sheaves his bosom.
Neither do they which go by say, The blessing of the Lord be
   upon you; we bless you in the name of the Lord."

"Out of the depths have I cried upon Thee, O Lord.
Lord, hear my voice: let Thine ears be attentive to the voice of
   my supplications.
If Thou, Lord, shouldest mark iniquities, O Lord, who shall
   stand?
But there is forgiveness with Thee, that Thou mayest be feared.
I wait for the Lord, my soul doth wait, and in His word do I
   hope.
My soul looketh for the Lord more than watchmen look for the
   morning—yea, more than watchmen for the morning.
O Israel, hope in the Lord; for with the Lord there is mercy,
   and with Him is plenteous redemption.
And He shall redeem Israel from all his iniquities."

IX

"SONGS OF ASCENTS"

THE one hundred and twenty-ninth and one hundred and thirtieth Psalms form a pair. They belong to the series of fifteen Songs of Degrees, which form a little Psalter by themselves. The Hebrew word *"Hammaaloth,"* translated "degrees," which is inscribed on them all, literally means *"ascents,"* and is rendered in the Septuagint by a word which means "the stairs," and in the Vulgate it is translated "stair song." There is an old Jewish tradition that there were fifteen steps leading up to the inner Temple Court. In relation to the future Temple at any rate, we read in Ezek. xl. 22-26 of "seven steps," and in vers. 31 and 37 of the same chapter, of another flight of "eight steps," making fifteen in all; the word translated there "steps" being the same as that inscribed over these Psalms, and here rendered "degrees," so that there may be something in the suggestion that these fifteen Psalms formed a kind of spiritual ladder, one being repeated in succession on each of the steps by those who ascended to the inner court to worship Jehovah. It is also probable that these Psalms were so called because they were used by the pilgrim bands on their "going up" three times a year, on the occasions of the three great festivals, to the "Mountain of the Lord's House"; and it has been rightly pointed out that the style and structure of these Psalms, as well as their contents, show their adaptation to such a purpose. But whatever truth there is in this, we must not overlook the fact that there is a strong prophetic vein running through this "Little Psalter"—that they speak chiefly of a time yet future, and describe some of the steps by which Israel will *"ascend"* out of the valley of national apostasy and humiliation in which they are, up to the Mount of God, in order to catch His glory and reflect it on all nations around.

Perhaps the two most important steps in Israel's future ascents are to be found in the two Psalms before us; the one telling us of the outward, and the other of the *inward* deliverance of that people, though of course the language, especially of Psa. cxxx., may be used also by the individual Christian now, and is capable of application to God's people in all times.

In Psa. cxxix., the speaker, as we see from the first verse, is Israel. It is the saved remnant of the Jewish nation at the conclusion of that awful day of their culminating national sorrow, the "time of Jacob's trouble" (Jer. xxx. 4-7), looking back upon their whole history and acknowledging that "Jehovah is righteous" (ver. 4) both in having permitted all the troubles to come upon them, and also in pouring out His wrath and fury upon their enemies, especially upon the final confederacy of the nations which will be gathered against them.

"Many a time [or, more literally, 'greatly'] have they afflicted me
    from my youth;
Yet they have not prevailed against me."

Israel's national youth, or childhood, was in Egypt, even as we find in Hos. xi. 1, which literally reads: "When Israel was yet a child [the word being the same as 'youth' in our Psalm] I loved him, and from the time that he was in Egypt, I called him My son"—that is, from the very beginning of their history when God began to love Israel, the nations began to hate them; and from the very time when God first called them "His son, His firstborn" (Exod. iv. 22), the nations began to "afflict them" (Exod. i. 12), and to lay plans for their extermination. Yes, from the very commencement of his history have the plowers mercilessly

"Plowed upon His back;
They made long and deep their furrows" (ver. 3)

—"yet," in spite of it all, *"they have not prevailed against me."*

This is Israel's final shout of triumph, even as in a sense it has been their national song and their defiant answer to the nations all through the ages.

To commence with Israel's "youth"—deep and terrible was the pain and laceration when Egypt plowed upon his back, but who came off worst in the end? Egypt was plagued; Pharaoh and his host were drowned, but of Israel we read, "the more they afflicted them, the more they multiplied and grew." Truly Egypt with all its world power did *"not prevail against him."*

Then, not to mention Canaanites, Philistines, Midianites, and other small powers, there came Syria, Assyria, Babylon, Persia Greece and Rome, each of whom in turn afflicted them much, and made deep and long their furrows; but where are all these powers? They have crumbled away and died, but Israel lives, and they have *"not prevailed over him."*

Then came the centuries of dispersion, when it might be supposed that a comparative handful of men scattered on the great ocean of humanity would soon be swallowed up of the multitude. As a matter of fact, every force was brought to bear against them with terrible severity. Their enemies were united, and seemed confident of success. The crusaders went from west to east with the cry, *"Hierosolyma est perdita!"* [1] and perpetrated wholesale massa-

---

[1] Or "Hep! Hep!" which is an abbreviation formed from the three initial letters of this Latin phrase; the English corruption of it is "Hip! Hip!"

cres of the Jews as a commencement of their "holy" wars.
Again and again apostate Christendom in the dark ages
showed its zeal for the Jewish Messiah, who teaches His
followers to love even their enemies, by burning whole
communities of Jews, numbering sometimes thousands of
souls, on one huge scaffold; but in spite of it all Israel
lives; "they have not prevailed over him"; for there are
more Jews in the world, after all the centuries of banish-
ments, massacres, and untold sufferings, than there have
been at any previous point of the world's history, and the
Jews at the present day, as is proved from official statistics,
in some parts of the world increase in proportion to their
Gentile neighbours at the ratio of three and four to one.
Well might the eloquent Michael Beer, in his "Appeal to
the Justice of Kings," make use of the following language:
"Braving all kinds of torments—the pangs of death, and
still more terrible pangs of life—we have withstood the
impetuous storm of time, sweeping indiscriminately in its
course, nations, religions, and countries. What has become
of those celebrated empires whose very name still excites
our admiration by the idea of splendid greatness attached
to them, and whose power embraced the whole surface of
the known globe? They are only remembered as monu-
ments of the vanity of human greatness. Rome and Greece
are no more; their descendants, mixed with other nations,
have lost even the traces of their origin; while a population
of a few millions of men, so often subjugated, stands the
test of revolving ages, and the fiery ordeal of eighteen
centuries of persecution. We still preserve laws that were
given to us in the first days of the world, in the infancy
of nature. The last followers of a religion which had
embraced the universe have disappeared these eighteen
centuries, and our temples are still standing. We alone
have been spared by the indiscriminating hand of time,
like a column left standing amid the wreck of worlds and

the ruins of nature. The history of our people connects present times with the first ages of the world, by the testimony it bears to the existence of those early periods. It begins at the cradle of mankind; it is likely to be preserved to the. very day of universal destruction."

Alas! the sufferings of Israel are not yet ended, and even in this twentieth century we read almost daily of Jewish massacres and atrocities worse than any which disgrace the annals of the dark ages, but Czardom and the corrupt bureaucracy of that unhappy empire will pass away, while Israel will still sing: *"Yet they have not prevailed against me."* And there is yet a future, or final, culminating "affliction," "trouble," or "tribulation," as the same Hebrew word is elsewhere rendered, awaiting Israel after a large portion of them are returned to their land in a condition of unbelief, when all nations will be gathered in a final siege of Jerusalem (Zech. xiii., xiv.)— but even then, when the nations cry, "Come, let us destroy them from being a nation, that the name of Israel be no more held in remembrance" (Psa. lxxxiii. 4)—one more blow and the Jewish nation will be no more—the answer of the saved remnant who are delivered by the sudden appearance of their Messiah, will be: "I shall not die, but live, and declare the works of Jehovah"—*"yet they have not prevailed against me."* Israel is indestructible. The bush may burn, but it cannot be consumed, because God has said: "Thou I make a full end of all nations whither I have scattered thee, yet will I not make a full end of thee." And the national, or collective life of the Jewish nation is a type not only of the Church as a whole, but also of the spiritual life of the individual believer, which is also indestructible, because it is born of incorruptible seed and is hid with Christ in God. In relation to Israel this is a fact attested by history as well as Scripture, that no man or nation which has lifted its hand against them has prospered, while those who seek to bless them, especially spiritually, are themselves blessed.

In the fourth verse we have, as already stated, a solemn acknowledgment on the part of Israel of the righteous character of Jehovah in all His dealings with them and with the nations.

> *"Jehovah is righteous!*
> *He hath broken asunder the cords of the wicked."*

The vindication of His own glorious character as the absolutely holy and yet loving God, which has been brought into question since the Fall, is the end towards which all His ways are directed; and when the mystery of God shall be finished, and sin and Satan shall be finally swept from the world, heaven and earth will join in the song of Moses and of the Lamb, "Great and marvellous are Thy works, Lord God Almighty, *just and true are Thy ways,* Thou King of the nations. Who shall not fear Thee, O Lord, and glorify Thy Name, for Thou only art holy?"

"Jehovah is righteous"; "Righteousness belongeth unto Thee," will Israel say in that day, "but unto us confusion of face, for we have sinned, and have committed iniquity, and have done wickedly, and have rebelled, even by departing from Thy precepts and from Thy judgments," and we have merited more than all the evil that has come upon us. Righteous also is Jehovah in His judgments on the apostate nations which have sought to crush us without regard to God or His truth, but the time has come for the cords of the wicked, by which we were held captive, to be 'cut asunder," so that we may go out free from our long bondage to the Gentile powers, to serve Jehovah. This is in keeping with Jer. xxx. 8, 9: "And it shall come to pass in that day, saith Jehovah of Hosts, that I will break his yoke from off thy neck, and I will break thy bands, and strangers shall no more serve themselves of him, but they shall serve Jehovah their God and David their King, whom I will raise up unto them."

The second half, verses four to eight of this short Psalm, gives us a prophetic vision of the final discomfiture of the enemies of Israel, who are also regarded as the enemies of God. "Ashamed and turned back shall be all the haters of Zion. They shall be [2] (to give a free rendering) as the grass growing on the flat eastern roofs—which is so feeble that scarcely does it spring up when it withers, and in consequence the mower has nothing wherewith to fill his hand, nor the binder of sheaves his lap; and seeing there is no blessing, but instead, Jehovah's curse, resting on such as are swept away in the great harvest of His judgments (Rev. xiv. 14-20), the passers-by say not according to ancient custom (Ruth ii. 4), The blessing of Jehovah be upon you," nor shall those engaged in the harvest of judgment answer: "We bless you in the Name of Jehovah";—and such is the destiny of all who hate God and help forward the affliction of His people.

From the outward deliverance of the Jews, and the terrible doom of their enemies, which is the subject of the preceding Psalm, we are next taken to the time when Israel's heart shall be humbled, and when as a nation they shall turn to the Lord.

The 130th Psalm is known as the sixth of the "Penitential Psalms," but there are very few who have seen in it the national repentance of Israel. The beginning is significant:

"Out of the depths have I cried unto Thee, O Jehovah,"

---

[2] The Hebrew allows of this rendering instead of "Let them be," as in the Authorised and Revised Versions.

and yet it is inscribed, as we have seen, as a "Song of Ascents." But there is no inconsistency here; there is no way of ascent to the Mount of God except by a steep descent, and the higher we would ascend the lower must we descend. Before we are fit for communion with God, or to enter into His thoughts, we must be brought to an end of ourselves; and the descent, as well as the ascent, is the result of the gracious work of His own Holy Spirit. *"The Lord killeth and maketh alive"*; He bringeth down very low, but only in order to lift us up (1 Sam. ii. 6). In the case of Israel, "the depths" of heart trouble on account of sin, and heart desire for God, will most probably be brought about by the depths of the outward sorrows and troubles of the culminating national "affliction," or tribulation, spoken of in the preceding Psalm. Blessed be God for these outward troubles, which drive us now, and will drive Israel by and by, into the arms and to the heart of God!

But when a man, or a nation, is brought into the depths, he is very much in earnest. It becomes a matter of urgency, and we want to be quite sure that we have God's ear. This is seen in the second verse:

"Lord, hear my voice,
Let Thine ear be attentive to the voice of my supplications."

It is also seen from the frequent use of the Name of God. No fewer than eight times are three different Names of God repeated in this short Psalm, as if the Psalmist, who in spirit here utters the soul of Israel, can do nothing else but wrestle with God, and cry: "'O *Jehovah*,' Thou Covenant, faithful God; 'O *Adonai*,' Thou sovereign Lord of all; 'O *Jah*,' Thou self-existent, living and eternal God"—conscious that it is in His own glorious Name that all their hope and strength lie.

"If Thou, O Jah, shouldest mark iniquities"

(literally, "watch"), or take note of iniquity, so as to call man to account, without finding Thyself a way of escape for him—

"O Adonai, who shall stand?"

This is a kind of challenge thrown down—let any son of Adam take it up. On the ground of sinlessness, on the ground of having no iniquity, there is not one who could stand before God. The blessings of innate purity and absolute innocence have never been tasted by the sons of man since the Fall, excepting by the One Holy One, in whom there was no guile, neither was deceit found in His mouth. But He who knew no sin took His stand before God as man's substitute, bearing all the load of our sin upon Him, and since then we too may stand before Him, not indeed on the ground of our own righteousness, but on the ground of sin forgiven, and iniquity not imputed. The word "Avon" (iniquity) describes sin more in the *radical* sense, not so much the outward effects as the inward cause; not what we do, but what we are. It is not merely by reason of conscious or unconscious *transgressions,* but on account of the innate sinfulness of his nature, that man cannot "stand" before God. But the same word is used in Psa. xxxii., where David speaks of the man to whom "the Lord *imputeth not iniquity";* but instead, in consequence of the work of his Redeemer, knows the blessedness of having righteousness imputed to him apart from works. (Rom. iv. 6). This is something which Israel must yet learn, for at present, ignorant of God's righteousness, they go about vainly seeking to establish their own righteousness, and think they can stand before God on the ground of their own merits or on the merits of their fathers. But by and by, when they behold Him who is "glorious in holiness, fearful in praises," and their eyes are opened to a sense of their own vileness, they

will cry: "Enter not into judgment with Thy servant, for
in Thy sight shall no flesh living be justified." Then they
will be glad to take their stand before God on the ground
of His grace expressing itself in forgiveness, as is seen in
the next verse:

> *"But there is forgiveness with Thee*
> *That Thou mayest be feared."*

This is one of three or four passages in the Old Testament where the word rendered "forgiveness" has a definite
article before it. "There is *the* forgiveness with Thee."
This will be a wonderful discovery made by Israel when
their eyes are opened to look upon Him whom they have
pierced, and, in the light of His wounded side, say, even
as we do now: *"In Him* we have redemption [or, literally,
'the redemption,' the redemption promised, the redemption
typified now actually accomplished] through His blood,
the forgiveness of sins, according to the riches of His
grace" (Eph. i. 7). There is only one way, and one
ground of forgiveness, and we only deceive ourselves if it
is not "according to the riches of His grace," and *"through
His blood."* And those who read forgiveness written on
the cross in the blood of Christ can no longer think lightly
of sin. Forgiveness after this manner, and at such a cost,
creates a holy dread in man's heart, a filial fear lest we
fall again into that which our Father hates, and which
the sacrifice of His only-begotten Son could alone remove.
The cross is a practical exhibition, not only of God's love,
but also of God's holiness. It is only in the light of Calvary that we can form a right estimate, either of the love or
of the justice of God. "With Thee is *the* forgiveness *that
Thou mayest be feared."*

It will have this blessed effect upon Israel; for we read
that by and by, when as a nation they seek and find Jehovah their God, and David their king, and are reconciled

and forgiven, that *"they shall fear toward the Lord and His goodness in the latter days"* (Hos. iii. 5).

We now come to the fourth verse, which is in keeping with what is told us in other prophecies of the attitude of the righteous remnant of Israel, when as a nation they are brought into "the depths":

> *"I wait for Jehovah,*
> *My soul doth wait,*
> *And in His Word do I hope."*

This may be understood in a literal, personal sense. In Isa. xxv. and xxvi., which also deal with the events of the last days, we have similar language: "Yea, in the way of Thy judgments, O Lord, have we waited for thee: the desire of my soul is toward Thy Name, and toward the remembrance of Thee. My soul longs for thee" (for Thy personal interposition) "in the night [of tribulation], yea, with my spirit within me will I seek Thee early" (compare Hos. v. 15), "for when Thy judgments overtake the earth, then the inhabitants of the world will learn righteousness." And when at last, in the hour of their extremity, the heavens shall be rent and Messiah shall descend, and Israel's eyes are opened to see in their deliverer none other than the long-rejected, crucified Jesus, they will cry in amazement and contrition: "Behold, this is our God; *we have waited for Him, and He will save us. This is none other than Jehovah, we have waited for Him,* we will be glad and rejoice in His salvation" (Isa. xxv. 9).

And this waiting will not end in disappointment; this hope will not make ashamed, because it has the Word of the God of Truth for its foundation:

> *"In His Word I hope."*

There is, perhaps, no other subject which has so much of God's Word for its basis, as the blessing and conversion of Israel. The whole Scripture is full of it, and God is not a man that He should lie, nor the Son of Man that He should repent: "In God will I praise His Word, in God I have put my trust," will the remnant of Israel then say, "and I will not fear what flesh can do unto me." "In His Word I hope." *"He will* turn again; *He will* have compassion upon us; *He will* subdue our iniquities; and *Thou wilt* cast all their sins into the depths of the sea. *Thou wilt* perform the truth to Jacob, and the mercy to Abraham, which Thou hast sworn unto our fathers from the days of old."

Let us take care that we too have God's Word for all our hopes and expectations, and let us too remember that we have to do with the same Jehovah, whose faithfulness to Israel is a strong pledge of His faithfulness to us individually in Christ Jesus.

The intensity of the waiting is described in the next verse:

"My soul is towards the Lord from [the time] of the watchers for
the morning."
"Watchers for the morning" (Hebrew).

I believe that this verse is explained by the custom in connection with the Temple ritual. The morning sacrifice in the Temple had to be offered at a point of time between the first indications of dawn and actual sunrise; and during the last hours of the night a party of Levites, known as *Shom'rim laboker*—watchers for the morning— used to take their stand on one of the higher pinnacles of the Temple to watch keenly for the first indications of approaching dawn. Meanwhile, at the altar of burnt-offering everything was prepared and the priests stood ready. At last the signal was given, in these words which are still preserved to us—"The sky is lit as far as Hebron!"—and when this cry was raised by the "watchers

for the morning," the morning sacrifice was slain, and
the daily routine of the Temple service commenced. Now
with the same intentness as these Levites watched for the
rising of the dawn, so, and "more than the watchers of
the morning," will the remnant of Israel, "out of the
depths" look out for the rising of the Sun of Righteousness, who is to bring them healing under His wings—
for the breaking of the bright morning without clouds,
which is to usher in the day of their national salvation,
when the tears of their long night of trouble shall be all
wiped away.

And this is our attitude also. We too are watching for
the morning. The grace of God which appeared bringing
salvation also teaches us that, denying ourselves in reference to ungodly or worldly lusts, "we should live soberly,
righteously, and godly in the present world, *looking for
that blessed hope, the appearing of the glory* of the great
God and our Saviour Jesus Christ, who gave Himself for
us that He might redeem us from all iniquity, and purify
unto Himself a peculiar people zealous of good works."
In this passage the results of the first Advent of our Lord
Jesus Christ are summed up in the words, "grace and
salvation," but we are looking "for the morning" when
grace shall be consummated in glory, when Israel's Messiah and Deliverer shall descend also as the long-absent
Bridegroom of the Church, and take His waiting people to
be for ever with Himself. "Amen, even so, come, Lord
Jesus."

The last two verses are, as it were, God's answer to
Israel's cry; they also show that the "I" in vers. 1 and 5
is Israel personified:

"Let Israel hope in Jehovah,"

their hope will not put me to shame, *"for with Jehovah,"*
the covenant God of their fathers, *"there is mercy."* Here

again before the word "mercy" or "grace" there is the
definite article—"*the* mercy"—the mercy stored up from
everlasting; "the mercy" displaying itself first of all in
"the forgiveness" (ver. 4), procured by the life blood of
the Son of God; it is with Jehovah waiting to pour itself
out on Israel on the first sign of repentance.

But you say, Has not the mercy of God already been
exhausted by the many and long-continued apostasies of
the gainsaying and disobedient nation? Oh, if you think
or speak thus you know not the heart of Israel's God,
whose mercy is infinite and everlasting, higher than the
heavens, and unfathomable as the ocean. "With Jehovah
there is mercy." Dear reader, is your heart in some
measure like unto the heart of God? *Is there mercy with
you for the people whose temporary fall has occasioned
your salvation, and the receiving of whom into God's
favour again shall be as life from the dead to the world?*
Have you ever shown your mercy or compassion for
Israel by pouring out your heart in prayer for their
salvation, and by helping to take to them the Gospel of
our Lord Jesus Christ—that message which gladdens
your own heart, and is the only message of peace to man?
If you have not, I can only say that you will be sorry
for it "in the morning," by not being able, in this respect,
to share the joy of your Redeemer whose heart has never
ceased to yearn for them that are His flesh (Rom. ix.),
and who will soon return as your Lord and Israel's King.

"And with Him is plenteous redemption."

The word translated "plenteous" means also "much" or
"many," so that it can never be exhausted. It is the same
word as is rendered "abundantly" in Isa. lv. 7—"Let the
wicked forsake his way, and the unrighteous man his
thoughts, and let him turn unto Jehovah, for He will have
mercy upon him, and to our God *for He will abundantly*

pardon." Yes, with Him is plenteous redemption—national and individual, temporal and spiritual. He redeemed Israel form Egypt, He brought a remnant back from Babylon, but He will again gather them from all parts of the world where they are now scattered, and better still, He shall redeem Israel *from all his iniquities.* "The Redeemer shall come out of Zion and turn away the ungodliness from Jacob."

At the end of the 25th Psalm there is a prayer of David, *"Redeem Israel, O God, out of all his troubles."* This is how we often pray. We see Israel's troubles and persecutions and we long and pray for deliverance, but God's answer puts the matter in the right way, "He shall redeem Israel *from all his iniquities."* The underlying cause of Israel's troubles are his iniquities, and when his iniquity shall be purged, and his relation to God is restored, then his troubles too will cease. Anyhow, it is well to note that God always puts that which is first first.

In Psa. ciii. 5 the chief mercies of God are, so to say, catalogued, but that which heads the list is *forgiveness*— "Who forgiveth all thine iniquity," because that is the first and greatest of our needs. All other things follow, for "He that spared not his own Son, but delivered Him up for us all, how shall He not with Him also freely give us all things?"

So it will be with Israel. Once they look at Him whom they have pierced, and wash at the fountain opened for sin and uncleanness, then all earthly blessings shall be added unto them, and the land that has so long been waste shall again yield her increase and become the beauty of all lands.

X

THE SUFFERING SERVANT OF JEHOVAH AND THE GLORIOUS FRUITS OF HIS MISSION

ISAIAH XLIX

"Listen, O isles, unto me; and hearken, ye people, from far;
The Lord hath called me from the womb;
From the bowels of my mother hath He made mention of my
    name.
And He hath made my mouth like a sharp sword;
In the shadow of His hand hath He hid me,
And He hath made me a polished shaft;
In His quiver He hath hid me close;
And He said unto me, Thou art My servant Israel, in whom I
    will be glorified.
But I said, I have laboured in vain, I have spent my strength for
    nought and vanity:
Yet surely my judgment is with the Lord, and my recompense
    with my God.
And now saith the Lord that formed me from the womb to be
    His servant,
To bring Jacob again unto Him, and that Israel be gathered to
    Him;
(For I am honourable in the eyes of the Lord, and my God is
    become my strength:)
Yea, He saith, It is too light a thing that thou shouldst be my
    servant,
To raise up the tribes of Jacob, and to restore the preserved of
    Israel.
I will also give thee for a light to the Gentiles,
That thou mayest be My salvation unto the end of the earth.
Thus saith the Lord, the Redeemer of Israel, and His Holy One,
To Him whom man despiseth, to Him whom the nation abhorreth,
    to a Servant of rulers:
Kings shall see and arise;
Princes, and they shall worship;
Because of the Lord that is faithful, even the Holy One of Israel,
    who hath chosen thee,
Thus saith the Lord, In an acceptable time have I answered thee,
And in a day of salvation have I helped thee:
And I will preserve thee, and give thee for a covenant
Of the people, to raise up the land, to make them
Inherit the desolate heritages:
Saying to them that are bound, Go forth;
To them that are in darkness, Show yourselves.
They shall feed in the ways,
And on all bare heights shall be their pasture;
They shall not hunger nor thirst,

Neither shall the heat nor sun smite them;
For He that hath mercy on them shall lead them—
Even by the springs of water shall He guide them.
And I will make all My mountains a way,
And My highways shall be exalted.
Lo, these shall come from far;
And lo, these from the north, and from the west,
And these from the land of Sinim.
Sing, O heavens;
And be joyful, O earth;
And break forth into singing, O mountains;
For Jehovah hath comforted His people,
And will have compassion upon His afflicted.
But Zion said, Jehovah hath forsaken me,
And the Lord hath forgotten me.
Can a woman forget her sucking child,
That she should not have compassion on the son of her womb?
Yea, these may forget,
Yet will not I forget thee.
Behold, I have graven thee upon the palms of My hands;
Thy walls are continually before Me.
Thy children make haste;
Thy destroyers and they that made thee waste shall go forth of
    thee.
Lift up thine eyes round about, and behold;
All these gather themselves together, and come to thee.
As I live, saith the Lord,
Thou shalt surely clothe thee with them all as with an ornament,
And gird thyself with them like a bride.
For, as for thy waste and thy desolate places,
And thy land that hath been destroyed,
Surely now shalt thou be too strait for the inhabitants,
And they that swallowed thee up shall be far away.
The children of thy bereavement shall yet say in thine ears,
The place is too strait for me; give place to me that I may dwell.
Then shalt thou say in thine heart,
Who hath begotten me these, seeing that I have been bereaved
    of my children,
And am solitary, an exile, and wandering to and fro?
And who hath brought up these?
Behold, I was left alone; these, where were they?
Thus saith the Lord God, Behold, I will lift up Mine hand to the
    nations,
And set up My ensign to the peoples;
And they shall bring thy sons in their bosom,
And thy daughters shall be carried upon their shoulders.
And kings shall be thy nursing fathers,
And their queens thy nursing mothers;
They shall bow down to thee with their faces to the earth,

And lick the dust of thy feet.
And thou shalt know that I am the Lord,
And they that wait for Me shall not be ashamed.
Shall the prey be taken from the mighty;
Or the lawful captives be delivered?
But thus saith the Lord,
Even the captives of the mighty shall be taken away,
And the prey of the terrible shall be delivered,
For I will contend with him that contendeth with thee,
And I will save thy children,
And I will feed them that oppress thee with their own flesh;
And they shall be drunken with their own blood as with sweet
    wine:
And all flesh shall know that I the Lord am thy Saviour,
And thy Redeemer the Mighty One of Jacob."

X

THE SUFFERING SERVANT OF JEHOVAH
AND THE GLORIOUS FRUITS
OF HIS MISSION

WITH the forty-ninth chapter begins the central section of the second half of the Book of Isaiah, which, as my readers will know, commences with the fortieth chapter, and ends with the sixty-sixth.[1] In the preceding section the foreground has for the most part been Cyrus, and the emancipation from Babylon, although by no means stopping short there; for the theme with which the prophet's soul is full, even in those earlier chapters, and to which his thoughts constantly recur, even while he deals with the minor deliverance, is the much grander redemption to be accomplished by One greater than Cyrus, even by Messiah—a salvation of which Israel is the centre, and all the ends of the earth the circumference.

From this chapter, however, and onwards, the foreground is altogether dropped; and, leaving Cyrus and the partial restoration from Babylon, we are introduced into the presence of the greater Redeemer, and to the universal redemption to be accomplished by Him.

The same Person who in the forty-second chapter is introduced by God the Father in the words: "Behold, My Servant whom I uphold, my Chosen in whom My soul delighteth, I have put my Spirit upon Him; He shall

---

[1] For the structure and sumblime character of the second half of the Book of Isaiah, I beg to refer my readers to Appendix III. in my book, "The Ancient Scriptures and the Modern Jew."

299

bring forth judgment to the nations. . . . I, Jehovah, have called Thee in righteousness, and will hold Thine hand, and will keep Thee, and will give Thee for a covenant of the people, and for a light of the Gentiles"—here speaks for Himself. That *it is* Messiah who is here speaking, there can be no doubt. Modern rationalism, both Jewish and Christian, tries indeed its utmost to rob Christ of His glory, by eliminating, or by explaining away, every reference to a personal Christ from the pages of the Old Testament Scriptures; but as long as the "scroll of the Book" remains—and it "shall stand for ever"—so long will it continue to testify of Him, who is its very life and substance. The favourite method among rationalistic writers is to explain this prophecy of Israel; but it is an impossible interpretation, for the speaker here is, as we shall see, most clearly distinguished from the nation of Israel—in fact He is introduced and described as *Israel's Saviour,* and therefore cannot be Israel. Besides which, what the subject of this prophecy says of Himself is expressed in such terms of individuality that it can only refer to a person.

The Jewish commentators interpret it of the prophet himself; but this is an equally untenable view. *It is not the manner* of the true prophet to put himself thus prominently in the foreground, and to call the attention of all men to himself; but, as is invariably the case in this very "book of consolations" (as the second part of Isaiah is called by the Rabbis), to retire entirely into the background, and to point men away from himself to Him, who is greater and mightier than the prophets, whose shoe's latchet, as they themselves confessed, they were not worthy to unloose. It would be not only hyperbole, but almost blasphemous, to apply what the speaker in this prophecy says of himself to any mere man. Was Isaiah—were any, or all, the order of prophets, "the covenant of the

people, the light of the Gentiles, and God's salvation unto
the ends of the earth"? In short, to adopt the language
of a great German theologian, "If the Church has Christ
at all, it is impossible that she should fail to find Him
here."

Messiah's Call and Qualifications

But let us now proceed to the exposition. In the first
six verses the servant of Jehovah announces the fact of
His call to the Messianic office, and sets forth His special
qualification for the great task entrusted to Him. The
prophecy begins with a call of attention to all men to the
important declarations which He has to make—

> *"Listen, O isles, unto Me;*
> *And hearken, ye peoples, from far"—*

and from the very form of the address we can already
gather the universal character of His mission, and the
fact that His salvation shall ultimately reach all lands
and all nations. It is not in vain that He calls the attention of all men to Himself. He speaks to all, because *He
only* has a message and a blessing for all—

> "Look unto Me, and be ye saved, *all ye ends of the earth;*
> For I am God, and there is none else."

The ground on which He claims the attention of all
to Himself is the fact that He has been "called," *i. e.*,
designated and appointed to His high office—

> "Jehovah hath called Me from the womb";

from My very birth did He separate Me for this mighty
task.

It may be of comfort to some of us to note that what
is here said of the Divine Master is true also of His
servants. Thus He said to Jeremiah: "Before I formed

thee in the belly, I knew thee; and before thou camest forth out of the womb, I sanctified thee. I have appointed thee a prophet unto the nations"; and thus Paul also could say that "it pleased the Lord who separated me from my mother's womb, and called me by His grace to reveal His Son in me, that I might preach Him among the Gentiles." Of course *we* are not Pauls or Jeremiahs, yet it is a blessed fact, that there is not one of us, with regard to whose life and path on earth the great God has not had some purpose from our very birth, and if by faith we could only realise this truth, there is a power in it to transform our lives. Is it possible, some may ask, that the daily drudgery in the obscure sphere in which my lot is cast can be part of God's purpose for me? But it is; and remember that it is not the drudgery, or "the sufferings of this present time" in themselves, that God has in view, but the perfecting of your character, and the training of your spirit, for the glory which is to be revealed in you. But this is a digression.

The next sentence—

"From the bowels of My mother hath He made mention of My Name"—

brings before our minds, as I believe, a beautiful historic fact. Christ's goings forth are from of old, even from everlasting (Mic. v. 2), and centuries before His incarnation, many of His *titles,* which describe His character and foretell His mission, were revealed. Thus Messiah is called in the Old Testament the "Shiloh," "Immanuel," "Wonderful," "Counsellor," "Mighty God," "Father of Eternity," "Prince of Peace," "Jehovah Tsidkenu," &c. But, among all these titles, that which might especially be called His *personal* Name, cannot be found, until just before His birth in time, literally "from the bowels of His mother," when God, His Father, made mention of it by sending Gabriel with the message: "Behold thou shalt conceive in thy womb, and bring forth a son, and shalt call His name *Jesus.*"   But immediately this secret is revealed, we see at once the suitability and applicability of this Name to the glorious Person who bears it—"Yeshua" —"God's Salvation"—"Saviour"—and in this precious Name all His titles, which but set forth different aspects of the great "salvation" which He is to accomplish, are included.

Jews sometimes ask, "If Jesus is the Messiah, why is not His Name found in the Old Testament Scriptures?" —but if we understand this prophecy correctly, the very fact that the personal Name "Jesus" is not found in the Old Testament is a proof in favour of the Messiahship of Christ, since, according to the prophecy, it was only just before His birth that the Name is to be made known, or "mentioned."

Another reason why the personal Name of the Messiah is not revealed in the Old Testament is, perhaps, that God in His infinite wisdom desired to prevent impostors from deceiving Israel by assuming that Name, after the manner of Bar Cochba ("Son of a Star"), which name was probably assumed in reference to Balaam's prophecy: "There shall come a Star out of Jacob" (Num. xxiv. 17), which, according to some, was to be the Name which Messiah would bear.[2]

---

[2] Delitzsch has a very suggestive note on the sentence, "From the bowels of My mother hath He made mention of My Name." He says: "It is worthy of notice that the great Coming One, though He is described in the Old Testament as One who is to be looked for 'from the seed of David,' is also spoken of as 'born of a woman,' wherever His entrance into the world is directly referred to. In the Protevangelium He is called 'the seed of the woman'; Isaiah, in the time of Ahaz, mentions 'the virgin' as His mother; Micah v. 23, speaks of her that should travail in birth to bring Him forth; and even the typical (Messianic) Psalms, as,

Having announced His call to the Messianic office, He next tells of His special qualifications for the accomplishment of the great task entrusted to Him:

> "And He hath made My mouth like a sharp sword:
> In the shadow of His hand hath He hid Me:
> And He hath made Me a polished shaft,
> In His quiver hath He concealed Me."

His mouth, or the word that issues from it, is like a sharp sword, able to cut through everything, so that no obstacle shall be able effectually to bar His way, or hinder Him in the accomplishment of His mighty task.

We may note in passing that this figure of the sword which proceeds out of Messiah's mouth, is used in Scripture in a twofold sense, corresponding with the twofold aspect of His mission on earth, or, we might also say, His two advents. Sometimes it is used in connection with His *merciful* work of breaking, or cutting, our hearts by His Word—of that "killing" which is with a view "to make us alive," as, for instance, in Heb. iv., where we read that "the word of God is quick and powerful, sharper than *any two-edged sword,* piercing to the dividing asunder of soul and spirit, and is a discerner of the thoughts and intents of the heart"—which "piercing" and "dividing" are with a view to lay our hearts bare to ourselves, so that in the consciousness of our own unworthiness and sinfulness we may cast ourselves before "the throne of grace," that mercy and healing may be ministered to our wounded hearts by "the great High Priest," who for this purpose has passed into the heavens on our behalf.

----

for instance, Psa. xxii. 10, 11, give prominence to the mother" (while, as the learned professor might have added, there is no hint or mention of a human personal father of the Messiah in the Old Testament Scriptures). "Is not this," he exclaims, "a sign that prophecy is a work of the Spirit who searches the deep things of the Counsel of God?"

And in connection with Messiah's work of judgment we find this figure in such Scriptures as Isa. xi. 4, and Rev. xix. 15, which foretell that at His glorious appearing He shall not only slay the wicked, or "lawless one," with the breath of His lips, but that with "the sharp sword which goeth out of His mouth He shall smite the nations, and rule them with a rod of iron, and tread the winepress of the fierceness and wrath of Almighty God."

But not only is His mouth like a sharp sword, but He Himself is "a polished shaft," or "cleaned," or "sharpened," arrow—the word here in singular form being the same as in Psa. xlv. 5, and reminds us of the time when He shall "pierce the heart of the King's enemies," and peoples shall be made "to fall under Him."

And the sword is "hid" under the shadow of God's almighty hand, and the shaft, or arrow, "is concealed in His quiver," kept there in safety and readiness until, "in the fulness of time," it should be drawn forth and wielded by the arm of Omnipotence with irresistible force.

THE TRUE ISRAEL

In the third verse Messiah makes known some of the converse in the *eternal* counsels between the Father and the Son. We are reminded of the Second Psalm, where He says:

> "I will tell the decree.
> Jehovah said unto Me, Thou art My Son;
> This day have I begotten Thee."

Here, however, it is not, "Thou art My Son," but—

> "He said unto Me, Thou art My servant
> Israel [or 'Thou art Israel'], in whom I will be glorified."

Some find a difficulty in reading this verse, and wonder how it can be applied to the Messiah, or how Christ can be called by the name of "Israel." The answer is to be found in the fact that in Him is to be seen the climax of realisation of the purpose which God had in the existence and high calling of the nation of Israel.

In reading the last twenty-seven chapters of Isaiah, we are struck by the fact, that the circle described by the term "Servant of Jehovah" keeps on continually contracting. Originally, and in its widest sweep, it is the whole nation of Israel which is called "the servant of Jehovah," as, for instance, in chap. xli. 8:

> "But Thou, Israel, art My servant
> Jacob, whom I have chosen—
> The seed of Abraham, My friend."

But the nation fails to respond to the purpose of God in its election, and the circle in some Scriptures contracts, and includes only the godly "remnant," or those who are of faith in Israel, and who form, so to say, the spiritual kernel in the nation. But even this little remnant fails fully to respond to God's thoughts, or to accomplish God's purpose, and has to confess, "We are all become as one that is unclean, and all our righteousnesses are as a polluted garment"—"We have, as it were, brought forth wind; we have not wrought any deliverance in the earth, neither have the inhabitants of the world fallen."

The circle, therefore, contracts still further, and meets in the end around one Person, the Messiah, who is not only the Head, but the *Heart* of Israel—"in whom the true nature of the ideal Israel is concentrated as the rays of light in the sun; in whom the history of Israel is coiled as into a knot for a further final development";

in whom Israel's world-wide calling to bring light and salvation to the nations is fully carried out.[3]

A parallel is to be found in the original promise of blessing for the nations which is bound up in the seed of Abraham. First, it is in Abraham and in his seed, which might be brought to mean the whole Jewish nation, that all the families of the earth were to be blessed. But as we read on we find the promise running through an ever-narrowing channel. "After Abraham the seed of promise was successively defined as the seed of *Isaac,* and the seed of *Jacob.* Then out of the twelve tribes descended from Jacob, only one, Judah, was to be the tribe from whom peace for the nations was to proceed. But still the circle contracted, and out of the particular tribe only one particular *family* was chosen; and finally every promise and prediction revolved for centuries round *one individual* of that favoured family, whose identity we can, without difficulty, trace in the various announcements of all the different prophets, and whose career and character is described with such minuteness of detail that

---

[3] "The idea of the servant of Jehovah assumed, to speak figuratively, the form of a pyramid. The base was Israel as a whole; the central section was that Israel which was not merely Israel according to the flesh, but according to the spirit also: the apex is the person of the Mediator of Salvation springing out of Israel. And the last of the three is regarded (1) as the centre of the circle of the promised kingdom—the *second David;* (2) the centre of the circle of the people of salvation—the *second Israel;* (3) the centre of the circle of the human race—the *second Adam.* Throughout the whole of these prophecies in chapters xl.-lxvi. the knowledge of salvation is still in its second stage, and about to pass into the third. Israel's true nature as a servant of God, which had its roots in the election and calling of Jehovah, and manifested itself in conduct and action in harmony with this calling, is all concentrated in Him, the One, as its ripest fruit. The gracious purposes of God towards the whole human race, which were manifested even in the election of Israel, are brought by Him to their full completion."— *Delitzsch.*

wilful blindness alone can deny that a personal Messiah is loudly and unequivocally proclaimed in the Old Testament Scriptures." [4]

But, to quote again a German master: "Israel was from the very first the God-given name of an individual. Just as the name Israel was first of all given to a man, and then after that to a nation, so the name which sprang from a personal root has also a personal crown. The servant of Jehovah is Israel in person, inasmuch as the purpose of mercy, upon the basis of which Jehovah made Jacob the father of the twelve-tribed nation, is brought by him into full and final realisation. We have already seen that Israel, as an entire nation, formed the basis of the idea contained in the term 'Servant of Jehovah'; Israel, regarded as a people faithful to its calling, the centre; and the personal servant of Jehovah its apex. In the present instance, where He is called distinctly 'Israel,' the fact is clearly expressed that the servant of Jehovah in these prophecies is regarded as the kernel of the kernel of Israel—as Israel's inmost centre, as Israel's highest head. He it is in whom (i. e., on whom, and through whom) Jehovah glorifies Himself inasmuch as He carries out through Him the counsels of His love, which are the self-glorification of His holy love—its glory and triumph."

We have also to bear in mind the adaptability of the name "Israel" to our Lord Jesus, and to remember the peculiar circumstances when the name was given. It was in that dark night of Jacob's experience, when, overcome by the angel, he clung to Him in his weakness, with his thigh out of joint, saying, "I will not let Thee go except Thou bless me!" It was then that by weeping and supplication he overcame, "and by his strength he had power

---

[4] "Rays of Messiah's Glory.

with God; yea, he had power over the angel, and prevailed" (Gen. xxxii. 22-32; Hos. xii. 3-5).

Now, of course, there never was any Jacob period in the life of that Holy One who is the only One born of woman who had no need of repentance, or to weep over His own sins. Yet may we not see in that mysterious transaction in Jacob's life a faint foreshadowing of Him, "who, in the days of His flesh, having offered up prayers and strong supplications, with strong crying and tears, unto Him that was able to save Him from death; and having been heard for His godly fear, though He was a Son, yet learned obedience through the things which He suffered; and having been made perfect He became unto them that obey Him the author of eternal salvation, named of God a High Priest after the order of Melchizedek"?

I have shown that the circle described by the term "the servant of Jehovah" keeps on contracting till it meets around one Person, namely, the Messiah, who is therefore designated as the true "Israel." But we note also that when the circle reaches its inmost centre it begins to *expand again,* and includes, first "the remnant," and finally *the whole saved Israel,* who, with their Redeemer-King at their head and in their midst, shall yet fulfil God's purposes of grace on this earth, and shall yet be the medium of His salvation for all nations.

"In whom I will be glorified."

This is the chief end for which "the servant of Jehovah" is called "from the womb," and qualified as described in the first two verses—to glorify God in the salvation and blessedness of His people, and by subduing all things to Himself. And once again we notice that that, which in the purpose of God was the aim in the high calling and election of the nation of Israel, is fully realised only in and through Christ.

Of the nation we read in chap. xliii.: "This people have I formed for Myself; they shall show forth My praise, . . . for I have created Him for My glory; I have formed Him; yea, I have made Him"; but hitherto the nation has not apprehended or responded to that for which it was apprehended of God; and only the one great and true Israelite, who is also the everlasting Son of the Father, could say: *"I have glorified Thee on the earth;* I have finished the work which Thou gavest Me to do"; but when the nation is, so to say, born anew in Christ, who is at once its heart and its head, God's purpose will be fully accomplished, and "this people, which He hath formed for Himself, *shall show forth His praise";* and Jehovah will not only be glorified in Israel, but Israel will be His glory, even as it is written: *"I will place salvation in Zion for Israel My glory."*

The Shadow of the Cross

In the fourth verse we see the distant shadow of the cross falling on our Saviour's path:

> "But I said, I have laboured in vain,
> I have spent my strength for nought and vanity."

He was called, and qualified by God for His great mission, but when He actually enters on it there seems no response. He was in the world, but the world which was made by Him knew Him not; He came unto His own, where He had every right to expect a welcome, but they that were His received Him not; and as the short years of His ministry on earth went by, it seemed more and more that, as far as the people were concerned to whom God sent Him, He was labouring in vain, and spending His strength

for nought. The nation rejected Him, and even the handful of His disciples on whom He had bestowed so much
tender care were ready at the critical moment to forsake
Him and flee.

Yet what did He do? Did He change His course? Did
He try more popular methods? Oh no—though all may
forsake Him, and though His path may lead to suffering
and humiliation, and end with the cross of shame, He
went steadily on. "The Lord God," He says, "hath opened
My ear and I was not rebellious, neither turned away
backward. I gave My back to the smiters, and My cheek
to them that plucked off the hair; I hid not My face from
shame and spitting." Even Peter, probably as the mouth-
piece of all the apostles, would have had Him change His
course, and said: "Be it far from Thee, Lord; this shall
never be unto Thee," showing how different the thoughts
even of His disciples were from His own, and how they
still minded the things not of God but of men; but He,
to whom alone God could point with complacency, saying, "Behold My servant whom I uphold, Mine elect in
whom My soul delighteth," *"had set His face like a flint,"*
seeking not applause or outward success, but perfectly to
accomplish the will of His Father, to whom with full confidence He committed Himself and His cause, as is brought
out in the last two lines of this verse:

"Yet surely [or 'nevertheless'] My judgment [or 'right'] is with
    Jehovah,
And My recompense [My 'reward'] with My God."

Thus it is that He became the Author and Finisher (or
the princely Leader and Perfecter) of faith, who for the
joy that was set before Him, endured the cross, despising
the shame, and is now held up before His believing people
as the great example, that they too may learn in the day
of darkness and outward discouragement to trust in the

Name of Jehovah, and to stay themselves upon their God
(Isa. l. 4-11).

But the apparent failure of Messiah's mission at first,
is in reality the occasion of greater triumph ultimately,
and the path of humiliation which He had to tread only
led to His greater glory, not only as King of Israel, but
as the Son of Man. This comes out in vers. 5, 6:

"And now, saith Jehovah that formed Me from the womb to be
    His Servant,
And that Israel may be gathered unto Him,[5]
For I am honourable in the eyes of Jehovah,
And My God has become My strength."

In the first part of this paragraph the primary object
of Christ's mission on earth is reaffirmed, as if it formed
the answer of the Father to the soliloquy of Messiah in
the fourth verse. That object was *"to bring Jacob again,
. . . and that Israel may be gathered unto Him."* Inci-
dentally we have a picture here of Israel from God's
standpoint.

Like the prodigal son, forward "Jacob" has left the
Father's home and presence, and has *wandered away* in
the far country to live a life of sin, which ends in humiliation and misery. But though he deserves it not, the
Father still loves him, and sends "His Servant" on the
errand to "bring" or "turn" him back, with the assurance
of a welcome; or, to pass over to another figure, "Israel"
is like a flock of "lost sheep . . . wandering from mountain to hill, having forgotten their resting-place" (*i. e.,*
Him who is the Dwelling Place of His people in all generations) ; and the Messiah, as the Good Shepherd, is

---

[5] The erroneous reading adopted by the A.V., "Though Israel
be not gathered yet shall I be glorious," &c., has long ago been
discarded by scholars, and is rightly rejected in the R.V.

sent to "gather" them. And not only is Jacob a wanderer, and Israel scattered, but "the tribes of Jacob" are *fallen,* oh so low! and the Mighty One is sent "to raise" them up. And even the "preserved" remnant of Israel is *lost* spiritually, and He is sent to "restore" them, not only to the land, but to fellowship with God.

Oh that Israel had known the day of their visitation and recognised Him who came to them on such a mission of love and mercy! But when He called "Repent," they refused to turn back; and when He would have gathered them, they would not.

"O Jerusalem, Jerusalem!" He had to cry at last—"thou that killest the prophets, and stonest them that are sent unto thee! How often would I have gathered thy children together, even as a hen gathereth her chickens under her wings, and ye would not." *"I would, and ye would not."* "Therefore, behold your house is left unto you desolate." But not for ever.

Man's unbelief and disobedience may *defer* to his own hurt the accomplishment of God's purposes; but man's unbelief and the very gates of hell *cannot frustrate them.* The first great item in Christ's commission has never been cancelled, though the fulfilment of it has, through Israel's disobedience, been postponed. Israel's "house" will not for ever remain desolate, for He who should be the life and joy of it—but whom they in ignorance shut out—will return to it, as is implied even in His parting words to the nation (Matt. xxiii. 37-39), when, after uttering the terrible word of judgment, "Behold your house is left unto you desolate," He added, "For I say unto you, Ye shall not see Me henceforth, *till ye shall say, Blessed is He that cometh in the name of the Lord."*

Yes, He whom they once put from them with shouts of "Crucify Him! Crucify Him!" will yet be hailed with "Hosannah! Blessed be He that cometh in the name of

Jehovah"; and then wandering Jacob shall be "brought back" to the Father's house, never again to turn away, and scattered Israel be "gathered," nevermore to go astray.

Meanwhile, through the temporary unbelief of Israel, another great purpose of God has come to light. This is brought out in the second half of the brief paragraph which we are considering:

"Yea, He saith, It is too light a thing that thou shouldest be My Servant,
To raise up the tribes of Jacob,
And to restore the preserved of Israel;
I will also give Thee for a light of the Gentiles,
That Thou mayest be My salvation unto the ends of the earth."

Yes, the partial fall of Israel has become "the riches of the world; and their loss, the riches of the Gentiles."

It was when the nation disobeyed and disbelieved the Word, that the larger commission was given, "Go ye out into *all the world,* and preach the Gospel to every creature"; and on this principle the apostles acted—as, for instance, in Antioch, when, after the Jews were filled with jealousy, and contradicted the things which were spoken by Paul, and blasphemed, Paul and Barnabas spake out boldly, and said: "It was necessary that the Word of God should first be spoken to you, but seeing ye thrust it from you, and judge yourselves unworthy of eternal life, lo, we turn to the Gentiles. For so hath the Lord commanded us, saying, I have set thee for a light of the Gentiles, that Thou shouldest be for salvation unto the uttermost part of the earth" (Acts xiii. 44-47).

Thus He, who was first of all sent as Israel's Messiah and King, has become also the Light of the Gentiles, and God's *Yeshua* (Salvation-Saviour—the Hebrew for "Jesus") unto the ends of the earth.

And oh! what a light that was which rose on the horizon of the Gentile world when Jesus appeared, and

when the "Mystery of Godliness" was preached among
the Gentiles, and believed on in the world! Masses in
Christendom at the present day are blinded by the light
to such an extent that they deny the very existence of the
Sun of Righteousness; but these very people owe almost
everything to the fact that they were born and live in
lands where, nominally at least, Christ and His Gospel
are acknowledged.

England is not, as a nation, Christian; but if we would
know something of the direct and indirect influences of
the Gospel, we need only compare the condition of England with the most advanced heathen or Mohammedan
country, and if we have eyes to see we shall note the
difference. Into whatever region of the earth, or in whatever human heart, the blessed quickening and healing
rays of the Sun of Righteousness have not penetrated,
there is nothing but darkness, coldness, desolation, and
death.

On the evening of that last day, the great day of the
Feast of Tabernacles,[6] after He had already stood and
cried in the Temple court, "If any man thirst, let him
come unto Me and drink!" Jesus again spake unto them
after the evening sacrifice—perhaps with reference to the
colossal lampstands by which the city was illuminated
every evening of the feast—*"I am the Light of the world;
he that followeth Me shall not walk in darkness, but shall
have the Light of Life."* And you, my dear Gentile
brethren and sisters, have experienced the truth of this
wonderful saying, which from mere human lips would be
blasphemy.

Christ has become your light; He has revealed to you
the only true God—He has manifested to you the Father.
He has also revealed to you your own selves, and dis-

---

[6] See the section on the Feast of Tabernacles in Chap. I.

pelled the darkness of sin and ignorance from your hearts. In His light alone you see light on your destiny, and by following Him, even though outwardly all may be dark, you have the "Light of Life," for He who is your light is also your salvation, and by His appearing "He hath abolished death, and brought life and immortality to light by the Gospel."

But the fulfilment of this prophecy so far has only been partial, both in its degree and in its extent. Multitudes indeed from among the Gentiles have, together with the remnant according to the election of grace from among Israel, since the appearing of Christ walked in His light, and rejoiced in His salvation; but when we look at corporate Christianity, we see, alas! much darkness, while the mass of the Gentiles—the great heathen and Mohammedan world—are still completely "under the shadow of death."

Not yet has the promise of the Father to the Son been fulfilled: "Ask of Me, and I will give Thee the Gentiles for Thine inheritance, and the uttermost parts of the earth for Thy possession"; but when Messiah's task in relation to Israel is fulfilled, when Jacob *shall* at last be brought back, and Israel *be* gathered—then the light of the knowledge of the glory of Jehovah shall fill this earth, even as the waters cover the sea. To this, psalmists, prophets, and apostles bear witness:

"Thou shalt arise and have mercy upon Zion,
  For it is time to have pity upon her.
  Yea, the set time is come; . . .
  So [then] the nations shall fear the Name of Jehovah,
  And all the kings of the earth Thy glory" (Psa. cii. 13-16).

"Arise, shine, for thy light is come,
  And the glory of Jehovah is risen upon thee [Israel]. . . .
  And nations [the Gentiles] shall come to thy light,
  And kings to the brightness of thy rising" (Isa. lx. 1, 3).

"O Zion, when thy Saviour came
    In grace and love to thee,
No beauty in thy Royal Lord
    Thy faithless eyes could see.

"Yet onward in His path of grace
    The Holy Sufferer went,
To feel at last that love on thee
    Had all in vain been spent.

"Yet not in vain—o'er Israel's land
    The glory yet will shine,
And He, Thy once-rejected King,
    For ever shall be thine.

"The nations to thy glorious light,
    O Zion, yet shalt throng,
And all the listening islands wait
    To catch the joyful song.

"The name of Jesus yet shall ring
    Through earth and heaven above,
And all His ransomed people know
    The Sabbath of His love."

THE SUFFERINGS OF CHRIST AND THE GLORY WHICH SHOULD FOLLOW

In the first division of this chapter, consisting of vers. 1-6, Messiah was the speaker, but in the second section— which we are now to consider—God is the speaker, and the whole may be briefly summarised as a promise from the Father to the Son, in the hearing of the universe, assuring Him of the ultimate success of His cause, and of the triumph of His kingdom.

In substance this has already been proclaimed in vers. 5, 6, but it is repeated as a solemn ratification, while in the repetition there is the additional unfolding of the glories of Messiah's Person and work more particularly in His relation to Israel.

"Thus saith Jehovah, the Redeemer of Israel,
And His Holy One,
To Him whom man despiseth,
To Him whom the nation abhorreth,
To a Servant of rulers."

The titles of God, which are arrayed by way of preface to this address, are like a solemn asseveration in pledge of the certain fulfilment of the word which proceeds out of His mouth.

"Thus saith *Jehovah*"—the everlasting faithful God of the history of redemption; and He is *"the Redeemer of Israel"*—who stands in special covenant relations to His people, and is therefore Himself infinitely interested in the accomplishment of the redeeming task with which His servant is entrusted; and He is *"the Holy One"*—the Father of Lights, with whom there is no variableness nor shadow of turning, and whose word shall come to pass, though heaven and earth may pass away.

In this verse we have a summary of all that the prophet says about the Messiah in chap. liii. Though in few words, we have here a comprehensive prophecy of the sufferings of Christ, and of the glory which should follow.

At first the condition of the "Servant of Jehovah" is to be one of deepest humiliation and suffering.

He is One *"whom man despiseth."* [7] The word is the same as in chap. liii.—"He is despised and rejected of men"—and well describes the attitude of men in general, to whom the very idea of a crucified Messiah is "foolishness," and who show their contempt of Him and His Gospel by turning their backs upon them, and by living as if there never were a Christ, or a God before whom they

---

[7] Or "despised from soul," as the words may be rendered, describing the depth of contempt as *from the very soul of man,* which He shall encounter.

shall give an account.   But while this is the attitude of
men generally, He is more particularly the One

"Whom the nation abhorreth";

and truly if, instead of a prophecy uttered centuries before
His advent, it had been a history, written subsequent to
the events, no more terse or graphic account could be given
of the attitude and feeling of men generally, and of "the
nation" in particular, to our Lord Jesus Christ.

No person in the history of the Jews has provoked such
deep-seated abhorrence as He who came only to bless
them, and who even on the cross prayed, "Father, forgive
them, for they know not what they do."   When on earth,
at the end of His three and a half years of blessed ministry
among them, they finally rejected Him, their hatred was
intense and mysterious.   "Away with this man;   release
unto us Barabbas: . . . crucify Him, crucify Him!" was
their cry.   And all through the centuries no name has
provoked such intense abhorrence among the Jews as the
Name of Jesus.

I have known personally most amiable, and, as men, very
lovable, characters, among the Jews; but immediately the
name "Jesus" was mentioned a change came over their
countenances, and they would fall into a passion of anger.
In the course of my missionary experiences these past
forty-four years, oh, how often has it been my lot to witness some of my people almost mad with rage—clenching
their fists, gnashing with their teeth, and spitting on the
ground, at the very mention of the Name which to the
believer "is as ointment poured forth"! Israel's attitude
to our Lord Jesus may be gathered also from their literature.   In the filthy legends about Him in the Talmud, and
more modern productions, the very names by which He is
called are blasphemies.   The precious name Yeshua

("Jesus"—Saviour) has been changed into *"Yeshu"* made up of initial letters, which mean "Let His name and His memory be blotted out." The Holy One who knew no sin, nor was guile found in His mouth, is often styled *"the Transgressor";* and another term frequently in the mouth of Jews is *"Tolui"*—"the hanged One," which is equivalent to "the accursed One." There are other lying and filthy designations, such as "Ben Stada," or "Ben Pandera," which imply blasphemies not only against Him, but against her who is "blessed among women."

But Israel's blind hatred to the Messiah does not stop short at His person, or His virgin mother, but extends to His words, and works, and particularly to those of their nation who are ready to take upon them His reproach and to follow Him. Thus His works are still ascribed to witchcraft and Beelzebub; His Gospel (the *Evangelium*) is called *Aven* or *Avon-gillajon*, "the sinful or mischievous writing"; while Rabbinic hatred to His followers (especially from among the Jews) was not satisfied with classing them as "apostates" and "worse than heathen," but rose to the height of instituting a daily public prayer in the most solemn part of their liturgy, that "the Nazarenes" may, together with all apostates, "be suddenly destroyed," without hope, and be "blotted out of the book of life"!

This may be painful reading to some Christians, and the Lord knows it is far from my thoughts to write anything which might tend to foster unchristian prejudice against my people, but it is necessary to show how literally the prophetic forecast has been verified, and how deepseated and mysterious Jewish hatred has been to Him, who, according to His human nature, is flesh of their flesh, and bone of their bone, and in whom is bound up all their hope and salvation.

Let it be remembered also that Jewish hatred to Christ and His followers, at any rate in more modern times, is partly to be traced to the sufferings which they have endured at the hands of so-called Christians, and also that it is not our Lord Jesus as we know Him that Israel in ignorance thus blasphemes, but the caricature of Him as presented to them by apostate persecuting Christendom in the dark ages. As I said elsewhere, "Often the only way left to the Jews to avenge their terrible sufferings and massacres was to write blasphemously of Him in whose Name they were ignorantly perpetrated."

Neither is it to be forgotten that if Christ has been, and, alas! to a large extent still is, *"abhorred of the nation,"* there has always been a remnant in the nation to whom He has been "the fairest of ten thousand and altogether lovely," and who, for the love of Him, counted not even their lives dear unto them. It was a man of Israel and a Pharisee who wrote: "But what things were gain to me, those I counted loss for Christ, yea, doubtless, and I count all things but loss, for the excellency of Christ Jesus my Lord; for whom I have suffered the loss of all things, and do count them but dung, that I might win Christ." And when the "blindness in part" which has befallen Israel shall be removed, and their eyes are opened to behold the true glory of Him whom they have pierced, then the whole nation shall show an example of love and zeal for their Messiah, such as has not been known in the world. But this has been partly a digression. There is still another item setting forth the humiliation of Him who is described as the One "whom man despiseth—whom the nation abhorreth"; and this is brought out in the expression,

"To a Servant of Rulers."

Though Maker and Ruler of the worlds, our Lord Jesus, during His life on earth, voluntarily subjected Himself to human laws and human authority, and at the end the Jewish hierarchy, Pontius Pilate, and Herod, treated Him as if He were wholly given over to their will. Did not Pilate say, "I have power to crucify Thee, and I have power to release Thee," as if He were his bond-servant? And our Lord used no restraint, but simply answered, "Thou couldest have no power against Me, except it were given thee from above," and submitted Himself to the authority of the tyrant. Thus did the Son of God, for our salvation, "empty Himself" of His Divine prerogatives, and "take upon Himself the form of a servant, . . . and being found in fashion as a man, humbled Himself, becoming obedient unto death, even the death of the cross."

But, as there is no humiliation like that into which the Son of God descended, so is there no glory to be compared to His; and this is brought out in the second half of this verse:

> "Kings shall see and arise,
> Princes, and they shall worship,
> Because of Jehovah that is faithful;
> The Holy One of Israel who hath chosen Thee."

Kings and princes *"shall see"* that the One whom man humbled God has exalted; that He who was despised of man, and abhorred of the nation, is, after all, He whom the Holy One of Israel hath chosen; that in spite of their vain counsels, and their individual and united efforts, His kingdom progresses, and is destined to triumph— and they shall *"arise"* from their thrones in token of reverence, and shall signify their submission and allegiance by prostrating themselves before Him in worship; and all this "because of Jehovah that is faithful" to His covenants and promises, "even the Holy One," who will never draw back from His word, and shall, by espousing and vindicating His servants' cause, make it manifest in the sight of the whole world that He hath chosen Him!

In a measure this has already been fulfilled. Because He hath humbled Himself, becoming obedient unto death, even the death of the cross, therefore also God hath highly exalted Him, and given unto Him the Name which is above every name; that in the Name of Jesus every knee should bow of things in heaven, and things on earth, and things under the earth, and that every tongue should confess that Jesus Christ is Lord, to the glory of God the Father.

Already before the crucified Nazarene kings must rise from their thrones, and princes fall in the dust, not, indeed, necessarily because their hearts have been subdued by His grace, or their eyes opened to His essential glory as the Son of God, but because they have found out from experience that it is no longer safe to resist His power. But even though the obedience be feigned, and the worship be outward, it is still a testimony to Christ's exaltation, and to the faithfulness of Jehovah, in lifting Him out of the valley of humiliation, and appointing Him His "First-born, higher than the kings of the earth." But we are looking forward to a fuller, more visible, and universal fulfilment, when He who was "despised and rejected of men; a man of sorrows and acquainted with grief," shall be the acknowledged King over the whole earth, and when—

"He shall have dominion also from sea to sea,
And from river unto the ends of the earth.
They that dwell in the wilderness shall bow before Him;
And his enemies shall lick the dust.
The kings of Tarshish and of the isles shall bring presents;
The kings of Sheba and Seba shall offer gifts;
Yea, all kings shall fall down before Him;
All nations shall serve Him" (Psa. lxxii. 8-11).

THE BLESSED RESULTS OF MESSIAH'S HUMILIATION

The next two verses set forth some of the glorious results of Messiah's humiliation, more particularly in relation to the land and the people of Israel:

> "*Thus saith Jehovah*
> In an acceptable time have I **answered** Thee,
> And in a day of salvation have I helped Thee;
> And I will preserve Thee,
> And give Thee for a covenant of the people;
> To raise up the land,
> To make them inherit the desolate heritages."

In the valley of humiliation and need in which He found Himself "in the days of His flesh," Messiah is represented as having cried to the Father, and His prayers were in accordance with God's good pleasure, for the time was an *êth-ratzon*—"a time of grace," or goodwill, and the day which is the synonym for "the time," was a *yom Yeshua*—a day when God occupied Himself with thoughts of salvation for His people; therefore "He was heard for His godly fear," and was "helped" and "preserved"— preserved from having His great mission frustrated or from being diverted from the path marked out for Him, which, through suffering, led to glory; and "helped," with a wonderful and mighty deliverance, when He was lifted from the "horrible pit," and demonstrated to be the Son of God with power, according to the spirit of holiness, by the resurrection from the dead. The truth of this part of the prophecy is more fully unfolded in Psa. xx. and xxi., where we have first the prayers of, and for, "the King," in the day of His "trouble," and then the joyous acknowledgment:

> "*Thou hast given Him His heart's desire,*
> And hast not withholden the request of His lips.
> For Thou preventest Him with the blessings of goodness;
> Thou settest a crown of fine gold on His head.
> He asked life of Thee, Thou gavest it Him,
> Even length of days for ever and ever.
> His glory is great in Thy salvation;
> Honour and majesty dost Thou lay upon Him;
> For Thou makest Him most blessed for ever:
> Thou makest Him glad with **joy in Thy presence**,
> For the King trusteth in **Jehovah**,
> And through the lovingkindness of the **Most High He shall
>   not be moved**."

But it was not for Himself merely that He was "answered"; and we may be sure that "the request of His lips" ranged not only over His own need "in the days of His flesh," but embraced His Church, and God's purposes in relation to the nations as well as the land, and the people, over which He yearned even unto tears.

Therefore the Apostle quotes these words in 2 Cor. vi. to remind believers that it is for them and as their representative that the Christ was accepted; and that because He was answered this is an acceptable time and the day of salvation to them also, only they are to take care not to use the grace of God in vain or to "no purpose." [8]

---

[8] "These words are often read as though they meant that the Corinthians were in danger of losing the salvation which they had received in Christ Jesus, if they failed to use their blessings aright. It is hardly needful to say that this is not the case. It is quite true that 'the grace of God' which they had received through the Apostle's ministry refers to the salvation of which their souls had become partakers; but the exhortation of the Apostle was not pointed by the desire to kindle in their hearts the fear lest they should lose that salvation, but the fear that they should neglect the privileges which they had received through it. 'We, then, as fellow-workers with Him, beseech you that ye receive not the grace of God *to no purpose.*'

"It will be observed that we have re-translated the last part of the text. The Greek words translated 'in vain' might be rendered 'as a light thing,' or 'to no purpose,' and they certainly refer here *to failure in service, and not to the loss of salvation.* 'The grace of God' refers especially to the precious privileges which a realised acceptance of the Gospel brings to the soul; and the words 'in vain' refer to the loss we should incur if we missed this ministry. If we know the preciousness of this privilege, we shall escape the danger of receiving it as though it were a matter of small value; but, if we receive salvation selfishly, and for our own souls alone, we might indeed be said to have 'received the grace of God in vain,' or 'to no purpose,' as regards the use we are enjoined to make of it for the good of others."

But here we see particularly what the issues of His humiliation and suffering will be to Israel. First we read—

"I will give Thee for a covenant of the people."

Thou shalt be the personal bond uniting My people and Myself in a new fellowship; not only the Mediator of the promised new covenant (liv. 10; lxi. 8; Jer. xxxi. 30-34; Ezek. xvi. 60-63), but the very embodiment of the covenant inasmuch as the promises and blessings are all centred in Him, and are to be realised only through a personal relationship to Him.[9]

"The people" *(am)* whenever used in the singular is always Israel, and in some passages in Isaiah this relation-

---

[9] "The Servant of God is called the personal and embodied Covenant, because in His appearance the covenant made with Israel is to find its full truth; and everything implied in the very idea of a covenant—all the promises flowing from this idea—are to be in Him, yea, and Amen. The Servant of God is here called the Covenant of Israel, just in the same manner as in Mic. v. 5 (*comp.* Eph. ii. 14) it is said of Him, 'This [man] is Peace,' because in Him peace, as it were, represents itself personally—just as in Isa. xlix. 6 He is called 'The salvation of God,' because this salvation becomes personal in Him, the Saviour; just as in Gen. xvii. 10-13 circumcision is called a covenant, as being the embodied covenant; just as in Luke xxii. 20 the cup, the blood of Christ, is called the New Covenant, because in it it has its root. The explanation 'Mediator of the covenant' is meagre, and weakens the meaning. The circumstance that the Servant of God is without further qualification called 'The covenant of the people' shows that He stands in a different relation to the covenant from that of Moses, to whom the name of the Mediator of the covenant does not the less belong than to Him. From Jer. xxxi. 31 we learn which are the blessings and gifts which the Servant of God is to bestow, and by which He represents Himself as the personal Covenant. They are concentrated in the closest connection which is to be established by Him between God and His people: 'I will be their God, and they shall be My people. It is only in the New Covenant, described in that passage of Jeremiah, that the Old Covenant attains to its truth."—*Hengstenberg.*

ship of Messiah to Israel is contrasted with what He is to be to the Gentiles; as, for instance, in chap. xlii. 6, where Jehovah says, "I . . . have called Thee in righteousness, and will hold Thine hand, and will keep Thee, and give Thee for a covenant of the people, for a light of the Gentiles."

And this is how the restored covenant relationship between God and His people will be made outwardly manifest—

"To raise up the land,"

which had been involved in the fall and ruin of the people.

Palestine in relation to Israel supplies a parallel to the manner in which this earth was involved in the fall of man. When Adam sinned, God said, "Cursed is the ground for thy sake; . . . thorns also and thistles shall it bring forth to thee," and ever since "the whole creation groaneth and travaileth in pain together until now"; and so when Israel fell, and broke the national covenant, ruin and desolation came as a consequence over the land, which for centuries has been lying under a double curse. This is the only way by which the long-continued desolations of Palestine can be accounted, for it is naturally a fertile and beautiful land. That Palestine would be thus involved in the sin of Israel is clearly foretold in the prophetic Scriptures. Thus Moses at the commencement of their history warned them that if they apostatised and turned away to other gods, not only would they themselves be scattered among the nations, but the generations to come, and "the foreigner that shall come from a far land, shall say when they see the plagues of that land, and the sickness wherewith the Lord hath made it sick, . . . even all the nations shall say, Wherefore hath the Lord done thus unto this land? What meaneth the heat of this great anger? Then men shall say, Because they forsook the covenant of Jehovah, the God of their fathers, which He hath made with them when He brought them forth out of the land of Egypt. . . . Therefore the anger of the Lord was kindled against this land, to bring upon it all the curse that is written in this book" (Deut. xxix. 22-27). But when the covenant relationship between God and Israel is restored, then the curse shall be lifted from the land too, and Messiah shall not only *"raise up the tribes* of Jacob" (ver. 6), but He shall *"raise up the land"* also (ver. 8), and the land of Israel shall, under His rule, be as never before—a land flowing with milk and honey, and "the glory of all lands" (Ezek. xx. 15).

But not only will He *raise* up the land from its ruin and desolations, but He shall *"make them inherit the desolate heritages"*—that is, the possessions which have been long desolate shall return to their rightful owners. Here Messiah is the greater than Joshua, who brings His people into the promised land, and apportions to each his inheritance—a hint, probably, of the future re-division of the land, which is to be accomplished under Messiah's superintendence (see Ezek. xlvii. 13-23).

The ninth verse continues to show in which way the new covenant relationship between God and Israel will be made outwardly manifest:

> "To say to them that are bound, Go forth;
> To them that are in darkness, Show yourselves."

The terms "bound" and "in darkness" describe primarily Israel's condition in captivity, and remind us of chap. xlii. 22, where the prophet laments:

> "But this is a people robbed and spoiled;
> They are all of them snared in holes,
> And they are hid in prison houses;
> They are for a prey, and none delivereth,
> For a spoil, and none saith, Restore."

And so Israel has remained for many centuries, and
will do so until, at His command, the prison doors of
their captivity shall open, and the fetters by which they
were held bound under Gentile oppression shall break,
and they shall "go forth" into light and liberty.   But it
is not merely outward liberation that these words describe;
for just as Israel's national captivity was the consequence
and outward symbol of the *inner* bondage of sin and
death, into which they had brought themselves by their
apostasy from Him who is the Fountain of light and life,
so will the future deliverance from the yoke of the Gentiles
be but the outward sign and accompaniment of the light
and liberty of the children of God, into which saved
Israel shall then be brought.

And into this spiritual light and liberty as many of us
as are "in Christ" have already entered; and as we read
these words in the prophecy, we feel that they describe
exactly what in the spiritual sphere has been accomplished
for us. *We* were bound; but His Word came and set us
free, and by His power *we* have been delivered from the
power and authority of darkness, and have been translated
into the kingdom of God's dear Son. *We* have been in
darkness; but God, who said light shall shine out of
darkness, hath shined into our hearts, to give us the light
of the knowledge of the glory of God in the face of Jesus
Christ.

The Shepherd's Tender Care for His Flock

In the lines which follow (vers. 9-12) we recognise
the familiar and beautiful figure of the Shepherd and
the flock, although it is true that in this part of the
prophecy the person of the Redeemer falls for the moment
into the background while the prophet is occupied in
describing the experiences of the redeemed:

"They shall feed in the ways,
And on all bare heights shall be their pasture;
They shall not hunger nor thirst,
Neither shall the heat nor sun smite them;
For He that hath mercy on them shall lead them,
Even by the springs of water shall He guide them."

The redeemed people on their way back home shall not need to turn aside into devious paths in search of necessaries, but He who fed their fathers forty years with manna from heaven, and gave them water out of a rock, will provide for them where they are, so that *"they shall feed in the ways"*—*i. e.,* on the trodden roads along which they shall have to go; and should these "ways" lead across *"bare heights"* (*shephayim,* bare sandy hills, steppes), even there shall they find pasture supplied for them. *"And they shall not hunger nor thirst"*; there shall be an end of the wilderness condition of privation and unsatisfied longing. Jehovah-Jesus shall be their Shepherd, and they shall not want. And not only will there be an end to the *want,* but also to the *dangers* which are incidental to a journey across the wilderness.

"Neither the heat nor sun shall smite them."

The "heat" is literally the *sharab,* the mirage, which in the hot sandy plains causes so much distress to the traveller by deceiving and leading him astray—that shall no longer be a source of danger to them; neither shall the hot rays of the sun smite them, because

"He that hath mercy on them"—

the One who, as the word implies, is by His very nature "full of compassion," and whose mercy has now been fully provoked by the long-continued sufferings and misery of His people—is Himself at their head, guiding them in safety, and *"gently leading"* them by springs of real and refreshing water, instead of the deceptive mirages which they might otherwise weary themselves to pursue—in the same manner as the Good Shepherd is described as causing His sheep to lie down in green pastures, and "tenderly leading them" by "the waters of rest" in ver. 2 of Psa. xxiii., where the same word is used.

And as we read this part of the prophecy and compare it with Rev. vii., where it is applied to the blessed condition of the redeemed in heaven, we are reminded of the fact that the condition of saved Israel by and by will be an earthly reflection, and a foretaste in time, of the eternal blessedness of "the multitude which no man can number" throughout eternity.

The Church, too, is now in the wilderness, the land of hunger and thirst—of danger and of the valley of the shadow of death: but the "Shepherd of Israel" is our Shepherd too, and "He goeth before" to deliver and provide for *His own,* guiding them with His counsel, until He shall receive them into glory, where "He that sitteth on the throne shall spread His tabernacle over them. And they shall hunger no more, neither thirst any more; neither shall the sun strike upon them, nor any heat—for the Lamb which is in the midst of the throne shall be their Shepherd, and shall guide them unto fountains of waters of life, and God shall wipe away every tear from their eyes."

And when the great day has come for the ransomed of the Lord to return back to their ancient home no obstacle shall be allowed to stand in their way, and every hindrance shall be removed:

"And I will make all My mountains a way,
And My highways shall be exalted.
Lo, these shall come from afar;
And lo, these from the north, and from the west,
And these from the land of Sinim."

The very mountains which naturally might be barriers are turned into roads, and the sandy paths of the desert are "exalted," or lifted up into properly made highways; and lest we should stagger in unbelief at the possibility of such a transformation, God says: *"My* mountains, *My* highways," to remind us that He who created can destroy, or change them, according to His good pleasure, and that He is almighty to remove every obstacle, however formidable, if it stands in the way of the progress of His people.

And now behold the various *bands* of exiles returning to their old fatherland: "These, they come from afar"— from some region in the far south or east, since the north and west are afterward mentioned; but wherever they may be, they shall not be forgotten in that day when "the Lord shall set His hand again the second time . . . to assemble the outcasts of Israel, and gather together the dispersed of Judah from the four corners of the earth." "Yea, if any of thine outcasts be in the uttermost parts of heaven, from thence will the Lord thy God gather thee, and from thence will He fetch thee; and the Lord thy God will bring thee into the land which thy fathers possessed, and thou shalt possess it" (Isa. xi. 11-16; Deut. xxx. 1-10).

"And behold these from the north and the sea" (which latter usually stands for the west in the Hebrew)—the regions where the great mass of the scattered people are to be found at the present time; "and these" from faraway "Sinim"—standing most probably for China, which, as is shown by Gesenius and others, was already known by the name of "Sin," or "Tchin," in Isaiah's time.

Thus from north to south, east and west—

> "The ransomed of Jehovah shall return
> And come with singing unto Zion
> And everlasting joy shall be upon their heads:
> They shall obtain joy and gladness,
> And sorrow and sighing shall flee away."

For the glorious results which issue from the restored covenant relations between Jehovah and His people Israel, brought about by Him who is Himself "the Covenant of the people" (ver. 8), as well as the Light of the Gentiles, and God's salvation unto the ends of the earth—the whole creation is called upon to join in a grand chorus of praise:

> *"Sing, O Heavens;*
> *And be joyful, O earth;*
> *And break forth into singing, O mountains;*
> *For Jehovah hath comforted His people,*
> *And will have compassion upon His afflicted"* (ver. 13).

In times past the heavens and the earth were often called upon as witnesses of Israel's apostasy and consequent punishment. Thus, this very prophet begins his book:

"Hear, O heavens; give ear, O earth: . . .
I have nourished and brought up children, and they have rebelled
    against Me."

Thus also Moses, at the very beginning of their history, "called heaven and earth to witness against them," that in case of their apostasy they would soon utterly perish from off the land whereunto they were going over Jordan to possess it (Deut. iv. 26).

But the same heavens and the same earth, which have been spectators of, and have shared in, God's sorrow over Israel's sin and long-continued sufferings, shall yet witness Israel's repentance and future blessing.

And not only as passive witnesses, but also as active participants, are the heavens and the earth called upon to join; for as it was involved in the curse in consequence of man's sin, so also will the blessing of God's people react reflectively on the whole universe; and, as we are more clearly taught in the New Testament, the consummation of redemption, and the glorious liberty of the children of God, shall become the focus from which the whole creation shall be glorified.

The joy and the song which will then permeate the universe will be the joy of the God of Israel in welcoming back His long-wandering national prodigal.

Thus we read in Zeph. iii. 17, "Jehovah, thy God, in the midst of thee is mighty; He will save; He will rejoice over thee with joy; He will rest" (or "be silent" in His love, as if it were too full and deep for utterance); *"He will joy over thee with singing"*—fervent and wonderful words, from which we can infer, in a measure, the sorrow which now fills the heart of God, because the "dearly beloved of His soul" (Jer. xii. 7) is absent and wandering from Him—a sorrow which found expression in the tears which Jesus shed over Jerusalem. But, just as on the return of the prodigal son, in Luke xv., the Father calls on all around "to eat and be merry," to rejoice in his joy; and just as the Good Shepherd, when His saving task is accomplished, cannot contain Himself in His joy, but "calleth together his friends and neighbours, saying, *Rejoice with Me,* for I have found My sheep which was lost," so also on the return of His beloved Israel will God call on the whole universe, saying, "Sing, O heavens; be joyful, O earth, and break forth into singing, O mountains!"

The ground and reason of this universal joy is this—

"For Jehovah hath comforted His people, and will have mercy upon His afflicted."

Sin has brought nothing but sorrow to Israel, and long has been the night of weeping which is to culminate in a yet future darker hour than they have ever yet experienced, but joy will come at the "breaking of the morning," and as one whom his mother comforteth, so will

Jehovah comfort them, and they shall be comforted in Jerusalem (Isa. lxvi. 13).

It is interesting to note how the future tense here alternates with the perfect: "He *hath* comforted His people and *will* [or 'shall'] have mercy upon His afflicted."

The act of consolation is spoken of as taking place once and for all; but the mercy, or compassion, which is the basis of it, continues for ever, and will follow them all through their days on earth. It is even so with us. When first, broken-hearted, we come to God by way of the Cross, we are comforted with His salvation; but, even after our conversion, we still need His mercy, and shall need it to the end, so long as we are in this body of sin and death; and blessed be His Name, "His mercy endureth for ever."

God's Infinite and Tender Love for His People

But from the mountain-top of the vision of Israel's blessedness in the future, the prophet returns for a moment to the period of Israel's captivity and suffering. Here, in the valley of humiliation, he sees the daughter of Zion sitting dejected and disconsolate, lamenting—

"Jehovah hath forsaken me, and the Lord hath forgotten me" (ver. 14).

In reply, there follow some words which are among the most beautiful and tender to be found in Scripture, by which the love of Jehovah for His people is shown to be as inalienable, and stronger and deeper than the love of a mother:

"Can a woman forget her sucking child,
  That she should not have compassion on the son of her womb?
  Yea, they may forget [or better, 'even though they may forget'],
  Yet will I not forget thee" (ver. 15).

The love of a mother for her infant child is supposed to be the strongest tie in nature; but, blessed be God, there is a tie even stronger than that, binding the Infinite God to those whom He has brought into covenant relation with Himself. It is the threefold cord of the faithfulness of the Triune God, which can never be broken; it is that everlasting love of Jehovah, which is stronger than death, and which all the many waters of our sins and apostasies cannot quench.

The same truth, under a similar figure, is brought out in Jer. xxxi. 3, which is really a dialogue, the word "saying," which is in italics in the middle of the verse, not being found in the original.

There also the prophet sees the daughter of Israel sitting desolate and saying to herself—

"Jehovah hath appeared of old [or 'afar off' in distance or time] unto me"—

as if to imply that now He is not near and hath forgotten her. But there breaks in the answer of God—

"Yea [or 'and'] I have loved thee with an everlasting love; therefore with lovingkindness have I drawn thee"—

as much as to say, "My love is the same to-day as 'of old,' when I first appeared unto thy fathers, for I am Jehovah, the God not merely of the past, but of the present, and I am ever at hand waiting to be gracious. It was thy sin which robbed thee of the *sense* of My love, and of the *consciousness* of My near presence."

There follows another figure which sets forth the intensity of Jehovah's love for Israel:

"Behold, I have graven thee upon the palms of My hands: thy walls are continually before Me" (ver. 16).

Orientals are fond of puncturing ornamental figures and mementoes on their hands and arms with an indelible dye; and this figure the great God condescends to use in order to show His inalienable affection for His people and His land.

On the inside of His hands, nearer and dearer to Him than any other object—yea, as near to Him as He is to Himself—is the picture of His beloved Israel; and as to the walls of Zion, they are indelibly graven before Him—can either ever be forgotten? "O Israel," He says—

"Thou shalt not be forgotten of Me."

"For a small moment, on account of thy sin, I may seem to have forsaken thee, but with great mercies will I gather thee; in a little wrath I hid My face from thee for a moment, but with everlasting kindness will I have mercy on thee, saith Jehovah thy Redeemer" (Isa. liv. 7, 8).

But I almost fear that some of you, my dear readers, will be disappointed in reading this exposition, for you have been used to apply these beautiful and precious promises to yourselves, and now I seem to take them all from you by applying them to Israel.

If this be your feeling, let me remind you that all things are yours, and that "in Christ" you are blessed with all spiritual blessings in heavenly places, of which no one in heaven or earth can rob or despoil you.

You can never be a loser but only a gainer by being shown the concrete connection and primary sense of Scripture; but remember that in these and all His words and acts to Israel the heart of Israel's God is opened up to you, whoever you may be, who have learned to put your trust under the shadow of His wings. For this God is your God for ever and ever—the Father of your Lord and Saviour Jesus Christ, who wants you to learn from

His infinite grace and faithfulness to His unworthy Israel, that His faithfulness to you, too, can never fail.

Or, need you be reminded that His love to you, too, is unchanging and inalienable, and that *He Himself hath said,* "I will in no wise fail thee, neither will I in any wise forsake thee"? Then let me commend you to Rom. viii. and to the grand climax reached by the Apostle—

"For I am persuaded that neither death, nor life, nor angels, nor principalities, nor powers, nor things present, nor things to come; nor height, nor depth, nor any other creature, shall be able to separate us from the love of God which is in Christ Jesus our Lord."

But this is a digression.

After the fervent outburst of God's heart of love to Israel there follows, in vers. 17-21, direct promise—

"Thy children make haste"—

i. e., to obey the signal to return to their ancient possessions, or, as the Targum and Septuagint version, by adopting another pointing, have it, "Thy *builders* make haste"—namely, to restore and rebuild the land: the word in the Hebrew for son and builder being the same.

They "make haste," for the set time for God to favour Zion has now fully come, and there must no longer be delay in the fulfilment of His promise. Neither shall any hinderer or obstacle be allowed to bar the way—

"Thy destroyers and they that made thee waste shall go forth of thee."

Now "the boar out of the wood" doth waste the maternal home of Israel's wandering sons, "and the wild beast of the field doth devour it." Jerusalem is trampled down of the Gentiles, who say, "The ancient high places are ours in possession," but it is only "until the times of the

Gentiles be fulfilled"; and then the command shall be given "to cast out the horns of the Gentiles which lifted up their horn over the land of Judah to scatter it" (Zech. i. 21).

And now Zion, or Jerusalem, as the mother, is to lift up the eyes that have been cast down for so long on account of the banishment of her children, for from all directions those whom she thought lost are coming back to her—

> "Lift up thine eyes round about and behold;
> All these gather themselves together and come to thee;
> As I live, saith Jehovah."

The expression *chai ani*—"as I live"—is the customary form of an affirmative oath when Jehovah swears.

It is an oath by His own existence. He, so to say, pledges His own life for the certain fulfilment of what He has just promised, which, in this instance, is the restoration and blessing of Israel; and yet—one almost shudders to think of it—there are many who, in spite of God's oath and promise, daringly deny that the Jews ever will be restored, or that there is any national future for Israel at all!

God's word is of itself certain; but when anything which He has promised is confirmed by Him with an oath, it becomes doubly immutable.

Not, however, as if an oath were needed to strengthen His purpose or determination to fulfil what He has promised, but "He swears by Himself," *in order to confirm faith in us,* so that *by two immutable things*—namely, His promise and His oath—in which it is impossible for God to lie, *we might have a strong consolation* [*or 'encouragement"*], who have fled for refuge, to lay hold upon the "hope set before us" (Heb. vi. 18).

But to return to our text. The glory of a mother is her children, and so Zion's returned sons will be to her like the ornaments with which women are fond of adorning themselves—

"Thou shalt surely clothe thee with them as with an ornament.
And gird thyself with them like a bride"—

"Like the ornamental girdle which a bride fastens round her wedding dress" (ver. 18).

As to the land, instead of being filled with ruins and desolation in the absence of its proper inhabitants, and because of the tyrants that have "swallowed it up," it shall not only be delivered from the rule of the oppressor, and be lifted out of its waste condition, but it shall even become too narrow for the restored and blessed people—

"For as for thy waste and desolate places,
And thy land that hath been destroyed,
Surely now shalt thou be too strait for the inhabitants;
And they that swallowed thee up shall be far away;
The children of thy bereavement"—

literally, "the children of thy desolate condition," the children that shall swarm around Zion after her long widowhood and her bereavement, more especially in the final great tribulation—

"Shall yet say in thine ears,
The place is too strait for me—
Give place to me that I may dwell" (vers. 19, 20).

These verses remind us of the jubilant exclamation in chap. liv.:

"Sing ['exult'], O barren—thou that didst not bear—
Break forth into singing, and cry, thou that didst not travail:
For more are the children of the desolate
Than of the married wife, saith Jehovah."

The words are addressed to Jerusalem, the counter-part of Sarah in her barrenness at first, and her fruitful-ness afterwards.   She is barren now—not, indeed, because she had never borne children, but because in her captivity and exile she had been robbed of her children, and as a holy city had all this time given birth to none.   But she is to awake and sing, because the children that shall gather around her after her long period of desolateness will be more than those in the time before her calamity came upon her she had as a married wife—yea, so great will be the increase of Zion's future population that, instead of bewailing her lonely and desolate condition, she shall even hear her children say "in her own ears" that the place is too strait, and the call to the surrounding nations: "Give place [literally, 'give way,' or 'fall back'], that I may be able to settle down."   I have elsewhere pointed out[10] that the land which God by oath and covenant promised to the fathers is about fifty times as large as the part which hitherto the Jews actually possessed, and that it is only pitiable ignorance which made the superficial Voltaire utter the blasphemy that the God of the Jews must have been a little God, because He gave His people a land no larger than Wales, and called it "a good land and large" (Exod. iii. 8).   Surely a land which includes within its boundaries an area at least one-third more than the whole of France may with right be called "a large land"; but it is possible that even the larger land, with its desert parts transformed into fruitful fields, will not suffice to hold the whole of blessed Israel in the millennial period, so great and rapid will be the increase of the saved remnant, as would seem from these verses in our prophecy, and from Zech. x. 8-10, where the Lord says: "I will hiss [or 'pipe'] for them, and gather them, and they shall increase

---

[10] See "The Jewish Problem."

as they have increased. . . . I will bring them again also out of the land of Egypt, and gather them out of Assyria, and I will bring them into the land of Gilead, and Lebanon, *and place shall not be found for them."*

All this is followed by an expression of surprise and astonishment on the part of Zion at the happy change of her formerly sad lot:

"Then shalt thou say in thine heart,
  Who hath borne me these, seeing I have been bereaved [or
    'robbed'] of children;
  And barren and an exile ['banished'], and wandering to and fro?
  And who hath brought up these?
  Behold, I was left alone. These, where were they?" (ver. 21).

The imagery of this verse is one of great beauty. It represents a mother who in the time of calamity and war is suddenly made a widow, bereft of all her children, and herself carried away captive and made to wander from land to land. Often had she sat and wept in hopelessness over her sad lot. Suddenly, however, she finds herself restored to her own ancient home, and surrounded by a large and happy family. Is it any wonder that she can scarcely believe her own eyes at what she sees, or her ears at what she hears, and that she breaks out in expressions of astonishment and glad surprise?

Lone and desolate Zion is that mother, and restored Israel her children. The description she gives of herself is significant. *Galmudah*—"barren," "one hard as stone," and utterly incapacitated from bearing children — like Sarah, who believed it not possible that she could bear Isaac. But again it shall be shown that "nothing is too hard for the Lord" (Gen. xviii. 14) ; who will make the barren woman [Zion] once again to keep house, and to be a "joyful mother of children. Hallelujah!" (Psa. cxiii. 9).

The Means of Israel's Restoration and the
Manner of Their Conversion

We now come to the last section of this wonderful chapter, consisting of vers. 22-26, in which the prophecy takes, so to say, a step backward in the vision of the future, and describes the *means* God will employ to bring the remnant of His people back to their ancient home, and the glory of Israel in the millennial period:

"Thus saith the Lord Jehovah,
  Behold, I will lift up Mine hand to the nations,
  And set up My ensign to the peoples;
  And they shall bring thy sons in their bosom,
  And thy daughters shall be carried upon their shoulders" (ver. 22).

The lifting up, or swaying of God's hand, in order to beckon and command, and the setting up of an ensign or standard as a signal to the nations to carry out His purposes, are familiar figures in the Book of Isaiah. It was at the lifting up of such a signal on the part of God, when the cup of Israel's apostasy was full, that the nations came and desolated their land, and carried the people into captivity; else all the forces of the universe could not have prevailed against them. Thus the prophet forewarns them in an earlier prophecy:

"And He will lift an ensign to the nations from far,
  And will hiss ['pipe'] for them from the end of the earth;
  And behold they shall come with speed swiftly;
  None shall be weary or stumble among them: . . .
  Their roaring shall be like a lion,
  They shall roar like young lions;
  Yea, they shall roar and lay hold of the prey,
  And carry it away safe: and there shall be none to deliver"
    (Isa. v: 26-30).

But He who used the nations to scatter Israel will also,

when His time to favour Zion comes, use them as His instruments to gather them:

"And it shall come to pass in that day
That the Lord shall set up His hand again the second time,
To recover the remnant of His people. . . .
And He shall set up an ensign for the nations,
And shall assemble the outcasts of Israel,
And gather together the dispersed of Judah
From the four corners of the earth" (Isa. xi. 11, 12).

And what a change will then be wrought by the power of God in the attitude and conduct of the nations in relation to Israel!

When in His righteous anger against His people He lifted up His standard to the nations, saying, "Go ye up upon her walls and destroy" (Jer. v. 10), they came like savage beasts, "roaring like lions, and taking hold of their prey, and carrying it away safe, so that none could deliver." And this savage cruelty has been characteristic of all the four great Gentile world-powers, who in prophecy are symbolised by wild beasts (Dan. vii.), who are permitted to tear Zion's sons, and to tread down Jerusalem "until the times of the Gentiles be fulfilled." Still it is "the *boar* out of the wood, and *the wild beast* of the field" (Psa. lxxx. 13), who ravage and devour Israel's land and people. But by God's power the "beast's heart" (Dan. iv. 16) shall be taken from their Gentile oppressors, who shall be subdued and awed by the sense that it is "the Most High who ruleth in the kingdom of men," and that the centre of His rule over the earth is Mount Zion.

Then, when His signal is given for His peoples' return, "They shall bring thy sons *in their bosom,* and thy daughters shall be carried *upon their shoulders,*" with all the tender care which parents and nurses lavish upon delicately nurtured children. And instead of being subjected to all sorts of indignities and humiliations, and often even hearing the tyrants' cry, "Bow down, that we may go over; and thou hast laid thy back as the ground, and as the street to them that go over" (chap. li. 23)—

"Kings shall now be thy nursing [or 'foster'] fathers,
And queens ['their princesses'] thy nursing mothers—
They shall bow down to thee to the earth
And lick the dust of thy feet.
And thou shalt know that I am Jehovah;
And they that wait for Me shall not be ashamed" ["or even He
    whose waiting ones are not put to shame"].

On reading this and similar prophecies we must bear in mind—

First, that they refer to a restoration in blessing subsequent to the dark cloud of Israel's final apostasy and final sufferings. Some seem puzzled at the apparent contradiction in the Scriptures in reference to this subject; for while some prophecies speak of a return of the Jews to Palestine in a condition of unbelief, there are other Scriptures which announce, in unmistakable terms, that Israel will be brought back in a condition of repentance and faith. The solution of the apparent difficulty is to be found, I believe, in the fact that the future restoration will be accomplished in different sections and at different stages, even as was the case with their dispersion. It seems from Scripture that in relation to Israel and the land there will be a restoration, before the second advent of our Lord, of the state of things as they existed at the time of His first advent, when the threads of God's dealing with them nationally were finally dropped, not to be taken up again "until the times of the Gentiles shall be fulfilled."

There was at that time a number of Jews in Palestine representative of the nation; but compared with the number of their brethren, who were already a diaspora among

the nations, they were a mere minority, and not in a politically independent condition.

So it will be again. There will be at first, as compared
with the whole nation, only a representative minority in
Palestine, and a Jewish state will be formed, probably
under a Gentile suzerainty. The nucleus of this politically
dependent Jewish state is already to be seen in the 120,000
Jews who have wandered back from all regions of the
earth to the land of their fathers.

Already Jerusalem is almost a Jewish city, while the
thirty and more Jewish colonies which dot the land "are
so many milestones marking the advance which Israel is
making toward national rehabilitation." And in no other
country in the world do the Jews, to the same extent,
represent the nation. If any one wants to see the whole
Jewish people in miniature, let him go to Jerusalem and to
the other Jewish settlements in Palestine. There you can
see them from east and west; from India and from the
burning plains of South Arabia; from the extreme north
of Siberia and the Caucasus: there you can hear them
speaking nearly all languages under heaven.

Around this nucleus a large number more, from all
parts of the world, will be gathered, and before long this
part of the Zionist programme may be realised, and Palestine may become the "openly recognised, legally assured
home" of the Jews.[11]

But what follows? After a brief interval of outward
prosperity there come a night of anguish. "Alas! for that
day is great, so that none is like it; it is even the time of
Jacob's trouble; but he shall be saved out of it" (Jer.
xxx. 7). The cause and occasion of the night of sorrow

---

[11] This was written in 1906 long before the war and the events
which have since transpired.

for Jacob is the yet future siege and final gathering of
the nations against Jerusalem.

In some of the prophecies this solemn event is set forth
with such clearness that it reads like history.   "Behold,
I will make Jerusalem a cup of reeling unto all the peoples
round about. . . . And in that day will I make Jerusalem
a burdensome stone for all peoples; all that burden themselves with it shall be cut to pieces, and all the nations of
the earth shall be gathered against it. . . . Behold, the
day of the Lord cometh, and thy spoil shall be divided in
the midst of thee, for I will gather all nations against
Jerusalem to battle: and the city shall be taken, and the
houses rifled, and the women ravished, and half of the
city shall go into captivity" (Zech. xii. 2, 3; xiv. 1, 2).

And not only will this be the case with Jerusalem, but
"it shall come to pass that *in all the land,* saith Jehovah,
two parts therein shall be cut off, . . . and I will bring
the third part through the fire, and will refine them as
silver is refined, and will try them as gold is tried."

It is the time of Jacob's greatest trouble—the very dark-
est hour of Israel's long night of sorrow.

The enemy thinks his end almost accomplished; he has
but to lift his hand for one final blow, and Israel will be
no more—when, suddenly, in the clouds of heaven, attended by His angelic hosts and "all the saints with Him,"
Israel's true Messiah and Deliverer appears, "and His
feet shall stand in that day upon the Mount of Olives,
which is before Jerusalem on the east."   The enemies'
hand stretched out to give the final blow becomes suddenly withered: "And the multitude of all the nations that
fight against Ariel, even all that fight against her and her
stronghold, and that distress her, shall be as a dream, a
vision of the night.   And it shall be as when an hungry
man dreameth, and, behold, he eateth; but he waketh,
and his soul is empty: or as when a thirsty man dream-

eth, and, behold, he drinketh; but he awaketh, and behold, he is faint, and his soul hath appetite: so shall the multitude of all nations be that fight against Mount Zion" (Isa. xxix. 7, 8).

But, simultaneous with their outward deliverance, there takes place also Israel's spiritual redemption: "And I will pour upon the house of David, and upon the inhabitants of Jerusalem, the spirit of grace and of supplication; and they shall look upon Me whom they have pierced: and they shall mourn for him as one mourneth for his only son, and shall be in bitterness for him as one that is in bitterness for his firstborn. . . . In that day there shall be a fountain opened to the house of David and to the inhabitants of Jerusalem, for sin and for uncleanness." [12] But though Jerusalem and Palestine will be the centre of these awful and solemn events, the whole world, especially the whole of Christendom, will be more or less involved in them.

When the final judgments of God are abroad in the earth, and when the anti-Christian rage and persecution will be everywhere directed, not only against the confessors of Christ, but against those in Israel who are faithful to the God of their fathers, there will be weeping and mourning and heart-searching among the scattered tribes of Israel in all the lands of their dispersion. And when at last, in the hour of their deepest need, their long-rejected, crucified Messiah appears for their deliverance—when His blessed feet "shall stand in that day upon the Mount of Olives"— they will be almost simultaneously made aware of it; for though they may not all at once behold Him with their eyes, the whole world, and nature generally, will be conscious of, and respond to, the visible Appearing and Presence of the Son of God. And the spared remnant of the dispersed of Israel will, like their brethren in Jeru-

---

[12] From "The Ancient Scriptures and the Modern Jew."

salem, hail Him—though at first, it may be, from a distance—whom they crucified, and turn to Him in true
repentance and love.   These will, at the lifting up of
God's standard to the nations, return in a condition of
faith, and such Scriptures as Deut. xxx. 1-10; Jer. xxxi.
6-13; l. 4, 5, which speak of their restoration *as subsequent to their conversion, and conditional upon it,* shall be
literally fulfilled.

And in this return in blessing the nations will not only
acquiesce, but will take an active part, and, as far as the
more distant nations are concerned, the prophetic Scriptures tell us how this will be brought about.   Among the
nations (or their armies) who shall be gathered against
Jerusalem, and who shall be overtaken by sudden destruction at the appearing of Christ, some shall be spared, even
as we read in the last chapter of Isaiah's great prophecy:

"I will gather all nations and tongues,
And they shall come and shall see My glory,
And I will set a sign among them;
And I will send such as escape of them unto the nations—
Unto Tarshish, Pul, and Lud, that draw the bow.
To Tubal and Javan—to the isles afar off.
And they shall declare My glory among the nations" (Isa. lxvi.
    18, 19).

They shall tell their peoples the awful and wonderful
things they had witnessed—the unspeakable majesty of
Him who descended from heaven as the Deliverer of Israel, and the relation which this heavenly King bears to the
despised Jews who are still in their midst:

"And they shall bring all your brethren out of all the nations,
For an offering unto Jehovah;
Upon horses, and in chariots, and in litters, and upon mules, and
    upon swift beasts,
To My holy mountain, Jerusalem, saith Jehovah,
As the children of Israel bring their offering in a clean vessel
    into the house of Jehovah" (ver. 20).

Secondly: When we read of the homage which shall be paid to Israel in the millennial period, and of the prosperity which they shall then enjoy, so that even kings and princes shall bow themselves down to the earth before them, we must remember that Israel will thus be honoured not for their own sakes, but because of the *Holy One* of Israel who shall be in the midst of them, and that they themselves, after the final ordeal of suffering through which they shall have passed, shall be a perfectly holy people, and the centre of blessing for the whole earth. "Do not imagine that any temporal glory or power will be entrusted by God to Israel as an unconverted nation. That would not be for the glory of God, nor would it be for the welfare of Israel and the world. They must be led through deep waters. They must be brought through fearful judgments. They must experience the wrath and the indignation of the Lord. They must be led into the valley of humiliation. Then will the Lord appear unto them, even as Joseph appeared unto his brethren, and the spirit of grace and of supplication will be poured out upon them; and there will be weeping such as this world has never heard; and there will be repenting and contrition more profound than the angels have ever witnessed upon earth, for they shall mourn over Him as over their only child; and then God, having cast them into the fire of His indignation, and having by the Holy Ghost worked in them repentance, and granted to them the remission of sin, shall fit them for the wonderful work that is before them in the future, for a nation that has come through such repentance and through such faith—a nation that has so tasted the bitterness of sin, and the sweetness of the infinite love of God, which is stronger than death—will then go on for a thousand years without ever looking back." [13]

---

[13] Adolph Saphir.

Yes, so much will Israel in the millennial period express the original Divine ideal of a Theocracy, so like will the congregation of the Lord be, both in purpose and manifestation one with its Divine Head, that for any among the nations to call themselves by the name of Jacob, and to surname themselves by the name of Israel, will be equivalent to saying, "I am for Jehovah" (Isa. xliv. 5) ; while hostility and antagonism to Israel will be rebellion against God. Therefore—

"That nation and kingdom that will not serve thee shall perish—
Yea, those nations shall utterly perish. . . .
And the sons of them that afflicted thee shall come bending unto thee ;
And all they that despised thee shall bow themselves down at the soles of thy feet ;
And they shall call thee, The city of Jehovah—
Zion of the Holy One of Israel" (Isa. lx.).

The last three verses of this great prophecy are God's answer to the question, "How can these things be?" and assure us that, however improbable this may appear looked at from the human standpoint, Jehovah shall show that there is nothing impossible with Him—

"Shall the prey be taken from the mighty?
Or the lawful captive [or 'the captive of the just'] be delivered?" [14]

---

[14] "*Shebhi*" (captive), though properly an abstract, is continually used as a collective term for captives. Its combination here with *Tsadik* (righteous) has perplexed interpreters. Houbigant, Lowth, Ewald, and Knobel read *aritz* (terrible one), as in the next verse, which is a mere subterfuge. Rosenmüller follows Albert Schultens in giving to *Tsadik* the sense of rigid, stern, severe; which is not in the least justified by Hebrew usage. Beck follows J. D. Michaelis in explaining it to mean victorious, according to the sense of vistory now commonly put upon *Tsadik*, notwithstanding the objection of Gesenius that there is no authority in usage for the application of this term to the successes of the wicked, without regard to its original import. Symmachus, Jarchi, Aben Ezra, and

These questions state the two great obstacles to the fulfilment of the promises of Israel's future great deliverance and blessing.

The first line emphasises the *might* of their Gentile oppressors, who are likened to a giant or mighty man of war who will not part with the prey ("malkoach"), into which his teeth are firmly set, ready to devour. The second line raises the question, How can they be delivered? seeing the tyrant who holds them is, so to say, justified in doing so, the captives having been lawfully delivered into his hands. Not, indeed (to use the figure of the next chapter), that Jehovah was obliged to sell His people, like a bankrupt' debtor, who sells his sons and daughters to his creditors, but by their iniquities and apostasies they had sold themselves (Isa. l. 1), and given their oppressors a certain right or claim to bear rule over them. The difficulties, both physical and moral, are indeed great, and to human probabilities insurmountable—

"But thus saith Jehovah:
  Even the captives of the mighty shall be taken away,
  And the prey of the terrible One shall be delivered;
  For I will contend with him that contendeth with thee, and I will
      save thy children;
  And I will feed them that oppress thee with their own flesh;
  And they shall be drunk with their own blood, as with sweet
      wine;
  And all flesh shall know that I Jehovah am thy Saviour;
  And thy Redeemer is the Mighty One of Jacob" (vers. 25, 26).

Hitzig understand the phrase to mean the righteous captives, *i.e.*, taken from the righteous. But this explanation of *Tsadik* is harsh, and the parallelism, as well as the analogy of ver. 25, requires that *Tsadik* should be referred to the subject, not the object of the action. The English version makes it agree directly with *Shebhi* in the sense of lawful captive, *i.e.*, one who has been lawfully enslaved, or one who deserves to be a captive. The simplest and most obvious construction of the words is that which makes them mean the captives of a righteous conqueror. The argument may then be stated thus: Shall the captives even of a righteous conqueror be freed in such a case?"

Thus are the two obstacles removed; for over against the *might* of the tyrant, who holds His people captive, over against *all the physical difficulties,* shall be matched the irresistible power of Almighty God, who "will contend with them that contend with thee," or, in the words of Jer. l. 34: *"Their Redeemer is strong,* Jehovah of Hosts is His Name, *He* shall thoroughly plead their cause, that He may give rest to the land and disquiet the inhabitants of Babylon"—who stand in some of the prophecies as the representatives of the oppressors of Israel in the latter days. Then, secondly, over against Israel's many sins and iniquities, which gave the enemy a certain claim and power over them, there shall be displayed *the infinite grace* of Jehovah, their "Saviour" and "Redeemer," who, in spite of their long-continued and grievous apostasy, has never broken His covenants, nor severed His relation with them as "the God of Israel" and "the Mighty One of Jacob," and who will soon demonstrate in the sight of all the nations that, as touching the election, they are still "beloved for the fathers' sakes," and that he that toucheth them toucheth the apple of His eye:

"Is Ephraim My dear son?
Is he a pleasant child?
For as often as I speak against him,
I do earnestly remember him still.
Therefore My bowels are troubled for him;
I will surely have mercy upon him, saith Jehovah"
(Jer. xxxi. 20).

And not only will He deliver His people, but the day of Israel's salvation is the day of doom of Israel's enemies, who are also the enemies of God and of His kingdom:

"And I will feed them that oppress thee with their own flesh,
And they shall be drunk with their own blood as with sweet [or
'new'] wine"—

of which one must drink much to become drunk, a figure indicating that all they that have devoured Israel shall now themselves be devoured (Jer. xxx. 16), or, in the striking language of Isaiah—

"Wherefore, hear now this, thou afflicted and drunken, but not
    with wine;
Thus saith thy Lord, Jehovah, and thy God, that pleadeth the
    cause of His people:
Behold, I have taken out of thine hand the cup of staggering,
Even the bowl of the cup of My fury;
Thou shalt no more drink it again.
And I will put it into the hand of them that afflict thee,
Which have said to thy soul, Bow down that we may go over,
And thou hast laid thy back as the ground,
And as the street to them that go over" (Isa. li. 21-23).

Thus the truth which may already be read in all history will be strikingly demonstrated—namely, that no nation or individual can lift up their hands against Israel and prosper, and that although He may permit this or that man, or nation, to rise up as His scourge against His people for a time, they are sure in the end to experience the truth of His ancient promise to Abraham: "I will bless them that bless thee, and him that curseth thee will I curse" (Gen. xii. 3).

Finally, as we read in these last verses of the prey being taken from the mighty one, and of the "lawful captives" delivered, we observe once again that the redeeming work of God on behalf of Israel nationally sets forth the great spiritual salvation through Christ for men generally. We, too, were by nature the possession and in the power of "a strong man, fully armed," having been taken captive by him in pursuance of God's will. "Satan and death are the mighty conquerors of man, upon whom his sin gives them their lawful claim." [15]

---

[15] See Dean Alford's notes on 2 Tim. ii. 26, in his Greek Testament.

O wretched man that I am, who shall deliver me out
of the body of this death? Blessed be God, there is One
mightier than the mighty, who entered his "court," and
overcame him, and took from him his whole armour
wherein he trusted, and divided his spoil (Luke xi. 21,
22), even our Lord Jesus Christ, "who through death
brought to nought him that had the power of death, that
is, the devil, and delivered all them who through fear of
death were all their lifetime subject to bondage" (Heb. ii.
14, 15), and who is now "ascended on high, leading captivity captive, and has received gifts among men, even
for the rebellious, that the Lord God might dwell amongst
them" (Psa. lxviii. 18). And not only has He by His
death freed us from the bondage of Satan and death, but
by His regenerating Spirit He also sets us free from the
oppression of the great enemy within. "For the law of
the Spirit of life in Christ Jesus made me free from the
law of sin and death; for what the law could not do in
that it was weak through the flesh, God sending His own
Son, in the likeness of sinful flesh, and as an offering for
sin, condemned sin in the flesh, that the requirement of
the law might be fulfilled in us who walk not after the flesh
but after the Spirit" (Rom. viii. 2-4).

APPENDIX I

The Arrangement of the Sacred Calendar

I.—NISAN

Spring Equinox, end of March or beginning of April

DAYS

1 New Moon.

14 The preparation for the Passover and the Paschal Sacrifice.

15 First Day of the Feast of Unleavened Bread.

16 Waving of the first-ripe Omer.

21 Close of the Passover.

II.—IYAR

1 New Moon.

15 "Second," or "a little" Passover.*

18 Lag-be-Omer, or the 33rd day in Omer, *i.e.,* from the presentation of the first-ripe sheaf offered on the second day of the Passover, or the 15th of Nisan.*

III.—SIVAN

1 New Moon.

6 Feast of Pentecost; or of Weeks—7 weeks, or 50 days after the beginning of the Passover, when the two loaves of first-ripe wheat were "waved," commemorative also of the giving of the law on Mount Sinai.

IV.—THAMUS

1 New Moon.

17 Fast; taking of Jerusalem on the 9th by Nebuchadnezzar (and on the 17th by Titus). If the 17th occur on a Sabbath, the Fast is kept on the day following.*

V.—AB

1 New Moon.

9 Fast (threefold destruction of the Temple).*

---

* All Feasts or Fasts in this list marked by an asterisk are of post-Mosaic and some of post-Biblical appointment.

357

VI.—Elul

1 New Moon.

VII.—Tishri

Beginning of Civil Year

1, 2 New Year's Feast.

3 Fast for the murder of Gedaliah.*

10 Day of Atonement; Great Fast.

15 Feast of Tabernacles.

21 Close of Feast of Tabernacles.

22 Octave of the Feast of Tabernacles. (In the Synagogues, on the 23rd, Feast of the Annual Completion of the Reading of the Law.)*

VIII.—Marcheshvan or Cheshvan

1 New Moon.

IV.—Chisleu

1 New Moon.

25 Feast of the Dedication of the Temple, or of Candles, lasting eight days, in remembrance of the Restoration of the Temple after the victory gained by Judas Maccabeus (B. C. 148) over the Syrians.*

X.—Tebeth

1 New Moon.

10 Fast on account of the Siege of Jerusalem.*

XI.—Shebat

1 New Moon.

XII.—Adar

1 New Moon.

13 Fast of Esther. (If it fall on a Sabbath, kept on the Thursday preceding.)*

14 Purim, or Feast of Haman.*

15 Purim Proper.*

APPENDIX II

The Actual Day of the Crucifixion and the Question of the "Three Days and the Three Nights"

It would be too large a question on which to enter here, and one on which there has already been much discussion by men more able and learned than I, as to the day of the week on which the 14th of Nisan (the day the paschal lamb was slain) fell in that year, and as to whether it was on that day, and at the very time, that the lamb, or lambs, were being slain in the Temple court that our Saviour was crucified, or whether it was on that evening at the very time that the Jews were eating their paschal supper that our Lord ate His last Passover with His disciples, during which He instituted the Supper of the New Covenant, when He took the bread and brake it, and said, "Take eat; this is My body, broken [or 'given'] for you," and again, the cup, saying, "This cup is the New Testament in My blood," and that the actual crucifixion did not take place till the 15th of Nisan. It must be admitted that the first of these views is bound up with more and greater difficulties in spite of the almost universal and ancient Christian belief, which is supported even by Jewish tradition and Talmudic sayings, that it was "on the eve of the Sabbath and of the Passover" that Jesus was led forth to death. On both sides of the controversy, and with the consent of all whose view on such a question is worth anything, it is admitted that "our Lord was crucified on the Friday, and that He rose on Sunday," but the question is, was the Friday in that week the 14th of Nisan, or the day of the paschal lamb, or was it the 15th, or the first day of the Passover feast? It seems clear, more particularly from the synoptic Gospels, that the paschal meal of which our Lord partook with His disciples was the regular paschal supper which could not legally be eaten before the evening of the 14th, and, as all the terrible and solemn events of the last night of our Saviour's life intervened between that Supper and His death, the crucifixion must have taken place on the 15th.

But there are difficulties also bound up with this latter view, arising chiefly from statements in the Gospel of John—as, for instance, that the priests and Pharisees when they led Jesus from Caiaphas to Pilate's judgment-hall would not themselves enter "lest they should be defiled, but that they might eat the Passover" (John xviii. 28); and again, "The Jews therefore, because it was the preparation, that the bodies should not remain upon the cross on the Sabbath (the day of that Sabbath was a great, or high, day), asked of Pilate that the legs might be broken, and that they

might be taken away" (John xix. 31). But these Scriptures Dr.
Edersheim and others have explained—

1. That the Passover referred to in the first of these two passages was not the paschal lamb, but the *Chagigah* sacrifices, which
were offered on the 15th of Nisan, and to the objection of Farrar
and others that "there was nothing specially paschal about this
Chagigah," he quotes Dr. Saalschütz, one of the most learned of
Jewish writers, to the effect that "the whole feast and *all its
festive meals* were designated as the Passover"—a view which is
supported also by a passage in the Talmud (Sebach. 99 b, and
Rosh. ha Sh. 5 a), where it is expressly said, "What is the meaning of the term Passover?" (Answer)—"*The Peace Offerings of
the Passover.*"

I must remind my readers that we have not to do in these passages with Bible statements, but with the interpretations and customs in reference to the Passover which existed among the Jews
in the time of Christ. As a rule the Chagigah was always brought
on the 15th of Nisan, and it required Levitical purity.

2. And as to John xix. 31, it has been replied by those who
hold that the day of the Crucifixion was the 15th of Nisan that
the expression, "the day of that Sabbath was a great, or 'high.'
day"—ην γαρ μεγαλη η ημερα εκεινου του σαββατου—does not necessarily imply that it was a double Sabbath, namely, because the
first day of the Passover, which was called a Sabbath, fell on the
ordinary weekly Sabbath, but because it was the second day of the
feast, when the Omer, or "sheaf" of first-fruits, was presented
in the Temple.

I have already stated that the question is too large a one to
enter on here, but the following two points which Dr. Edersheim
quotes from Wieseler are important as showing that St. John, like
the synoptists, places the date of the Crucifixion on the 15th.

1. "Not only the synoptists, but St. John, refers to the custom
of releasing a prisoner at 'the feast,' or, as St. John expressly
calls it, 'at the Passover.' Hence the release of Barabbas, and
with it the crucifixion of Jesus, could not have taken place on the
14th of Nisan, the morning of which could *not* have been designated
as 'the feast,' and still less as 'the Passover.'"

2. "When St. John mentions that the accusers of Jesus went not
into Pilate's judgment-hall 'lest they should be defiled, but that
they might eat the Passover,' he *could not* have referred to their
eating the paschal supper. For the defilement thus incurred would
only have lasted to the evening of that day, whereas the paschal
supper was eaten *after* the evening had commenced, so that *the
defilement of Pilate's judgment-hall in the morning would in no
way have interfered with their eating the paschal lamb. But it
would* have interfered with their either offering or partaking of the

Chagigah on the 15th Nisan." (See the whole important Appendix on the subject in "The Temple and its Ministry.")

But whether on the 14th, when the paschal lamb was actually slain, or on the 15th, which was the first day of the Feast of Passover, the synchronisation of type and antitype in the fulfilment in point of time, as pointed out on pp. 45-47, is sufficiently near. It should also be borne in mind that the paschal lamb was sacrified "between the evenings" of the 14th and 15th of Nisan, namely, before the close of the 14th and the beginning of the 15th, and that the paschal supper which followed later took place on the 15th itself, that is according to Jewish reckoning, which is not as in the West, of day and night, but of "the evening and the morning," that is, the night and the day (the day beginning as the first stars become visible), so that if we accept the 15th as the day of crucifixion, the Jewish paschal meal, our Lord's Last Supper, and the Crucifixion and Burial, were all included within that one "day," consisting of the night of what we should call the 14th and the day of the 15th.

But a question which the writer is continually asked is, How can we make out the "three days and three nights" (Matt. xii. 40) which the Lord said would intervene between His death and resurrection if the crucifixion took place on Friday, the 15th, and His resurrection on the morrow after the weekly Sabbath, or early on the 17th Nisan? On which I would observe:

(*a*) That the expression "three days and three nights" is an Old Testament idiom carried over into the New Testament, and means not necessarily three whole days and three whole nights, but in round numbers a period of about three days. In the case of Jonah, to whose typical experience the Lord refers, we have no means of accurately ascertaining what actual measure of time he was in the belly of the whale, but in the other places where this idiom is used, or implied, we have strong reason to believe that it *could* not have meant literally three days and three nights. Exactly the same expression as in the case of Jonah is found in Sam. xxx. 12-14, when on David and his men's return to Ziklag on "the third day" (ver. 1), to find the place devastated in their absence, and their families and property carried off as spoil by the Amalekites, they found an Egyptian slave who had "eaten no bread nor drunk water three days and three nights" (ver. 12), but in the 14th verse we read that it was "three days ago" that he fell sick, and the impression left on the mind is that it was a period of *about* three days. In Esther vi. 16 we read that after Esther had been sufficiently roused by Mordecai to the imminent danger which was threatening, she sent a message to him: "Go, gather all the Jews that are present in Shushan and fast ye for me, and neither eat nor drink *three days —night and day; I also and my maidens will fast in like manner"*; but "it came to pass *on the third day*" (chap. v. 1), and evidently early on that day, that she appeared before Ahasuerus and on that same day we find her already at the "banquet" to which she had invited him and Haman.

(b) It is to no purpose to try to push back the day of the Crucifixion to the Thursday, or even the Wednesday in that week, as some have without basis, either historical or biblical, endeavoured to do, so as to get in three whole days and three whole nights between His burial and the resurrection, since, according to the express words of Christ, and of the apostles, the resurrection took place "on the third day."

Thus, to take only the Gospel of Matthew, we find that from the sixteenth chapter and onwards, when "Jesus began to show His disciples" with increasing clearness and fulness of detail the experiences which were awaiting Him in Jerusalem—how "the Son of Man shall be betrayed unto the chief priests and unto the scribes, and they shall condemn Him to death, and shall deliver Him to the Gentiles to mock and to scourge and to crucify Him,"—these statements always end with the confident prediction, "and on the third day He shall rise again" (Matt. xvi. 21; xvii. 23; xx. 18, 19). And with these predictions as to the time of His resurrection corresponds the historic fact.

To take only the testimony of one or two passages; we have in Luke the beautiful classic account of the meeting and conversation of the Christ with the two disciples on their way to Emmaus after His resurrection had become a glorious accomplished fact, and then, after their telling Him in their simplicity, as if He were "only a stranger," how He, whom they had trusted would have redeemed Israel, had been delivered by the chief priests and rulers to be condemned to death and crucified, but of whom the as yet incredible report had now reached them that He had risen from the dead, they add, "And besides all this to-day is the third day since these things were done."

The Apostle Paul, therefore, in summarising the great foundation facts of the gospel which he preached, and which were universally believed in the Churches, says, not only that Christ died for our sins, and that He was buried, but that "He rose again from the dead the third day according to the Scriptures (1 Cor. xv. 4).

I might point out also the fact that the Jews who heard the Lord use the expression did not understand it to signify literally "three days and three nights," for after the Crucifixion they came to Pilate saying, "Sir, we remember what that deceiver said while He was yet alive, After three days I will rise again. Command therefore that the sepulchre be made secure until the third day" (Matt. xxvii. 63, 64).

(c) According to Jewish law part of the day stands for the whole, for "if a day had been once entered on, even for a few minutes, the whole twenty-four hours were reckoned to the person who had so entered on the day." If a child is born in the last hour or even in the last few minutes of a day it is counted as a whole day of the period of time within which he must be circumcised. Thus *legally,* according to Jewish reckoning, the crucifixion and burial of our Lord having taken place before the 16th Nisan actually commenced, He may be said to have been in the grave "three days and three night," viz., *Friday,* to which legally belonged the might of what we should call Thursday; *Saturday,* consisting of the night of Friday and the day of Saturday; and *Sunday* to which belonged the night of Saturday and the very early morn of Sunday.

Further books available through:

Keren Ahvah Meshihit
P.O. Box 10382
91103 Jerusalem, Israel
Visit our Website: www.kerenahvah.org

Books from **Different Authors**

Books from **Unknown Authors**